MARKETING TO THE
NEW NATURAL CONSUMER

Marketing to the New Natural Consumer

Understanding Trends in Wellness

Harvey Hartman
with David Wright

The Hartman Group, Inc.
Bellevue, Washington

The Hartman Group, Inc.
Bellefield Office Park
1621 114th Ave SE, #105
Bellevue, WA 98004
425-452-0818 • Fax: 425-452-9092
e-mail: info@hartman-group.com
www.hartman-group.com

Library of Congress Cataloging-in-Publication Data
Hartman, Harvey.
        Marketing to the new natural consumer:
    understanding trends in wellness / Harvey Hartman
    with David Wright. -- 1st ed.
        p. cm.
        Includes bibliographical references.
        ISBN: 1-929027-00-1

        1. Green marketing--United States. 2. Consumer
    behavior--United States. 3. Consumers--United
    States--Attitudes. 4. Health products--Marketing.
    I. Wright, David, 1962- II. Title.

    HF5413.H37 1999   658.8'34
                                   QBI99-911

.

In loving memory of my daughter
Emily Marie Hartman
June 5, 1976–November 15, 1995

My "Beautiful" . . .

CONTENTS

ACKNOWLEDGMENTS

The Hartman Group has been in existence since 1989. Over the years a number of talented individuals have contributed in research, writing, and in building the collective entity which now makes up the company. Cindy Robideau has been instrumental in building the company, and thus the findings that make up this book, from the very beginning. Thanks go to Gary Lewis for his early contributions and his work on *The Evolving Organic Marketplace*, Mark Sten for all his efforts, and Jack Whelan and Bill Shepard for their contributions on the *Food and the Environment* studies. Tanya Pergola and Jarrett Paschel have helped us to learn more and more about social change, consumer lifestyles, wellness and Natural Sensibility. Laurie Demeritt, Bill Gottlieb, Stephanie Gailing, Charlie Curtis, Robert Hashizume and Joelle Chizmar have all been instrumental in one way or another in growing The Hartman Group. Help in building our research studies came from Monica McGuire at NFO. Finally, many thanks to Bob Samuels, a man of strong and unique intuitive beliefs, unwavering trust, conviction, and a friend.

All in all, this book is both a point of departure—in that it represents the distillations of over ten years of work—and a point of arrival, as we are just beginning to understand what wellness means to the consumer and thus what wellness means in terms of market potential. The diversity of consumers that shop and use various wellness products and services, combined with their evolving lifestyles, ensures that The Hartman Group has its work cut out for it in the years ahead. We welcome your thoughts on this book.

Introduction

MARKETING TO THE NEW CONSUMER

When The Hartman Group originally became involved in studying what it then called "green consumers" nine years ago, much of the company's efforts were focused on how environmental achievements, such as production enhancements made to apparel manufacturing that decreased environmentally damaging chemicals and processes, could be studied in relation to the consumer and turned into market opportunities. Some very successful projects proved that this approach worked,[1] and at the time, the environment was still a hot topic: In the 1980s, corporations and nonprofits thought that the consumer was willing to purchase *anything* with environmental enhancements.

This was only partly true. In actuality, consumer interest in purchasing and using green products was inconsistent, underscoring the chasm between attitudes and behavior. Consistent purchase of green products was much closer to home and hearth: Food, water, and

---

[1] Wrangler *"Green Initiative: Environmental Improvements and Strategic Positioning for Wrangler Rugged Earth Wash Green Jeans,"* The Hartman Group, 1992

many of the goods and services central to nutrition and health were to become the focus of consumers seeking all things natural in the 1990s. In the late 1990s, a new focus on personal health and wellness, that is the consumer's individual environment, appeared as a driving force behind purchasing behavior. The physical protection of nature and the environment, while idealized, came next. Wellness shoppers, made up of individuals embodying an ideal that had been evolving since the 1960s, were entering the mainstream. Today, market opportunities abound for both mainstream and natural marketers to capitalize on the win-win scenario of consumers satisfying an individual drive for health while simultaneously using products better for both themselves and the environment. To create natural products that consumers seek out, trust, and purchase consistently, however, requires in-depth understanding and analysis of how and why a constantly evolving consumer is shopping the natural category.

Figure I-1. Recent Consumer Trends

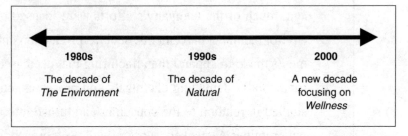

1980s	1990s	2000
The decade of *The Environment*	The decade of *Natural*	A new decade focusing on *Wellness*

Studies undertaken in 1996 and 1997 by The Hartman Group that assessed consumer attitudes toward food, agriculture and the environment established the importance of the personal and natural environment as issues of concern to more than 50 percent of the U.S. population.[2] This half of the population still sees a connection between the health of the environment and their own well-being, as re-examined in 1998.[3]

Following the studies in the food and beverage category, in 1997 and 1998 The Hartman Group undertook detailed attitudinal and behavioral studies in consumer purchase and use of dietary supplements, complementary and alternative medicine, and natural personal care and household products. Based on this continuous research, The Hartman

---

[2] *Food and the Environment: The Consumer Perspective: Phases I and II*, 1996 and 1997, The Hartman Group. See Appendix I.
[3] *Food and the Environment: Phase III*, January 1999, The Hartman Group. See Appendix I.

Group now projects that the segments made up of "green consumers" (those who express concern for the environment and the effect that its degradation will have on their lives) will expand to the point that over 85 percent of the U.S. population is participating, or willing to participate in one way or another, in what we call natural product worlds. The green consumer is now mainstream, and natural products and services are firmly in place as a trend—not just as a fad.

Natural product worlds, as currently defined by The Hartman Group, make up five product and service categories:

Key Drivers of Natural Market Opportunities
• The aging population is focused on health, nutrition and fitness. By the year 2000, 76 million Americans will be over the age of fifty, more than twice the population of Canada. By 2020, 117 million Americans will be over fifty, more than one-third of the U.S. population. At the same time, 75 percent of all assets (about $3 trillion) will be held by people fifty and older.
• Over 68 percent of the population is using vitamins and minerals while over 25 percent are using herbs and related supplements
• Over 86 percent of the population is using various alternative medicine products and services.
• Over 50 percent of the population is open to purchase or try sustainably produced food and beverages. 11 percent are actively buying organic food and beverages.
• Mainstream and natural companies are building infrastructure to supply the $29 billion functional food category.
• Price, quality and availability of natural products are meeting more and more consumer criteria.

1. **Natural and Organic Food and Beverages:** Some 53 percent of the U.S. population indicates an interest in or purchases natural and organic food and beverages.[4] Eleven percent of consumers represent the core of the earth-sustainable marketplace and are actively paying a premium for earth-sustainable products, including organic foods and beverages. The organic market alone, estimated at $4 billion in sales in 1997, is experiencing double-digit growth and widespread penetration onto mass market shelves.

2. **Vitamins, Minerals, Herbs and Dietary Supplements:** Currently over 68 percent of Americans supplement their health and wellness with vitamins and minerals, while a full 25 percent of the country takes herbs and other dietary supplements. The U.S. supplement market, projected at over $10 billion in sales in 1998, is growing at double-digit rates.[5]

---

[4] *Food and the Environment: Phase III*, January 1999, The Hartman Group. See Appendix I.
[5] Natural Products Census: *Supplement Report* (third quarter 1998 data), The Hartman Group. See Appendix I.

3. **Complementary and Alternative Medicine:** More than 86 percent of Americans currently report using one or more of twenty-three different health modalities considered to be alternative medicine.[6] U.S. consumer expenditures on alternative health services provided by health care professionals in 1997 were recently estimated at $21.2 billion.[7]

4. **Natural Health and Beauty Aids:** Natural health and beauty aids are currently purchased and used by a small segment of consumers. Cosmoceuticals, the new category of beauty and personal care products with specific active ingredients added to bolster the preventive health aspect of the products used, are relatively unformed as a specific category in the consumer's mind. Potential purchasers consistently voice a strong interest in purchasing if quality, efficacy, availability and price factors are addressed. Consumers in general are somewhat confused about how to define this category.

5. **Natural Household Products:** These products are currently purchased and used by a small segment of consumers. Potential purchasers consistently voice a strong interest in purchasing, if quality, efficacy, availability and price factors are addressed.[8]

The one underlying conceptual key to understanding the size and impact of these product worlds lies in recognizing that growing numbers of consumers participate unpredictably and experimentally in many of these product and service categories. *American consumers are constructing new personal wellness regimes.* They are integrating a broad array of experiences and natural health products and services into their lives. Undeniably, the size and breadth of impact of these forays into various health-promoting and nutrition-related consumer product categories is potentially enormous. New market frontiers, created at the intersection of the mainstream and the natural market, will continue to expand with increasing consumer adoption of natural products and services (see figure I-2).

---

[6] *Integrated Health Care: Consumer Use and Attitudes*, Fall 1998, The Hartman Group. See Appendix I.

[7] Eisenberg, D et al., "Trends in Alternative Medicine Use in the United States: 1990–1997." Journal of the American Medical Association 280 (1998): 1569–1575.

[8] Product worlds 4 and 5 were analyzed in consumer studies reported in *Natural Sensibility: A Study of America's Changing Culture and Lifestyle*, Fall 1998, The Hartman Group. See Appendix I.

Figure I-2. Key Factors Forming New Market Frontiers: Natural and Mainstream Markets and Brands[9]

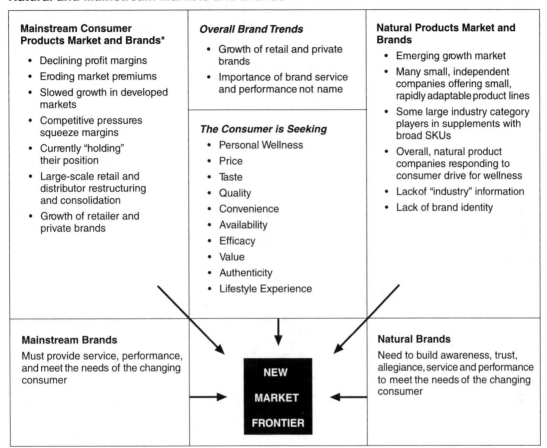

Mainstream Consumer Products Market and Brands*

- Declining profit margins
- Eroding market premiums
- Slowed growth in developed markets
- Competitive pressures squeeze margins
- Currently "holding" their position
- Large-scale retail and distributor restructuring and consolidation
- Growth of retailer and private brands

Overall Brand Trends

- Growth of retail and private brands
- Importance of brand service and performance not name

The Consumer is Seeking

- Personal Wellness
- Price
- Taste
- Quality
- Convenience
- Availability
- Efficacy
- Value
- Authenticity
- Lifestyle Experience

Natural Products Market and Brands

- Emerging growth market
- Many small, independent companies offering small, rapidly adaptable product lines
- Some large industry category players in supplements with broad SKUs
- Overall, natural product companies responding to consumer drive for wellness
- Lack of "industry" information
- Lack of brand identity

Mainstream Brands

Must provide service, performance, and meet the needs of the changing consumer

NEW MARKET FRONTIER

Natural Brands

Need to build awareness, trust, allegiance, service and performance to meet the needs of the changing consumer

Currently, the trend of consumers seeking products, services and lifestyle experiences which stem from concerns about individual health and wellness shows no sign of slowing. This trend exhibits a growing impact on core consumer product and service sectors, especially in retail food and pharmacy as well as health care delivery settings. For marketers of various consumer products and services, understanding what drives consumer experimentation and motivates consistent use of natural product categories is a key to understanding where long-term consumer trends—and market frontiers—are headed.

---

[9] Mainstream market and brand information adapted from *The Future of Brand Management: New Frontiers in Building a Learning Organization Attuned to 21ˢᵗ Century Customer and Consumer Needs*, Deloitte & Touche Consulting Group, Deloitte & Touche L.L.P. as published in Progressive Grocer, July 1998, pp. 21–32.

INTERPRETING THE NEW CONSUMER

Building upon years of experience in analyzing the natural consumer, The Hartman Group provides a fact-based platform from which strategic decisions can be made for marketing and branding consumer products and services for both mainstream and natural food and beverage, dietary supplement, pharmaceutical, health care, and personal care categories.

Figure I-3. Growth of the Natural Products Industry

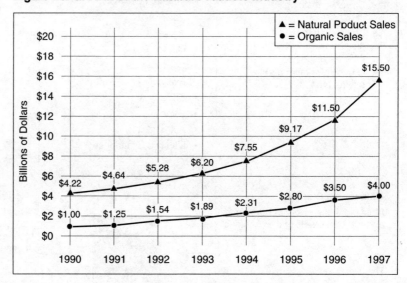

The Hartman Group has ten years of experience analyzing and advising on how consumer participation in the natural products market can be understood and transformed into market growth opportunities. The Hartman Group:

- was the first U.S. research firm to strategically analyze U.S. consumer perceptions toward food, the environment and sustainable agriculture.
- is the first to develop and provide accurate monthly information on consumer use and purchase behaviors in the over $10 billion dietary supplement category.

- is the leading authority on cultural lifestyles and changes as they
relate to U.S. consumer involvement in natural and organic food
and beverage, dietary supplement, alternative and integrated
medicine, and natural personal care categories.

Background

Founded in 1989, The Hartman Group develops, collects, and strategically analyzes consumer and trade information for companies and organizations that seek to produce and market natural, nutritional,
health-promoting or environmentally enhanced consumer products and
services. The Hartman Group specializes in analysis and interpretation
of consumer participation in the natural products marketplace, the results of which are available either as proprietary consulting engagements
to leading natural and mainstream consumer products companies or in
various publicly available formats (such as printed publications and
electronic data).

The Hartman Group is positioned as a window through which conventional consumer products companies look in on an explosively evolving natural market. The Hartman Group also serves the strategic
information needs of thousands of natural products companies in their
emerging markets. While small in comparison to the $500 billion con-
ventional food and beverage market, overall sales of natural food, beverage, personal care, dietary supplement, and related consumer products
rose to over $15.5 billion in 1997, up 28.7 percent from 1996 sales of
$11.5 billion.[10] This phenomenal growth is being fueled by an increas-
ing consumer emphasis on health, fitness, and nutrition, coupled with
higher-quality products available through a large number of natural and
conventional retail channels.

---

[10] The Hartman Group/New Hope Natural Media, "Annual Market Overview," *Natural Foods Merchandiser*, June 1998. Note: Since June 1998, these figures have been adjusted to represent market projections derived from The Hartman Group's Natural Products Census *Supplement Report* which, based on monthly consumer purchase and use of vitamins, minerals, herbals, and dietary supplements, projects a total U.S. supplement market size of $10 billion. Thus, the cor-rected estimate on the "natural market" is $5.51 billion (natural food, beverage, organic and personal care products) plus $10 billion (supplements), representing a $15.5 billion market.

The Emerging Market Opportunity

Based on nine years of consumer and trade research, The Hartman Group has determined that the "natural" or "green" consumer is now mainstream. The natural market is not a fad, but instead is a manifestation of deep-rooted cultural and lifestyle changes occurring within the U.S. population.

In total, with mainstream and natural retail channels added in, current sales for natural, nutritional and alternative health products and services annually exceed $65.7 billion.[11]

Some of the greatest indicators of this trend, based on The Hartman Group's analysis of consumer purchase and use of natural food and beverage, dietary supplement and alternative medicine categories, are evidenced by large segments of the population who shop and eat healthier, self-treat medically, and seek overall general wellness both pro-actively and as a result of dissatisfaction with the current health care system. This is most evident in the dynamic upswing of interest and consumer participation in consumer products categories which intersect with individual health, fitness, and nutrition concerns. Such interests have led to dramatic increases in consumer awareness and active purchase of such product categories which interest the individual.

Consumer products and services meeting natural criteria are now available through nearly all conventional retail channels including but not limited to pharmacies and supermarkets, warehouses, direct mail, health food stores, and the Internet. The Hartman Group's analytical studies of consumer participation in natural food and beverage, dietary supplements, alternative and conventional medicine, organic products, natural apparel, household products, and natural personal care categories show that with increasing availability, more than fifty percent of the U.S. population is purchasing from and participating in, to different degrees, these emerging natural categories.

In the context of this significant consumer demand, the natural market can currently be classified as an emerging market with high frag-

---

[11] This figure represents a compilation of numbers taken from the $5.51 billion natural and organic products market (as determined in the 1998 Hartman Group/New Hope Natural Media 17th Natural Products Market Overview, *Natural Foods Merchandiser*, June 1998).; $10 billion sales in vitamins, minerals, herbals and dietary supplements (projected from The Hartman Group's Supplement Census); $29 billion in functional food sales (Decision Resources, Waltham, MA); and $21.2 billion in alternative health services and product sales (Eisenberg et.al. See footnote 7). These figures totaled exceed $65 billion.

mentation and dynamic growth, yet little brand power and recognition among natural market manufacturers.

Concurrently, conventional food and beverage, pharmaceutical, health products and agricultural life science companies are eyeing consumer participation in the $65.7 billion natural market with great interest. As a consequence, monthly developments impacting the natural market include announcements by major conventional corporations that outline the establishment of divisions that focus on producing natural foods, nutritional foods, medical foods, fortified foods, nutraceuticals, and cosmoceuticals. At the same time, the double-digit growth of the natural products and services industry introduces hundreds of new consumer products into conventional and natural channels each year. The success of these new products in both natural and conventional settings depends almost entirely on understanding *why* and *how* consumers are increasingly demanding these goods and services and what marketing and branding strategies can be applied to gain maximum opportunity.

Simultaneous to the gathering consumer demand, mainstream companies such as Bayer, SmithKline Beecham, Warner-Lambert, Monsanto, DuPont, Arthur D. Little, American Home Products, and Archer Daniels Midland have announced product developments *in 1998 alone* which focus on capitalizing either on the $15 billion natural market or the $29 billion functional food market. These events should be considered in tandem with developments in the health care arena, where alternative medicine and conventional medicine are combining to form new integrated practices and services.

The Hartman Group's Consumer Market Research and Trade Analysis

The Hartman Group offers consulting services through The Hartman Group Strategic Consulting group, and category-specific data, analysis, and reports through its Strategic Business Units focusing on supplements, food and beverage, personal care, and alternative health.

1998 has seen implementation of *The Natural Products Census*, the main component of which is *Supplement Report*, a state-of-the-art market research vehicle that tracks 11,000 individual consumers and their weekly purchase and use of products and services in the over $10 billion vitamin, mineral, herb, and supplement category.[12] Similar research vehicles are planned in food and beverage, personal care and integrated medicine categories.

The Hartman Group's consumer market research and trade analysis focuses on both annual and continuous consumer market research studies as well as specialized projects that answer specific corporate branding, product development and natural product category questions.

Most major consumer studies conducted by The Hartman Group are fielded in partnership with NFO (National Family Opinion) Worldwide, the ninth largest market research company in the world. NFO's panel membership is the largest in the United States and consists, in total, of some 525,000 U.S. households. NFO panels are balanced and controlled to be representative of the forty-eight contiguous states, based on U.S. Bureau of Census data, nationally and within each of nine Census divisions. Demographic information on each panel member is available from over 133 selected variables representing eleven major categories.

Annual and continuous research studies, each available for corporate participation, focus on the following natural product sectors and areas:

- **Vitamins, Minerals, Herbals, and Dietary Supplements**—Supplement Census; Annual Supplement Reports; Corporate syndication in national studies; Custom research
- **Food and Beverage**—Annual studies (*Food and the Environment reports, Hartman Organic Monitor*); Corporate syndication in national studies; Planned for 1999: Continuous studies on consumer use of organic food, nutritional foods/nutraceuticals, sports nutrition; Custom research
- **Personal Care**—Planned for 1999–2000: Continuous studies, via the Natural Products Census on consumer use of natural personal care products and cosmoceuticals; Corporate syndication in national studies

---

[12] All Supplement Report information is collected in partnership with NFO Worldwide. See Appendix I.

- **Integrated Medicine and Health Care**—Annual Studies (Integrated Medicine reports). Planned for 1999: Continuous studies on consumer use of alternative modalities as well alternative practitioner trends; Corporate syndication in national studies
- **Cultural Studies**—The Hartman Group's cultural analysis group *N/sight* uses unique research methodologies to study the behavior of consumers who use natural products and services. Traditional and cutting-edge methods from the fields of sociology, anthropology and social psychology are combined into an eclectic and powerful analytical toolbox. Cultural studies complete or underway include:

Natural Sensibility: A Study of America's Changing Culture and Lifestyle. This study lays the foundation for a comprehensive explanation of long-term change in American culture and lifestyles. Specifically, Natural Sensibility considers how changes in the broad, cultural sphere get translated by individuals into everyday actions—and, reciprocally, how these changes in individual behavior eventually culminate to changes in cultural trends in purchase and use of natural products and services.

How Americans Are Understanding Wellness: An Ongoing Study. This ongoing study utilizes a linked series of consumer and industry research explorations which seek to explain how consumers are currently understanding the concept of wellness and how they differentially explore this lifestyle in relation to the products and services they purchase.

HISTORY OF THE NATURAL AND ORGANIC INDUSTRY

Until a few short years ago, the competitive environment in the organic and natural products industry consisted of a small community of farmers, processors, marketers, and more recently, certifiers, who developed innovations together, debated, competed, and achieved product distribution based on personal relationships and sales ability. The consumer base was quite small and was comprised mostly of people who were on the deep-green or "True-Natural" fringe. Virtually all of the companies making up the industry were small, and few participants were formally trained in business or marketing. But these people had intelligence, drive, and determination. Almost all the members of this community cared personally about the land and its natural health.

Some of this has already changed, and more changes will occur in the next few years. As the natural market gains momentum and intersects with conventional consumers and retail settings, it will undergo rapid change. As this evolution occurs, it is worth understanding that the organic and natural market of the recent past required *trailblazers*—people and companies who could:

- Develop and test new growing methods with few resources to support them
- Sell the harvest, mainly through personal sales skills and relationships
- Service the needs of health food retailers, most of whom were local stores or small chains
- Maintain fairly consistent quality standards
- Assemble new processing procedures or simple factories
- Manage the finances of small enterprises
- Create a basic yet attractive product package
- Work with a diverse network of people to solve problems
- Manage a handful of full-time employees
- Persevere and innovate amidst great obstacles and seemingly low public interest
- Struggle by trial, error, brainstorming, and debate to create a standard of integrity that could be certified (organics)
- Convince a very select market that health and the environment merited paying a premium

The trends, opportunities, and pressures shaping the organic and natural products industry have worked to create an expanded market where the above critical success factors are generally still necessary, but certainly inadequate by themselves. A number of cultural and business trends are also shaping the natural and organic products industry now and for the future. The most significant of these changes are discussed in the following sections and summarized in figure I-4.

Changes in the Public

Evolving Cultural Values

As demonstrated by The Hartman Group's research, most Americans are growing to more deeply value health and wellness in many realms of life. This yearning expresses itself in new attitudes, changing behaviors, and a deeper appreciation regarding nutrition, exercise, community involvement, nature, spiritual connection, femininity, and ecological health.

Figure I-4. Key Trends Revolutionizing the Natural and Organic Products Industry

Changes in the Public

1. Evolving Cultural Values emphasizing health, nature, community, spirituality.
2. Demographic Changes involving aging baby boomers with more children.
3. Growing Awareness about health, the environment, and even organic issues.

Changes in Natural and Organic Products

4. Better Quality Products in terms of taste, appearance, packaging, convenience.
5. Reduced Price Premiums due to better production methods and economies of scale.
6. Ever-Increasing Product Offerings within existing categories and new categories.
7. Growth of "Suborganic" Natural Products with health and "eco" improvements.

Changes in the Conventional Food Industry

8. Conventional Retailing with consolidation, automation, category management, etc.
9. Conventional Production with farm buyouts, corporate expansion, biotech, etc.
10. Conventional Food Distribution with consolidation, third-party warehousing, etc.

Changes in the Organic Industry

11. Expanded Retail Availability in natural foods and conventional supermarkets, etc.
12. Mergers, Acquisitions, Joint Ventures, and Outside Investor Interest among organic retailers and producers.
13. Entry by Mainstream Food Companies via acquisition or new product development.
14. National Certification Standard to regulate organic claims and verification.
15. Growing "Professionalization" and Competitive Sophistication among companies.

Source: *The Evolving Organic Marketplace*, The Hartman Group, Fall 1997

These values have waxed and waned as influences throughout the history of America and Western Civilization, but have usually been confined to minority subcultures. After the widespread diffusion of modern chemical-based agriculture following World War II, these minority cultural values first began to influence attitudes about food and farm practices in the late 1960s with the rise of the counter-culture and a "back to the land" movement. Since then, they have been slowly percolating through the culture and into an ever larger percentage of American minds. As illustrated in figure I-5, The Hartman Group's study *The Evolving Organic Marketplace* reveals that by now, most Americans are moving to adopt the kinds of natural, healthful, "caretaking" values that are the raison d'être of the organic movement. The Hartman Group predicts that these "organic" values will continue their diffusion through the hearts, minds, and motivations of Americans—mainly because they reflect basic human needs for connection, meaning, security, and permanence which "inorganic" conventional and industrial-consumer culture does not necessarily provide.

Figure I-5. Consumer Organic Purchase Interest

"I am not very interested in buying organic products."

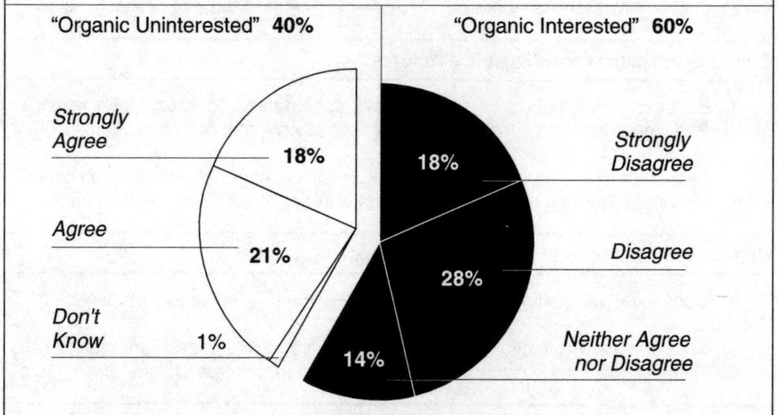

"Organic Uninterested" **40%**   "Organic Interested" **60%**

Strongly Agree — **18%**

Agree — **21%**

Don't Know — **1%**

18%

28%

14%

Strongly Disagree

Disagree

Neither Agree nor Disagree

* Because they have a potential interest, the "Organic Interested" category includes those ambivalent respondents who neither agreed nor disagreed that they were not interested.

Source: *The Evolving Organic Marketplace*, The Hartman Group, Fall 1997

Demographic Changes

The large and influential Baby Boom generation has entered its middle years, and its members' concern for preventing health problems and maximizing physical vitality and longevity are becoming a paramount trend. Most in this generation are also raising children, and thus concern for family health is equally compelling to them.

The development of the post-World War II Baby Boom generation is widely recognized because it is frequently featured in the general news media. People born during the late 1940s through the late 1950s are beginning to confront the "natural developments" incurred with aging, and a large percentage of them are highly motivated to maintain their energy and health as long as possible. Perhaps because this generation grew up with a sense that limits either did not exist or could be overcome, it has become the first generation in America to turn in large numbers toward foods and remedies that promise to defeat or defer the natural limits of aging bodies.

The "Baby Boomlet"—which represents the surge in births to families of the Baby Boom generation—is another fundamental demographic factor which appears to be raising demand for healthier products. As detailed in the 1997 *Hartman Report* on food and the environment, 88 percent of environmentally oriented Americans (who themselves comprise 52 percent of the U.S. market) believe that the health of the environment is important for the future health of their children. Importantly, almost half (47 percent) of the respondents surveyed were more concerned about the food their children ate than about their own diets. Notwithstanding a probable regression toward junk food during the Baby Boomlet's adolescence, we believe the health food orientation being taught to the children of many Baby Boomers will keep the migration toward healthier products and services alive for the next several decades.

Growing Awareness

New knowledge about health, diet, toxins, the environment, and even organic principles themselves is being produced and more widely disseminated than it was a few years ago (see figure I-6). Organic products and production methods have been highlighted in articles and stories in the mainstream press and even on television programs. As the subjects of health, diet, toxins, and the environment have become standard fare in mainstream media, consumer concerns are becoming wedded with better awareness.

Figure I-6. Appearance of Topic "Organic Food" in 2,591 U.S. Magazines and 70 Major U.S. Newspapers, 1988–1998.

Year	Magazine	Newspaper
1988	2	5
1989	16	51
1990	20	71
1991	25	39
1992	12	64
1993	13	80
1994	21	65
1995	16	77
1996	30	108
1997	49	221
1998	109	305

▲ = Newspaper
● = Magazine

Source: Lexis-Nexis

As the scientific debate and public awareness evolve regarding the true health benefits of organic foods compared to conventional products or "sub-organic" alternatives, would-be organic customers can be expected to become more discerning shoppers. While most people involved in the production and marketing of organic products are probably convinced that their products represent the most healthful choices available, the scientific jury is still out on how much organic production methods by themselves improve the health impacts of a food. For example, many scientists argue that eating more fruits and vegetables, even if they are conventionally grown using pesticides, will positively benefit health. And yet evidence has accumulated that, especially for children, agricultural biocides in foods can impair health. Given current research funding priorities and the need for long-term toxicological studies to fully assess the acute and chronic impacts of toxic chemical residues in conventional foods, it will probably be years before any compelling evidence emerges to resolve the scientific debate. In the meantime, a large proportion of people will probably continue to view agricultural biocides to be "guilty until proven innocent."

Changes in Products

Better Quality Products

Both the perceived and actual quality of organic and natural products has improved substantially over the last several years. Many companies selling organic products have adopted higher standards and employed research, development, product testing, and new production or distribution methods to improve the taste, appearance, packaging, and convenience of their products. The image of natural and organic products has also improved immensely: For example, many up-scale restaurants and high-end chefs are beginning to feature natural and organic ingredients in their meals.

In the early 1990s, Hartman Group consumer focus groups revealed that many environmentally concerned people held very negative images of the *quality* of organic products. This image developed from seeing bruised or over-ripe organic produce in grocery stores. Since then, quality control, greater supply, and better inventory turnover appear to have improved the visual appeal of typical organic produce, and many stores (both natural and conventional) have learned how to display these products more attractively. At the same time, more packaged organic foods have become available and package quality has progressed to a high standard. In the meantime, many manufacturers of organic, processed foods have focused considerable resources on developing and testing products to ensure better taste. More natural and organic foods featuring convenient preparation have also appeared. Hartman Group interviews conducted with several organic product manufacturers indicate that the trend toward improving quality in organic foods will continue: It is a key development priority.

Reduced Price Premiums

The premiums associated with many organic and natural products have fallen in the last couple of years.

Several factors are driving down the cost of organic items. Farmers have developed better methods, which yield higher or more consistent yields with less expense. For many commodities (for example, cotton), organic pest controls utilizing improved monitoring, crop rotation, beneficial insects, revised planting or harvesting schedules, and companion planting have produced excellent results at an equivalent cost to pesticide use. Machines have been better utilized to lower costs as well. In other areas such as weed control, however, the cost of organic farming has tended to remain higher than conventional spray methods.

Ever-Increasing Product Offerings

In the last few years producers have added hundreds of new organic products in categories spanning virtually the entire grocery store. Not only have entirely new categories been developed (e.g., Organic Pasta Sauces and Salsas), but most categories have experienced an explosion of new variations of a given product class (e.g., Organic Black Teas, Organic Herbal Teas, Organic Medicinal Teas and Organic Coffees).

Growth of "Sub-Organic" Natural Products

A vast continuum of products in potential competition with organic foods has arisen to satisfy people's desires for a healthier or environmentally responsible lifestyle, and to take advantage of cultural shifts toward "natural" values. These range from products of very questionable health or beneficial status (e.g., "natural" sodas comprised mainly of water and standard corn syrup), to products incorporating and promoting substantive yet "sub-organic" improvements in ecological or health qualities (e.g., produce grown without pesticides or with reduced spray).

Changes in the Conventional Food Industry

Conventional Retailing

Key trends potentially impacting organic and natural food marketing in the retail arena include intensified competition, mergers and acquisitions, new department developments (e.g., ready-to-eat, segregated natural sections, food service), category management, the expansion of private labeling (including generic and premium lines), and increased automation in inventory management.

Conventional Food Production

Key trends in the production arena include buyouts and consolidations of small and medium-sized farms, the expansion of corporate ownership and business methods, the continuous development of new agricultural chemicals, an increase in the amount of chemicals used in many agricultural categories, advances in biotechnology, and continued low attention to workers' rights for farm laborers.

Conventional Food Distribution

Key trends in the distribution of foods include mergers and consolidations, the growing use of third-party warehousing, and the data automation that has helped both the operations of distributors and their interface with food producers and retailers.

Changes in the Organic and Natural Food Industry

Expanded Retail Availability

Growing beyond the classic health food store channel, more and more categories of organic products are becoming increasingly available in four additional retail channels:

1. The explosively expanding natural foods supermarkets sector, which tends to offer the largest selection of organic and natural products (including private label products) of any channel.
2. Conventional grocery stores and supermarkets, many of which are moving beyond produce to offer organic dairy and shelf-stable products.
3. Gourmet and specialty stores, including "discount" gourmet chains such as the rapidly growing Trader Joe's
4. Catalog mail-order, home delivery and Internet sales.

Mergers, Acquisitions, Joint Ventures, and Outside Investor Interest

Industry consolidation and new partnerships are being created among producers, distributors, and retailers of organic and natural products. This trend looms largest in the retail arena, driven through acquisitions by Whole Foods Markets and Wild Oats Markets. Additionally, Whole Foods' recent acquisition of supplement manufacturer and catalog marketer Amrion is an important example of mergers across industry sectors. While currently very active among retailers, distributors, and to some extent manufacturers, the trend toward mergers, acquisitions, and joint ventures is expected to continue across the value chain. At the same time, capital resources are starting to flow toward the organic and natural products marketplace in the form of investments from Wall Street.

Entry by Mainstream Food Companies

Conventional food marketers whose size and distribution power dwarf their largest organic or natural competitors have been examining the consumer interest and premium margins of organic products with increasing attention and activity. To date, most of their market activities have focused on purchases of existing organic food or natural products companies. Recently, however, the move has begun for mainstream food companies to initiate their own branded organic products such as General Mills' recent introduction of Sunrise organic cereal. The implications of this potential power shift are profound, since many conventional organizations either dominate in terms of financial clout or own brands that have developed equity through decades of marketing.

National Certification Standard

Since the 1990 passage of the Organic Foods Production Act, the U.S. Department of Agriculture (USDA) has undergone years of dialogue with organic industry leaders.

In 1997, the USDA released for public comment a proposed set of standards for organic food labeling. This initial version of the proposed rules met with an overwhelmingly negative response because of key issues that flew in the face of traditional understandings of what organic had traditionally meant.

Organic farming and trade organizations along with consumer advocacy groups created a media furor to raise awareness about the offending components of the impending legislation. Town hall meetings with USDA representatives and industry representatives were conducted in Boston, Seattle and Los Angeles. The resulting publicity generated over 275,000 comments to the USDA.

It is expected that a revised set of standards that do not contain the offensive issues will be released in 1999. This new version will in turn be submitted for public comment, creating another opportunity for increased awareness and attention to organic practices.

Implementation of the final National Organic Program is predicted to require an additional two or more years, but the impending publication of the new regulations will expand certification, shape certification practices, and offer consumers a more credible, simple standard by which to evaluate organic products. But it will also generate a firestorm of controversy within the organic movement—indeed this has already begun—at a time when the open market window and impending competition make these least affordable.

Organic growing methods were developed independently by various innovators under diverse conditions The biological subtleties of farming (not to mention new unprecedented developments) make it difficult for a simplistic organic standard to easily emerge. Organic farmers will differ on what should and should not be considered organic, as this is a controversial topic. Nevertheless, the value of an organic standard has been recognized by virtually all people in the industry. Nationally, the rule-making process by the USDA has been quite drawn out—mostly because the National Organic Standards Board, which was created to advise the Secretary of Agriculture on setting standards, asked to hear all sides so as to form an industry consensus on the standards. In the meantime, a semi-de-facto standard has arisen: compliance with California's organic act.

Growing "Professionalization" and Competitive Sophistication

The organic and natural products industry is becoming more complex, and competitors are responding with increasing sophistication and professionalism in the sense of more structured, disciplined business processes and practices.

This trend is occurring both among long-time organic companies, many of whom are hiring MBAs with mainstream brand-management experience, for example, and among conventional corporate entrants to the industry. These entrants may be large multi-national corporations, or new companies made up of former mainstream corporate executives.

How the Industry and Market Have Co-Evolved

Through the synergy of these trends functioning in the organic and natural products market, consumer and company responses to one another have engendered a mutual evolution. This evolution has led to the current state of the industry which stands on the brink of phenomenal growth and realignment. As with any industry, major changes in customer base or competitive dynamics require strategic re-assessments and a reconstitution of new skills required by the emerging environment. Certainly this emerging market will require an above-average focus on understanding not only consumer purchase behaviors, but especially the underlying lifestyles driving such behaviors.

PART I

The New Consumer

THE SOCIAL CONTEXT

Natural products and services have arrived in the market-place. What was once an eclectic smattering of people with myriad visions and ideals is now a full-fledged industry. Estimates suggest sales in excess of $16 billion dollars in 1998, with projections recast daily as venture capitalists, financiers, established corporations, market analysts, and retailers—as well as consumers—consumers continue to join the natural products and services market.

Americans are individuals at heart. Our cultural recipe—equal parts participatory democracy; the Protestant work ethic; a pioneering, go-west spirit; and Horatio Alger mythos—translated through institutions such as work, religion and family, has assured the individualist spirit a secure home in nearly every sphere of modern life. We aren't fond of admitting that larger forces (things outside of individual control) may be responsible, so we nominate individual heroes to shoulder the weight. For instance, solutions to complex problems (for example, slavery) are easily and quickly attributed to the genius of a single individual (Abraham Lincoln).

Researchers in new markets, excited by the prospect of uncharted terrain, target the individual consumer with a well-honed collection of research strategies and methods. Given the cultural heritage described above, the theoretical foundations underlying these research approaches are often derived from individual perspectives on human behavior. Traditional accounts of consumer behavior in economic and business literature focus on the individual consumer, often neglecting the role that important, societal-level forces play in patterning consumer behavior.

Economists, for example, typically model consumer behavior in a starkly individualistic, utilitarian world of costs and benefits. It is as if consumer behavior takes place in a vacuum, without influence from the outside world. When pressed on thornier issues such as the origins of tastes, preferences, fads and fashions, economists typically pass the buck to psychologists. Similarly, much business literature—applied as well as academic—relies heavily on psychology and related studies of the individual to better explain consumer behavior. Literature on branding, for example, is marked by discussions of emotion, personality, identity, and attachment—all psychological constructs. To the degree that larger processes (e.g., fads or trends) are considered, they are often presented as the product of soothsayers, with no formalized research apparatus grounded in a field of theory (e.g., business, economics, sociology, and psychology).

Consumers are individuals with goals, preferences, and attitudes, but consumers are also real people responding to a host of pressures, influences, and constraints, many of which emanate from larger societal forces. These forces include culture, institutions (e.g., economy, family, religion, work) and trends (e.g., fads and fashions), all of which have the power to modify and direct consumer behavior.

Chapter 1 begins by examining how changes in the larger organization of the economy have impacted specific consumption patterns and practices in the late twentieth century. Chapter 2 considers several threads from evolving cultural changes that are specifically relevant to the natural products industry. Chapter 3 introduces a specific frame (Natural Sensibility) developed to describe consumer involvement in the natural products industry, and also considers three relevant subthemes—ideology, authenticity, and experience—that provide a key insight to the "big picture" of consumer involvement in natural products and services. Finally, Chapter 4 concludes with a discussion of five product worlds that play a prominent role in the natural products market: vitamins, minerals, herbals and dietary supplements; alternative health care; organic foods; natural health and beauty aids; and natural household products.

CHAPTER 1

Structural Change

BACKGROUND

Most of us have an intuitive sense that there are profound changes occurring in the world's economic order. Reliance on temporary workers, once only encountered in light-industrial and secretarial sectors, has spread to nearly every job classification imaginable—including physicians, managers, and professors. For many, the traditional nine-to-five workday now seems like an ancient relic from a not-so-distant past; flex-time is now routine. Advances in microprocessor technology have led to changes that previous generations could only dream about—for example, the cellular phone.

While we all have some exposure to the dramatic changes going on around us all, it is often difficult to step back and assess the impact of these developments. To do so properly requires a serious look at the organization of the economy (as well as the linkages to the economy of the larger world) while at the same time keeping a reflexive eye on the individual. For brevity's sake, we will limit our discussions to structural changes in the organization of production and consumption, which provide specific insight into the natural products industry. This is intended to provide a brief overview of a complex set of ideas and to provide context and setting for the development of the natural products marketplace.

Current work by sociologists and economists is concerned with global changes in the organization of production and consumption.

Specifically, some argue that fundamental changes in the *organization* of production and consumption activities will have powerful, long-lasting effects on consumer activities.

HOW TRADITIONAL MODELS ARE CHANGING

In traditional models of production, the creation and manufacturing of goods typically took place under one roof, under the auspices of a single corporation. Similarly, classical and neo-classical economics tended to emphasize production (supply) while viewing consumption (demand) as an essential but unproblematic feature of an economy (see figure 1-1). Finally, the causal logic flowed from back to front (left to right in our model). That is, production (supply) was seen as the driving force in these models.

Figure 1-1. The Traditional Economic Model

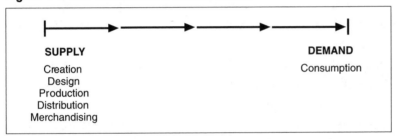

However, the close of the twentieth century has brought about significant changes in the economic landscape. Many use the term globalization to refer to an entire subset of related processes responsible for these changes: the decline of statist economies in the East, the growth of high-tech industries, the dissolution of cultural barriers, the increasing affordability and omnipresence of global shipping networks, as well as the expanding role of flexible production networks and their related by-products (flexible specialization, outsourcing, etc.). Whatever the diverse causes, these assorted processes have led to a change in the traditional model of production. Specifically, the *creation* of goods has been separated from manufacturing and consumption. In such a world, designers, merchandisers, branding consultants, and super-discount houses—all firms without physical factories—play key roles in the creation of goods.

At the same time, manufacturing has become a truly global activity, largely carried out by networks of Original Equipment Manufacturer (OEM)-dedicated manufacturing houses in, most prominently, Southeast Asia and the Pacific Rim. In such a scenario, economic power shifts away from production and into the realm of creation. Manufacturers fade into the background as designers, merchandisers, and branding experts increasingly dominate the economic landscape. Compared to the traditional model, the *interaction* between consumption and creation—the lifestyle experience—is the driving force in this model. Pottery Barn, for example, doesn't need to worry about manufacturing products—that's all taken care of by a series of OEM houses in the Pacific Rim. Instead, their designers and branding consultants can focus on what the merchandise looks like, what it means, and how it is used—all lifestyle experiences.

Due to the flexible "realignment" of these processes, consumers are no longer stratified by class position. Rather, they are loosely organized into lifestyle categories, or "product worlds," where they are free to move about. Thus, one no longer needs to be wealthy to afford some of the finest things in life. Instead, all one needs is an interest in the lifestyle associated with that particular product world. For example, while a $250 Avalanche Rescue Beacon from Patagonia may prove too costly for most financially-strapped college students, this could be received as a Christmas gift from Mom and Dad. While many in poor urban areas struggle to afford the basic necessities, athletic shoes remain a high-status, lifestyle item.

This new organization of consumers also reflects a more intimate, direct relationship with the creation process than was possible in traditional, manufacturing-centered models. Designers and merchandisers can now interact on a more personal level with the consumer to create more customized lifestyle worlds. These lifestyle worlds are interpretive arenas centered on a specific product and its associated method(s) of consumption. In such worlds people come not only to identify themselves, but also to promote the identities they adopt within the associated lifestyle world.[1] This was evident in a recent Recreational Equipment Inc. (REI)

---

[1] From correspondence, drafts, and discussions with Gary Hamilton, Professor of Sociology at the University of Washington.

"Basement Sale" at the flagship headquarters in Seattle. Hundreds of devoted REI members camped out—complete with all of their associated REI gear—for the opportunity to buy more REI "stuff" at clearance prices.

It is important to recognize that although merchandisers create the lifestyle associated with a particular product, consumers are still the ones who organize themselves into specific product worlds. For example, Starbucks created a "coffee culture" surrounding the consumption of their products, but consumers (and other business owners) organize themselves into their own social networks centered around the consumption of coffee. A long-term goal is to be able to shed light on *how* people come to differentiate themselves into specific product worlds.

While those in the ivory tower work on refining their explanations, many commercial firms are already actively engaged in this evolving economic landscape, often with demonstrable results. Most noticeably, firms such as Nike and REI have benefited significantly from concentrating their efforts in merchandising and design, while outsourcing production to OEM shops in the Pacific Rim. Their dynamic, interactive, retail environments—where the product and the experience merge to create a true lifestyle experience—are benchmarks against which others are judged. Likewise, as previously noted, Pottery Barn utilizes an integrated set of artists, designers, and buyers to create a largely "mail-order lifestyle" out of what used to be plain old home furnishings. Closer to home in the natural products arena, one finds the likes of Whole Foods, Wild Oats, and Trader Joe's all working toward a more complete lifestyle experience in the retail setting.

There has been a fundamental, progressive reorganization of the global economy, and part of this reorganization has had profound effects on the creation, design, production, merchandising, and consumption of goods. These changes are all-encompassing and impact many facets of the consumer world, including the natural products and services arena. These changes require a new orientation for marketers, one that stresses concepts such as lifestyles and product worlds over previous models of economic action based on more straightforward assessments of attitudes, opinions, values, and beliefs. In behavioral analysis of consumers, The Hartman Group's interest is to approach the world with a true lifestyle perspective informed by the ideas expressed above.

One of the key questions concerning the rise of the natural products and services market is whether or this represents simply a fad or a long-term trend. To properly address this question, we need to consider both individual and institutional factors. Social scientists use the term institution to describe a larger, social unit of analysis distinct from the individual, such as religion, law and family. This book seriously considers the relationship between the natural products consumer and the larger social world, where institutions are said to reside.

CHAPTER 2

Cultural Change

"And I just think that I took personal responsibility for my well-being. That was the big major point. [I] just said, 'You know what? If you want to do all this stuff, if you want to have an athletic body, if you want to do this, you want to have energy, you want to always look great, you want to look fresh—it starts from within.'"

—Female, 30s, New York

·•·

Interviewer: "What do you think is bringing you back into the natural products world?"

Respondent: "It's probably just more stress in my job or my life—life with a five-and-a-half year old—and [I'm] just trying to maintain my health, well-being and sanity."

—Female, 40s, San Francisco

·•·

"And after the treatment [chiropractic] I feel more invigorated . . . and again, I respect her. She doesn't tell me what to do. She kind of lays out alternatives, you know, diets, all this— 'You may want to walk, not run,'—I respect her."

—Male, 40s, San Francisco

*Interviewer: "It's interesting . . . you mentioned that your
other doctor told you what to do and it sounds like you don't
like it that much."*

*Consumer: "I'm tired of it. I am. I respect him a lot, I've
had him 20-something years, but now I'm starting to question
his method about treatment of the body."*

—Male, 50s, San Francisco

BACKGROUND

Our discussion of structural change in the previous chapter highlighted
changes in the organization of the economy and discussed the impacts
of those changes on consumption and production practices. By nature,
this economic approach emphasizes material processes and tends to de-
emphasize the role of cultural values and beliefs. This chapter brings
those values and beliefs back into the picture with an examination of
larger, cultural change and its intersection with the growth of the natural products industry.

We offer the following definition of culture: *Culture may be taken
as constituting the way of life of an entire society, and this will include
codes of manners, dress, language, rituals, symbols, norms, meanings,
beliefs, values and lifestyles.* Culture encompasses everything there is
to know about a given society. Additionally, culture is a *collective* phenomenon. While it certainly takes an assortment of *individuals* to produce culture, the end product remains analytically distinct from the
individual level of analysis. Thus, when people make witty observations regarding the differences between Americans and Canadians, they
rely on generalizations based on differences in culture. Since they are
generalizations based on collective properties—aggregations of attitudes,
beliefs, values and behaviors—it is not necessarily true that these observations apply to any particular individual. So as we examine elements of cultural change with specific applicability to the natural
products industry, remember that we are talking about a collective property of a society and not the specific attitudes, beliefs, and behaviors of
a subset of individuals. The German term *Zeitgeist* is useful in illustrat-
ing this point. While the literal translation is "time ghost," the more
applied meaning is "spirit of an era." In this sense we could think of
culture as capturing the "general mood, spirit and feeling of an era."

NATURAL PRODUCTS AND WELLNESS

The most consistent theme to emerge from The Hartman Group's collective body of consumer research—a theme that encompasses broader aspects of cultural change related to the natural products industry—is **wellness**. Hence, we use the term "wellness" to designate a cultural shift in the larger, social world favoring a general state of well-being across physical, emotional and spiritual dimensions. In their search for wellness, individuals come to participate—in varying degrees—in different segments of the natural products market. Often this participation takes the form of a lifestyle experience. The term **Natural Sensibility**™ represents an individual orientation to the pursuit of wellness which holds natural products and services—along with their accompanying lifestyle experiences—to be the appropriate course of action. In terms of broader cultural change, the move toward wellness frames much of the increased participation in purchasing and using natural products.[2]

We've identified three larger, societal-level factors driving the trend toward wellness, many directly related to the general evolution toward modernity:

- Generalized loss of control
- Compressed sense of time
- Increasing differentiation

Loss of Control

One of the distinguishing features of the modern condition is the large, impersonal, bureaucratic nature of social, economic and political institutions. Many recall the poignant image from Charlie Chaplin's classic film "Modern Times" (1936) in which Charlie, dressed in working-class garb, perches atop a giant gearwheel.[3] "Charlie's real enemies are no longer the Cop or the Boss, with whom he can always enter into some human relation, but a vast impersonality," argue Griffith, Mayer, and Bowser in *The Movies*.[4] Not surprisingly, consumers whom we interview often report a sense of alienation and frustration with the perceived unresponsiveness of larger institutions.

> **Culture may be taken as constituting the way of life of an entire society, and this will include codes of manners, dress, language, rituals, symbols, norms, meanings, beliefs, values and lifestyles.**

---

[2] *Natural Sensibility: A Study of America's Changing Culture and Lifestyle*, The Hartman Group, Fall 1998. See Appendix I.

[3] *Modern Times* (United Artists, 1936).

[4] Richard Griffith, Arthur Mayer, and Eileen Bowser, *The Movies* (New York: Simon and Schuster, 1981), pp. 67

In political circles, for example, many argue that the federal government has grown too large and is unresponsive to constituent interests. With regard to health care, many bemoan the demise of the traditional health care model (long-term, one-on-one doctor–patient relationships) which is rapidly being replaced with more impersonal, bureaucratic models (i.e. managed care). Consumers in the natural products arena respond proactively to this resulting sense of alienation and diminished control by pursuing wellness. In this view, the pursuit of physical, mental and emotional well-being is a means of wrenching control back from larger institutions—medicine, science, and regulatory agencies—and empowering the individual. For example, some consumers interviewed report that their interest in alternative health care is motivated, in part, by a desire to have a say in how their body is treated.

Note that the use of natural products as a way of regaining control over one's physical and emotional self is *not* contingent upon efficacy. So, for example, it is not necessary that a treatment (such as reflexology) or a regular maintenance plan (taking vitamin C) necessarily works. Simply engaging in these behaviors brings a regained sense of control to the individual.

Cultural anthropologists make a very similar argument, suggesting that the body is the last remaining part of the self that isn't yet under some form of institutional control in modern, Western societies. In this view, individuals participating in body-modification rituals—tattooing, piercing, scarification—attempt to reclaim part of their self from the larger institutional structure. Among other things, this implies that the recent popularity of tattooing and body piercing may not be a fad, but instead, a larger trend linked to the evolution of modernism.

Compressed Sense of Time

As we approach the millennium, time seems more compressed than at any previous point in world history. The rapid spread of information technology over the last twenty years has dramatically shortened project lengths, production schedules and deadlines. As little as twenty years ago, collective projects staged in separate cities were routinely delayed for several days by use of the U.S. Postal Service to transfer documents. Ten or so years ago, the fax machine closed up that time gap. Similar advancements with technologies such as electronic paging, cellular phones, electronic mail, and video conferencing—combined with the full-steam-ahead expansion of a truly global, capitalist economy—have left many the victims of a "time famine." Whereas workers in the industrial age could, at minimum, look forward to the factory's whistle as signaling the end of the workday, the workday for today's knowledge worker often has no clearly defined end.

Thus, consumers in the natural products arena pursue wellness as a coping strategy—as an antidote if you will—to the stress and hustle and bustle of the modern experience. In some cases, the pursuit of wellness is a holistic, all-encompassing strategy integrated into a lifestyle experience. In these scenarios consumers integrate natural products and services into many spheres of their daily life—alternative health care, proper nutrition, VMHS supplements—as a method of ensuring physical and emotional well-being.

Others utilize wellness as a concrete, pragmatic solution to the hectic pace of the modern work experience. Here the approach is less holistic and less ideologically driven. Instead, consumers turn to wellness because it "gets them through the day."

Once again, as discussed above with regard to issues of control, it isn't a requirement that participation in the natural products arena is an effective counter—in any objective sense—to the frenetic pace of the modern world. The mere pursuit of wellness may be, in and of itself, an effective counter measure.

Increasing Differentiation

The larger, macro-level changes in the organization of the economy discussed earlier have also played a significant role in the push for wellness. A host of material factors related to the organization of production—such as the spread of work process technologies, the evolution of information-technology systems, the accelerated speed of new consumer-product development, an increasing reliance on flexible-specialization processes, expanded retail channels and a truly global shipping infrastructure—have made highly specialized, differentiated products available to more consumers than at any previous point in U.S. history. Today, specialized, even customized niche-market products are the norm and not mere curiosities in the economic landscape. This shift is of fundamental importance for the pursuit of wellness.

Consumers in the natural products arena pursue wellness as a coping strategy—as an antidote if you will—to the stress and hustle and bustle of the modern experience.

One often unrecognized feature of differentiation and highly specialized niche markets is that they allow people to more easily come together, meet and interact in a lifestyle setting.

Twenty years ago, consumers seeking out natural products had few opportunities or alternatives. While there were pockets of swelling interest in the natural products arena—especially around the west coast and a smattering of college towns elsewhere—most found participation difficult, if not impossible. Today, natural products have become mainstream to the point that information, products and services are easily accessible in or near even the most remote geographic regions. The rising popularity of the Internet will likely assure that geographic barriers to participation all but disappear in the near future. Yet, while larger economic changes have facilitated the push for wellness through basic product and service availability, the story is largely incomplete without considering the cultural component.

One often unrecognized feature of differentiation and highly specialized niche markets is that they allow people to more easily come together, meet and interact in a lifestyle setting. These lifestyle settings become interpretive arenas centered on a specific product or product category and its associated methods(s) of consumption. In such worlds, people come to not only identify themselves, but also to promote the identities they adopt within the associated lifestyle world.[5] For example, it is difficult to find any shared, collective meaning around use of canned goods purchased from a supermarket. We could say the same of camping gear purchased at Sears. But consider highly specialized climbing gear found at Patagonia. Merely inquiring about such items brings one in contact with similar, like-minded people—and with mountaineering clubs, public demonstrations, climbing schools, etc.

The natural retailers Whole Foods Market and Wild Oats Markets provide landmark examples in the natural products market. The retailers' unique combination of high-quality specialty departments, information seminars, cooking demonstrations and community outreach programs have transformed traditional grocery retailing into a true lifestyle experience. Thus for many, the ability to even pursue wellness has been facilitated by the spread of highly differentiated, specialized, niche market products—in this case, products and services in the natural arena. This represents how changes in larger economic processes have helped propel a general cultural shift toward wellness.

---

[5] These insights arose from discussions with Gary Hamilton, Professor of Sociology at the University of Washington, and reflect current work in progress by Hamilton and his colleagues.

DEMOGRAPHIC CHANGES

As discussed in the introduction, the impact of the Baby Boom generation and their large-scale movement toward purchase and use of wellness products is part of the driving force behind the success of natural products and services. While certainly the children of the Baby Boom generation (the Baby Boomlet) are also an important second wave of natural consumers currently purchasing and using health and nutrition products, The Hartman Group now recognizes that there is extensive demand for environmentally enhanced or health and nutrition products and services at many age levels and demographic types. Alternative health services are being added at a rapid rate to traditional health service organizations based on demand from a wide range of consumer demographics. The American Association of Retired Persons (AARP) has gradually added more and more dietary supplements to supply demand from their enormous senior membership, and faddish elixirs and herbal tonic beverages are popular with teenagers.

Another development related to children is that they themselves are much more educated about health and the environment than ever before, and increasingly seem to be more influential in the grocery purchases their families make.

Another development related to children is that they themselves are much more educated about health and the environment than ever before, and increasingly seem to be more influential in the grocery purchases their families make. In focus groups conducted among elementary and junior high school classes in 1992, and in a survey among high-schoolers in 1993, The Hartman Group found that many children speak with their parents about making more environmentally-oriented purchasing choices, and some have gone as far as to replace items their mother had placed in the shopping cart. In more recent focus groups among pre-schoolers, The Hartman Group found that many of them are learning not only about recycling, but about more complex topics such as composting. Such early education in ecological and environmental issues points to large numbers of potential consumers seeking organic or other natural products in the years ahead.

CHAPTER 3

Natural Sensibility: Ideology, Authenticity and Experience

BACKGROUND

As mentioned previously, we use the term "wellness" to refer to a cultural shift in the larger social world that favors a general state of well-being across physical, emotional and spiritual dimensions. In the search for wellness, individual participation often takes the form of a *lifestyle experience*. The term Natural Sensibility™ represents an individual orientation to the pursuit of wellness that holds natural products and services—along with their accompanying lifestyle experiences—to be the appropriate course of action.

Natural Sensibility represents something more than an *individual* attitude, opinion, preference or value favoring natural products. It also takes seriously the set of lifestyle experiences related to participation in the natural products arena. To our knowledge, no other work has examined the role of lifestyle experiences in the natural products arena. We will discuss this topic in greater detail in Chapter 4 as we discuss five individual product worlds relevant to the natural products and services industry: vitamins, minerals, herbals and dietary supplements; alternative health care products and services; organic food and beverages; natural health and beauty aids; and natural household products. Below we discuss four key themes related to the Natural Sensibility.

IDEOLOGY

Ideology is a tough issue to tackle in the natural products arena. Clearly, some of the natural markets' founding entrepreneurs were driven by deeply held values, beliefs and ideologies. Likewise, some of the earliest adopters of natural products and services shared in these ideologies—be they political, spiritual, ecological, philosophical or otherwise. Today, these beliefs have diffused into the mainstream. The consumer base for natural products and services is becoming broader and more diffuse. Changes are underway in the larger organization of consumption and production processes. In short, it remains unclear how much consumer participation is directly related to ideological concerns.

We do know that while consumers will express interest in the ideological foundations of consumption practices, they rarely match that interest with behavior. Likewise, if we take our lifestyle-driven model seriously, we have reason to believe that ideology will fade into the background as consumers engage pragmatically in routine lifestyle experiences. An example from the world of leisure research nicely illustrates this point.

For many years, researchers examined wilderness hikers in an effort to deduce the meaning of a true wilderness experience. As one would predict, wilderness hikers have a long history of expressing—via attitudinal questions on survey instruments—deeply held values and ideologies favoring solitude, isolation in the wilderness, etc. Likewise, they are also the quickest to complain to park rangers and researchers about crowding and other detracting conditions on wilderness trails. What researchers didn't anticipate, however, was what they found when they left the confines of the laboratory and headed out on the trails to observe and interact directly with wilderness hikers. As it turns out, crowding per se isn't such an issue with wilderness hikers. While they express ideologies and values favoring isolation and solitude, these don't become an issue *so long as the wilderness hikers are around other people like themselves.* As long as they encounter other wilderness hikers of roughly the same age, ethnicity, and class, they don't report any conflict with their ideological commitment to isolation. In this manner, we suggest that for most consumers, a routine of lifestyle activity in a given product world quickly replaces the need for ideological commitment.

We do know that while consumers will *express interest* in ideological foundations to consumption practices, they rarely match that interest with behavior.

Frustrated by the predictability and uniformity of mass-produced goods and services of the industrial era . . . [natural product] consumers actively seek out alternatives, and the key differentiating factor for these alternatives is authenticity.

As long as the activity is routine, predictable, and patterned, there is never a need to relate ideology directly to behavior.

AUTHENTICITY

Extensive qualitative research conducted by The Hartman Group demonstrates that natural product consumers desire authenticity. Frustrated by the predictability and uniformity of mass-produced goods and services of the industrial era, these consumers actively seek out alternatives, and the key differentiating factor for these alternatives is authenticity. Some consumers, for example, find authenticity in the curious taste of Tom's of Maine toothpaste, suggesting "This is the way toothpaste is *supposed* to taste." Others find authenticity in the highly personalized, less bureaucratic nature of alternative health care. Finally, some consumers view natural products as "the real thing . . . the natural stuff." Whatever the case, these consumers are looking for authenticity, and they find it in the natural products arena. We will turn to this issue more concretely in later sections concerning branding strategies.

EXPERIENCE

One of the ironies of the modern condition is the degree to which consumers desire authentic experiences. As depicted in the film *City Slickers*,[6] people are willing to pay top dollar for the chance to engage in what most would consider grueling physical labor because the experience is seen as authentic. Compared to the perceived artificiality of the modern existence—where successes and failures are measured by tiny bits of electronic information—cattle drives, archeological digs, winemaking and gold mining all represent authentic experiences, within which people have the opportunity to show "who they really are." Often, authenticity and experience interact as mutually reinforcing processes. In fact, one of the key contributing factors to a legitimate lifestyle experience is authenticity.

---

[6] *City Slickers* (Columbia Pictures, 1991).

CHAPTER 4

Natural Product Worlds

*"I think some people are very fanatical about it . . . every-
thing that they have must be organically grown and everything
must be natural and they would never take a prescription drug
and they're vegetarian—they're quite serious. Then you have
people like myself who dabble in it and think it's a good thing
and there's good parts to it and there's bad parts to it. But I also
use Scott Tissue and I will eat a hamburger. I'm not a fanatic
about it."*

—Male, 40s, Chicago

*"Like a jigsaw puzzle—part of it I do, other parts I don't. I'll
lick butter off the floor of a movie theater . . . I have no morals
whatsoever when it comes to this. But I don't know—I've found
stuff with the organic, like Tom's of Maine, this organic toothpaste.
I always know people who go out and buy this Tom's of Maine—I
can't stand the stuff! It's like brushing with Vaseline. It's just awful.
I can't do it. So some of the stuff I don't like because it's flavorless
or tasteless or doesn't seem to perform the way this really good
flavored stuff does. . . . I find I choose this way for a variety of
reasons. I've never really thought of that. If I'm going for an environmentally sound world, you'd think I'd go all the way, but I don't!"*

—Male, 40s, Seattle

This chapter presents general observations regarding consumer involvement in five significant product worlds that The Hartman Group studies
within the natural products marketplace. These observations are based

on extensive ethnographic analyses of qualitative research data. In this case, the data include more than 800 hours of personal interviews with consumers in four regions of the U.S., as well as a series of supplementary focus groups held in significant metropolitan markets. These observations are meant to highlight the general culture and context within which consumers come to participate in the natural products marketplace.

WELLNESS AND PRODUCT WORLDS

One of the most interesting observations with regard to wellness and an accompanying Natural Sensibility is the relative scarcity of true, ideological converts. Many assume there is a core group of individuals, however small, who display ideological and behavioral commitment to what we now label Natural Sensibility. Besides actively participating in most, if not all, of the natural market's product and service categories, one would expect these people to offer detailed value- and ideology-driven explanations for their involvement in these product worlds. Instead, a very different picture emerges.

With some exceptions, most consumer participation in the natural products arena reflects a pragmatic, piecemeal approach, integrating natural products and services in some sectors of their lives and not others. Looking at the five product and service categories mentioned in Chapter 3—vitamins, minerals, herbals and dietary supplements (VMHS); alternative health care; organic foods; natural health and beauty aids; and natural household products—we found many consumers enter and exit from these worlds, participating more heavily in some arenas and not others. We use the term **product worlds** to refer to this type of selective participation.[7]

Movement within these product worlds is frequently not uniform—at times unpredictable—and often subject to other, more pragmatic concerns associated with the demands of everyday living (cost, availability, convenience, place, efficacy and other lifestyle issues). Few consumers appear to be heavily involved in all five categories.

---

[7] Per conversations with Professor Gary Hamilton, Department of Sociology, University of Washington.

Similarly, values and beliefs, while certainly present, don't seem to significantly drive participation and involvement in the natural products arena. While most consumers certainly express a larger concern for pro-natural values as part of the lifestyle associated with Natural Sensibility, many readily admit that these values and beliefs take a backseat to pragmatic, individual concerns.[8] Consider the following example regarding use of health and beauty aids:

> *"I have boughten [sic] Tom's toothpaste. But I don't buy it on a regular basis. I used to use Tom's toothpaste a lot, but I got kind of sick of the flavor. I like the fact that it is natural, but I didn't really like the flavor."*
>
> —Female, 40s, Seattle

This statement is an example of consumers putting pragmatic, self-interested concerns (e.g., taste preferences, delivery vehicle) ahead of values and ideology (e.g., "I like the fact that it's natural"). Simply put, this consumer didn't like the flavor or packaging of the toothpaste in question. When dealing with larger, societal level concerns—such as the impact of chemicals and phosphates on the environment—consumers indicated similar behavior patterns. They could acknowledge the importance of the issue, yet their behavior still reflected a pragmatic, self-interested approach to daily living:

> *"I considered buying the biodegradable detergents, just because I am concerned about the environment. But it's just so— it's harder to get, the access is harder, you have to go to the organic store, you can't just pick it up at the drugstore, it's more expensive, it doesn't smell as nice. I don't like putting toxic things in the earth—it's important, it really is—but I don't do it even though I know it's important."*
>
> —Female, 50s, New York

This sort of consumer behavior reflects the general mainstream acceptance of natural products and services. While broader audiences may indeed be sympathetic to pro-natural messages (emphasizing environmentally sound, promoting the wellness of the planet, etc.), they may not be

---

[8] Note, we don't suggest that values and beliefs have no relationship to consumer behavior. Rather, our evidence suggests that participation in natural product worlds *primarily* relates to pragmatic, self-interested concerns and lifestyle issues, and only secondarily relates to attitudes, beliefs and values.

willing to put forth the perceived extra effort to integrate these products into their everyday lifestyle. Put another way, as the natural market matures, marketers will have to promote appropriate branding messages while keeping a keen eye focused on consumer requirements such as quality, value, convenience, efficacy, and availability.

VITAMINS, MINERALS, HERBALS AND DIETARY SUPPLEMENTS (VMHS)

Interviewer: "Help me understand the difference [between Long's and GNC]. Why GNC?"

Consumer: "GNC specializes in supplements, vitamins, minerals, and I feel that I'm kind of leaving that up to them that they will only carry the best brands, brands that are safe, brands that are good brands."

—Male, 40s, San Francisco

"Echinacea . . . I learned about it through a friend who learned about it through someone else."

—Female, 40s, Seattle

"Well, I kind of look at the bottle and see what that says, but I may also look at whatever I'm getting my information from . . . magazine article or whatever. I take more chromium based on what the diabetic study did rather than what they say on the bottle."

—Female, 50s, Seattle

The world of vitamins, minerals, herbals and dietary supplements is far and away the most active product world in the natural products and services marketplace. In fact, 68 percent of American households take vitamins, while of this group a full 30 percent purchase herbals and dietary supplements.[9,10] We should, however, temper this observation with a note of caution: the traditional definition of the VMHS category

---

[9] *U.S. Consumer Use of Vitamins, Minerals, Herbals and Dietary Supplements: Phase I,* The Hartman Group, March 1998. See Appendix I.

[10] *Supplement Report,* The Hartman Group, Natural Products Census, 1998–1999

includes everything from standard multivitamins (e.g., Flintstones chewables, Centrum, One-a-day) to more recently popularized herbal supplements (e.g., kava kava, St. John's wort, echinacea).

Generally speaking, VMHS use is intrinsically a social activity for many consumers. VMHS users enjoy sharing information and swapping stories with friends, co-workers, and relatives regarding their VMHS participation. This sharing of information brings with it a certain amount of power and independence as consumers seek to take back a certain amount of personal control over health issues. These consumers devour information from all sources—popular media as well as academic research—and information tends to travel quickly across loose social networks. Additionally, the unusually social nature of activity within this product world creates a sense of shared purpose and meaning. As consumers come to more easily identify with the nature of the activity at hand, participation is reinforced through a lifestyle experience. When consumers are busy participating in this world (using products, sharing recommendations, swapping stories, etc.) a little bit of "who they are" gets tied up into this activity. As they move about their day, participation becomes a seamless, natural activity. This is the hallmark of a fully developed product world.

As consumers come to more easily identify with the nature of the activity at hand, participation is reinforced through a lifestyle experience.

Origins and Entry

Entry into the VMHS product world varies according to the nature of the product in question. In the case of vitamins and multivitamins, many take such products simply as part of their daily routine—a behavior they learned as a child (often from mom) and continued as they grew older. Some begin taking specific mineral supplements—such as folic acid or calcium—based on the advice of a health care professional or on the advice of information presented by the mass media.

Entry into the world of herbal and dietary supplements, however, proves very different. While there is no consistent pattern, most consumers purchase and use herbals and dietary supplements following the advice of friends, relatives, co-workers, magazine articles, books, television reports or some combination of these sources. Likewise, information regarding herbals and dietary supplements travels quickly through loose social networks of friends and relatives.

While some consumers are skeptical about herbal and dietary supplements in general, most appear willing to trust their friends as reliable information sources. Similarly, most consumers are reasonably trusting of information from popular magazines and network television programs. For currently popular herbal supplements such as echinacea and St. John's wort, many cite articles in *Time* or *Newsweek* as well as high-profile media events (network news stories, television newsmagazine segments, etc.) as notable sources of information drawing them into this world.

There does appear to be a noticeable segment who feel reasonably skeptical of information claims from the mass media. Yet rather than become disinterested, this group turns to more "authoritative" media sources such as *Prevention Magazine, Prescription for Health*, and *Life Extensions*.

Dosage and Efficacy

VMHS users demonstrate no clear pattern in terms of regulating dosage levels. The users most likely to follow dosage guidelines are typically introduced to the supplement in question by a trusted health care professional. In these instances, their usage is likely targeted to a specific problem (e.g., calcium deficiency) and they adhere to the recommended dosage levels quite closely. Other supplement users exceed dosage recommendations dramatically—sometimes four- or five-fold—based on the recommendations of friends and relatives. Occasionally, VMHS users justify this behavior with the belief that many herbal supplements are "flowers" and, thus, not as potentially harmful as other substances. Others experiment to find their own, unique, optimum dosage level. Even though some report negative effects from a recommended dosage that they felt was too high, most simply lower the dosage rather than cease taking the vitamin, mineral, herbal or dietary supplement.

Finally, while consumers are increasingly aware of the inconsistency between recommended dosage levels (per product labels as well as various information sources), this issue doesn't appear to contribute negatively to consumer involvement in these arenas. Consumers respond pragmatically by sharing experiences and information with each other and conducting their own "experiments" in order to achieve optimal dosage levels.

Concerning efficacy, we've been surprised in interviews by the number of consumers who continue to be actively involved in the VMHS world despite a lack of clear evidence that their VMHS regimen is in any way "effective." In these instances, participation is based as much on the added value of "peace of mind" as it is on concrete results. For these consumers, simply taking a VMHS product brings a sense of "peace of mind" which, in turn, makes them feel better. VMHS products are just one part of a healthy lifestyle for these people.

Purchasing Habits: Place and Place Branding

Consumer purchase and use of dietary supplements is still very much an emerging marketplace. As such, consumer purchasing habits are not yet solidified, leaving large, uncharted terrain for future branding efforts. While we will address branding themes—brand recognition, brand loyalty and brand recall—more concretely later in this book, we now examine a series of larger observations regarding the nature of consumer behavior in the context of place branding.

Fieldwork and interview data suggest that consumer behavior is, generally speaking, not centered around brand identity in the VMHS marketplace. Unlike the product worlds of, say, athletic footwear or soft drinks—where brand identity and brand equity figure prominently in the ordering of consumer behavior—consumers in the VMHS world are presently responding to other, larger forces. Specifically, consumers are much more likely to orient their activity around a *specific place* than they are a brand. In fact, we predict that this phenomenon, to which we apply the label "place branding," is crucial to any comprehensive understanding of consumer behavior in the natural products marketplace.

The role of place can take slightly different forms. For example, we find that many consumers unfamiliar with manufacturer's brands are quite familiar with store brands. An example is Trader Darwin, a line of VMHS products distributed and sold through Trader Joe's. Similarly, consumers are more likely to demonstrate allegiance to a specific retail outlet (e.g., Wal-Mart, Fred Meyer, Trader Joe's or Costco) than to a specific product. This phenomenon is indicative of the nature of lifestyle experiences in a product world centered on places. People move through lifestyle experiences and product worlds as they move through their day, so it is only logical that those places become significantly associated with consumption practices.

The Role of Place: Specialists, the Price-Conscious and the Lifestylers

This is a discussion of the culture and context within which consumers come to use natural products. We mention this because next we will introduce a three-part typology of VMHS consumers. While similar in nature to market-segmentation analyses based on survey instruments, this model is offered as a way of thinking about the VMHS consumer, and cannot necessarily be generalized to the larger consumer world. Later in this book we present other consumer segmentations on dietary supplement users. Those result from different studies.

Based on our sociological research and observation of consumer participation in the VMHS product world, consumers generally fall into three, sometimes mutually overlapping, categories: the Specialists, the Price-Conscious and the Lifestylers (see figure 4-1).

Figure 4-1. Distribution of the Specialists, the Price-Conscious and the Lifestylers

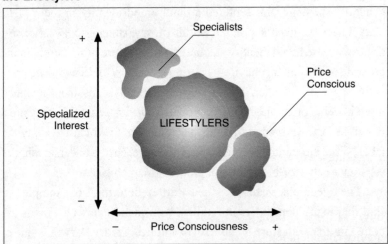

Source: *Natural Sensibility*, The Hartman Group, Fall 1998

Specialists demonstrate no consistent pattern of brand loyalty. They tend to leave that decision up to the buyers for assorted specialty stores such as The Vitamin Shoppe or GNC. These consumers generally take their involvement in the VMHS product world more seriously and prefer to utilize the assistance of store personnel to guide their decisions. The Specialists appear to be smallest in number and some are currently migrating to larger, specialty retailers such as Whole Foods and Trader Joe's (an issue we will address later).

As one might surmise, the **Price-Conscious** express most concern with cost. Perhaps most important, they don't associate the best prices with specific brands, but with specific *places*. While Costco and Trader Joe's lead the pack, many consumers cite local and national drug retailers such as Fred Meyer, Wal-Mart, Rite Aid and Walgreen's. Consumers in this group tend to view products within specific VMHS categories (such as ginseng) as "all the same" and most show no apparent interest in brands. As one consumer suggests regarding his first purchase of St. John's wort:

> *"Well, this was the first time I ever took it, so I looked at the biggest bottle at the cheapest price. I think I went to one of those places . . . I don't know . . . like a Wal-Mart, a drug-store sort of chain . . . St. John's wort is St. John's wort."*
> —Male, 30s, Seattle

Some in the Price-Conscious category also include trust as a relevant factor—in this case, the trust of branded, national chains to offer a safe product at a competitive price. For example:

> Consumer: *"It's important because I know—I trust—Walgreen's. A big chain like that. I don't know if I'd go to a store in Chinatown and pick random vitamins in a bag just to save money. [Walgreen's is] a store, a reputable store, and I save money."*
> —Female, 40s, San Francisco

Finally, we refer to our third—and largest—category as Lifestylers. By using the term Lifestylers we suggest that these consumers integrate VMHS products into their routine lifestyle experiences. In essence, they buy VMHS products at specific locations not due primarily to price or quality considerations, but because they find themselves at these locations as part of their day-to-day lifestyle. Let's consider the following excerpts:

> *Interviewer: "Do you remember what brand it is you buy?"*
> *Consumer: "It's the Trader Joe's brand."*
> *Interviewer: "Why that brand?"*
> *Consumer: "I don't think there's that much difference. And it's an excuse to go to Trader Joe's and buy it!"*
> —Male, 40s, San Francisco

Convenience and price undoubtedly remain significant features of a lifestyle experience. We cannot overstate the importance of the ability of a given consumer to visit a single retail destination and find most of the products that accompany his or her lifestyle—at reasonable prices.

Note carefully the last phrase: "It's an excuse to go to Trader Joe's and buy it!" *This is the essence of what we refer to as a lifestyle experience*—as if "going to Trader Joe's" supersedes the need for a specific product.

Whereas a few years ago, it might have taken several trips to specialty retailers to satisfy cooking, personal health, and VMHS needs, one can now find everything in one place. Convenience and price undoubtedly remain significant features of a lifestyle experience. We cannot overstate the importance of the ability of a given consumer to visit a single retail destination and find most of the products that accompany his or her lifestyle—at reasonable prices:

> *Interviewer: "And a while back you say you'd go to the health food stores? What made you shift [to Trader Joe's]?"*
> *Consumer: "Well, one of the things is price and sometimes it's just convenience. Whichever place I'm at first when I need it, and I seem to go to Trader Joe's a lot, so I tend to get them there if I'm there. I noticed over the last year I've been getting most of my stuff there."*
> —Male, 30s, Seattle

The previous excerpt also highlights a final pattern among many consumers. Increasingly, retail environments geared toward the Lifestylers are broadening their appeal and, in the process, capturing rising numbers of consumers from the Specialist and Price-Conscious sectors. Consider the following excerpt:

> *Consumer: "You know, I think I've been getting that [gingko] at Trader Joe's too."*
> *Interviewer: "Is that where you go for..."*
> *Consumer: "Actually recently I've been going there, yeah, I've been going there a lot. I used to go to the health food stores, but I tend to get a lot of stuff now at Trader Joe's because I think they're sort of on top of whatever the media says is good, so they keep coming out with the same stuff. Because a couple of years ago you couldn't get omega-3 fish oil there, but now you can get all the stuff that I guess is sort of 'in' for people to take. So whoever is doing their marketing I guess is doing a good job!"*
> —Male, 40s, Seattle

We found similar patterns as we moved from specialty retailers such as GNC to general, discount retailers such as Fred Meyer.

> *"I went to the health food stores initially. I guess I hadn't been into buying things like that [echinacea], I didn't know you could get things like that [echinacea] at Fred Meyer at all. And I just bought a small bottle at the health food store at Crossroads. And then when I needed more, I just happened to notice that Fred Meyer had it . . . it was quite a bit cheaper, and I'm always there for other stuff, so I got it there."*
>
> —Female, 50s, Seattle

We see repeated evidence that Specialists have begun to migrate in the direction of lifestyle-oriented retail environments. We predict this trend will only continue as specialty retailers such as GNC face stiff competition on lifestyle fronts from the likes of Whole Foods, Costco, and Fred Meyer.

As in the excerpts above, we see repeated evidence that Specialists have begun to migrate in the direction of lifestyle-oriented retail environments. We predict this trend will only continue as specialty retailers such as GNC face stiff competition on lifestyle fronts from the likes of Whole Foods, Costco, and Fred Meyer. Current research conducted by The Hartman Group seeks to identify which types of people become Lifestylers—that is, how and why they come to purchase in this fashion. Answers to these questions would yield insights into the potential growth of lifestyle/experience retail environments.

Observations and Insights

Brand managers and marketers face a unique set of challenges selling vitamins, minerals, herbals and dietary supplements to the American consumer. Probably the most daunting task—as detailed above—lies in reconciling the role of place and the power of the retail shopping environment with typical elements of a successful branding strategy.

The Hartman Group has observed that consumers appear to pay more attention to the retail environment than the brand largely because many tend to view the actual vitamin, mineral, herbal or dietary supplement ingredients as brands in and of themselves. Just as many consumers would be hard pressed to identify the brand of lettuce or peaches they buy, most cannot identify the brands of VMHS products. Consider the following examples:

*"It's [the bottle of gingko] got a green top on it but I usu-
ally don't look at the brands actually. Because you sort of look
for the supplement and I never look at the brand."*

—Female, 40s, San Francisco

·—·

"The brand actually is the ingredients that you look at."

—Male, 40s, San Francisco

These comments mirror those of many consumers we've interviewed
and reflect the general state of brand recognition in the VMHS product
world. As we know from past successes in such scenarios—such as
Sunkist in produce—branding is still possible. We found two points of
consideration that should assist marketers in these efforts.

1. Delivery Format—In interviews, consumers refer to the difficulty involved in swallowing supplements in the form of pills or
   tablets. These consumers actively pursue brands that offer supplements in the form of smaller caplets (ideally) or capsules. The
   standard-size gelatin capsules utilized in most herbal supplements
   are seen by many as too large and too quick to dissolve in the
   throat.

2. Recommended Dosage—Consumers mention that when choosing between brands they opt for the brand whose recommended
   dosage requires fewer pills simply because they dislike taking
   large numbers of pills. These consumers never make any mention of dosage levels in milligrams, standardized extracts, or
   efficacy. Instead, they simply dislike taking numerous pills.

ALTERNATIVE HEALTH CARE

*Consumer: "He's an Eastern-style physician, he does acu-
puncture, I presume. He gives me these herbs. . . . His little tool
kit is different than a westerner's tool kit. His remedies are different too. Instead of giving you a shot of penicillin or something like that, he gives you these herbs. So it's a parallel medical
universe, if you will, using different tools. You know, if you folks
had called me a month earlier I wouldn't know any of this stuff.
And I had this experience and it's not because I'm in the mood
to have an alternative medicine experience, it's because I hold*

my arm—he says gallbladder—boing! And I said, wow, that's interesting, what was that? And you would too. Anybody would."
—Female, 30s, Chicago

.◆.

"Something I was very impressed with and indicated to me that it's not as far out of the mainstream as maybe it was a few years ago, from my perception, which tends to be somewhat conservative, is that I went up to North Western Memorial which I consider to be probably as fine or finer than any other hospital in the country, and I went up for a flu shot to one of their satellite things, and there was a very interesting doctor there, a woman, who told me they were opening a Western style and alternative medicine clinic, side by side, so that you could have both."
—Female, 30s, Chicago

.◆.

"Like I was saying before, I think there's a real place in our society for—I think it's real important to combine the traditional medicine world with chiropractic—like going to a chiropractor, doing massage therapy, and I think that there are just a lot of benefits. A chiropractor isn't going to be who I go to if I think I'm having appendicitis. But I think it's real important to look for the most non-invasive solution to a problem and oftentimes I think doctors are real ready to do surgery. And it's not necessary."
—Female, 40s, Seattle

Much like the dietary supplement world, alternative health care[11] is currently experiencing tremendous growth. The Hartman Group's *Integrated Health Care* study conducted in late 1998 shows that 86 percent of U.S. households have utilized some form of alternative health care. The results from our sociological interviews suggest a very similar picture. A strong majority of the consumers interviewed participated in at least some form of alternative health care, and most are quite familiar with the assorted healing practices falling under this rubric. Many are regular users, and a few even utilized these resources for their children and pets! Finally, only a very small number express no interest at all in alternative medicine.

Participation in the alternative medicine product world appears less ideological and more experience-driven than expected.

---

[11] Since there is currently some debate over the correct terminology used to refer to "non-conventional" forms of medicine we use the terminology our respondents favored.

Consumers usually find one or two methods and practitioners they trust and tend to stick with them. This further highlights the current power of word-of-mouth referrals in alternative health care arenas.

Many consumers interviewed consider participation within the world of alternative health care crucial to the pursuit of wellness. For many, alternative health care practitioners provide consumers with a source of much-needed relief from problems for which, in their views, "conventional medicine offers no solutions." Although such health concerns vary in both scope and intensity, the most common include chronic conditions such as pain, asthma, stress, arthritis and allergies. Participation in the alternative medicine product world appears less ideological and more experience-driven than expected. While many respondents express frustrations with the over-all philosophy of the conventional medical approach, few express a deep ideological concern or commitment to a specific form of medicine—alternative or otherwise. Finally, most consumers favor a true integration of conventional and alternative medicines in their pursuit of wellness.

Origins and Entry

Consumers come to utilize the services of alternative health care practitioners through a variety of informal channels, including adult education seminars, magazine articles, word-of-mouth, physician referrals, advice of co-workers and advice of family members. Of these, word-of-mouth from family members and trusted friends plays the most significant role in bringing consumers into the world of alternative health care. For some, this occurs in a straightforward, pragmatic manner—discussions with friends concerning success with a perceived "unusual" or "new" form of health care treatment. In these scenarios, alternative health care often enjoys a honeymoon status—consumers tend to express less criticism of alternative health care than of the established, institutionalized practices of conventional medicine. For others, word-of-mouth testimonials and referrals resemble the fervor of a religious revival. These consumers report learning of alternative medicine through friends who had undergone powerful, transformative, life-changing experiences which they attribute to alternative medicine.

For consumers expressing no interest in alternative health care, most of their disinterest appears agnostic (e.g., don't need any health care) rather than antagonistic (e.g., alternative health care is inferior to western medicine) in nature. Finally, once drawn into the world of alternative health care, consumers appear to have little trouble moving from one branch of medicine to another.

As suggested above, most consumers have no real antagonistic or oppositional feelings toward alternative health care. In fact, the two significant barriers that inhibit further participation—lack of insurance coverage and industry regulation—are most often mentioned by those already active in the alternative health care arena. The former should come as no surprise and probably needs little discussion. In short, consumers say they would be much more likely to utilize the services of an alternative health care practitioner if such services were covered by their insurance plan. Even more intriguing, *most* of the consumers we have interviewed who use the services of an alternative health care practitioner on a regular basis do so without the help of an insurance plan that covers these services.

Consumers haven't abandoned their conventional, managed-care facilities and physicians. Instead, they appear to integrate alternative practitioners where they perceive the most efficacy (holistic care, long-term well-being, chronic conditions) and retain conventional medical professionals for more serious, acute care.

The perceived lack of regulatory power over most of the alternative health care industry also serves as a barrier to extended participation. In general, alternative health care consumers express awareness that some practitioners "could be practicing quackery" and feel the assorted professional designations, regulatory bodies and licensing agencies appear less credible in the world of alternative medicine. Generally, these concerns tend to *inhibit* rather than *prohibit* participation—consumers usually find one or two methods and practitioners they trust and tend to stick with them. This further highlights the current power of word-of-mouth referrals in alternative health care arenas.

Specific Themes in Alternative Health Care Use

The following sections bring together several loosely connected themes we see running through consumer involvement in alternative medicine. Increasingly, consumer attitudes and behavior appear to be reflecting a more general, cultural frustration with the nature and efficacy of the current U.S. health care system. Consumers specifically report dissatisfaction with the impersonal, bureaucratic nature of managed-care systems. Likewise, they're equally frustrated with the *perceived* arrogance of conventional health care professionals, especially when faced with a host of chronic conditions—such as colds, asthma, allergies, arthritis, and stress—for which Western medicine appears incapable of offering any long-term

**Consumers appear
less interested in
the ideas and
philosophy behind
the experience
than they are
the outcomes.**

solutions. We should add that, dismay and frustrations aside, consumers **haven't** abandoned their conventional, managed-care facilities and physicians. Instead, they appear to integrate alternative health care practitioners where they perceive the most efficacy (holistic care, long-term well-being, chronic conditions) and retain conventional medical professionals for more serious, acute care.

Experience

Curiosity regarding the *experience* of alternative medicine rates highly among the factors engaging consumers in the world of alternative health care. For many, visiting an alternative health care practitioner is "something new," "exciting" and "interesting." Most important, the interaction appears more personal—especially in lieu of recent changes in the nature of managed care. Finally, consumers appear less interested in the ideas and philosophy behind the experience than the outcomes. The following conversation exemplifies this thread:

> Respondent: *"Well, it's an experience that you probably haven't had before. . . . I have no idea what it means, but I know that the experience happened and I know that Western-style medicine doesn't give you experiences like that. So do I think there's something—in addition to the 5,000 years of history— do I think there's something to it? Yeah. Do I know how it works? No. Does it matter? I don't know how penicillin works either."*
> —Female, 30s, Chicago

Here the experience and results clearly take center stage to ideas and philosophies. After the consumer openly admits that she has no real idea how acupuncture works, she reflects critically on the foundations of Western medicine.

Pragmatism and Frustrations with Conventional Medicine

Here we consider a most significant finding in our sociological studies of alternative health care: Many consumers turn to this approach simply because conventional treatments fail to prove effective. Indeed, a key factor directing new patients toward naturopaths and acupuncturists is the general inability of the conventional medical community to provide consistent relief from allergy and asthma-related symptoms. Again, these decisions seemed motivated out of a desire for "something that works" rather than a conscious rejection of conventional ideals and philosophies. In fact, many alternative health care consumers initially seek the help of conventional medical professionals, yet eventually turn to alternative practitioners when conventional solutions prove ineffective.

Of course, the issue of efficacy is quite complex. One of the facets of wellness that we alluded to earlier is that efficacy cannot always be measured in clear-cut, objective terms. Sometimes simply visiting an alternative health care specialist provides a regained sense of control or spirit. Positivistic thinking in conventional medicine would likely explain this phenomenon by pointing to "the placebo effect" and get on with the business at hand—measuring efficacy with traditional "objective" measures. We contend that the world of alternative health care would benefit substantially from future research into this curious notion of efficacy. Specifically, these efforts should not start with the a priori notion that efficacy is an objective, measurable construct. Instead, we should take all accounts of efficacy seriously—positivistic, constructed, imaginary, and/or otherwise.

Many alternative health care consumers initially seek the help of conventional medical professionals, yet eventually turn to alternative practitioners when conventional solutions prove ineffective.

Ideology (lack thereof)

Keeping on the theme of pragmatism, many consumers appear uninterested in the philosophical underpinnings or logic behind the specific course of alternative health care treatment. Instead, they just acknowledge that "it seems to work." This is especially relevant to current discussions regarding the increased popularity of alternative health care among U.S. consumers. For example, some critics suggest the American Medical Association has for years ignored "alternative" medicine practices out of a belief that Americans would never come to understand or embrace the foundations and philosophies underlying these approaches. Our evidence suggests that this isn't a significant hurdle for most consumers. As long as alternative health practitioners can make good on their claims, consumers aren't particularly interested in getting to the bottom of "how things work." Thus, it appears that professions such as science and medicine are beginning to lose some element of jurisdictional control as consumers are increasingly disinterested and unimpressed by the positivistic nature of western scientific claims.

Consumers seek a harmonious balance between conventional medicine and alternative health care.

Integration

Not coincidentally, consumers seek a harmonious balance between conventional medicine and alternative health care. They recognize that conventional practitioners have their "place" right beside alternative practitioners. Just as it is important to choose the "right tool for the job," consumers understand that some practitioners are appropriate for some treatment regimens and not others. This is a powerful, consistent statement voiced by many.

ORGANIC FOODS AND BEVERAGES

> *Respondent: "Well, I don't drive. I live in the city and I work in the city so for me to go to a Whole Foods store is a big hassle. But if for example I were visiting somebody in the suburbs and buying food and [they were] giving me a ride home or something, I'd go into a Whole Foods store, it would be great. I'd prefer to do shopping there. I like this organic foods notion."*
> —Female, 40s, San Francisco

> *"I picture something organically grown, it's in your backyard in a garden, you're obviously not using pesticides, it's not highly processed foods. It's like you got out and you just pick it out of the garden. But I can't really believe that really and truly happens in a grocery store. But it may."*
> —Female, 30s, Seattle

> *"I should start using organic foods because I know pesticides are bad and all. But it's kind of a pain . . . if I'm at the Cali-Foods up the road, why should I go to another store to get organic produce—it's just kind of inconvenient to go get them."*
> —Female, 40s, San Francisco

Based on sociological interviews, the organic food and beverage product world lies somewhere in the middle in terms of natural product consumer activity. While the VMHS and alternative health care product worlds carry significant consumer participation, only a slight majority of consumers are engaged in a pattern of regular purchase and use of organic foods and beverages. As one Hartman Group analyst has suggested, consumer interest, knowledge, and behavior within this world resembles a "most confusing hodgepodge." Likewise, of the five product worlds detailed in our sociological studies, the world of organic foods was far and away the most chaotic, muddled, and fragmented.

To generalize, consumers appear reasonably interested in the idea of organic foods. Put into practice, however, this interest does not always correlate with behavior. Some of the most important issues yet to be resolved include availability, cost, definition, quality, appearance, and flavor. Most consumers operate as part-time participants in the organic foods product world. Some purchase organic foods only occasionally when they happen to be in their favorite retail destination for such goods, while others chose organic only in certain categories, such as fruits and root vegetables. Few consumers use organic foods exclusively.

Consumers appear reasonably interested in the idea of organic foods. Put into practice, however, this interest does not always correlate with behavior.

Origins, Entry and Barriers

For most consumers, introduction to the world of organic foods is an easily accomplished task. Simply shopping in many retail grocery stores exposes the consumer to a varied selection of organic foods. Likewise, articles and sound-bites in the mainstream media familiarize consumers with organic product offerings. Few consumers report learning about the organic category from friends or word-of-mouth; people don't talk about organic foods as they do alternative health care and VMHS use. While exposure is easily accomplished, consistent retention isn't. In this product world, the barriers to sustained activity include cost, availability and quality.

Cost

The perceived cost difference between regular and organic produce far and away poses the most significant barrier to regular, continued participation within this product world. While many in the industry are keenly aware of this, we remain baffled by the wide range of perceived price differences cited by consumers. Few consumers can offer concrete examples, and many estimate costs that show their inaccurate perceptions of the price differential. Note the unusual math in the following examples from personal interviews:

Consumer: "I would like to eat more organic, but it's the cost frankly. Doesn't seem to be worth the price for what they're charging . . . I know it's a little more costly, but it doesn't justify the price they're charging."

Interviewer: "Just as an example, how much do the prices vary between the organic and non-organic?"

Consumer: "I would say the organic seems to be twice as much. Fifty percent more, sometimes twice, sometimes three times. I don't feel like I'm a fanatic about eating that healthy, you know, try to get fresh vegetables, but probably if I was making more money I would probably go for it. But I don't have that expendable income."

—Male, 40s, Seattle

·◆·

Interviewer: "So you said you'd really be there if it weren't for money. Now how much more expensive is buying organic food versus the regular food? Is there a big difference?"

Consumer: "A little less than half. I mean it's almost half, it's expensive but not quite. What is that, a fourth? Yeah, it's a lot more expensive."

—Female, 40s, New York

·◆·

Consumer: "Oh, if it were the same price I'd probably lean toward it. I mean, why not?"

Interviewer: "Price isn't worth it?"

Consumer: "That's the dramatic part, if you ask me, is how much the cost difference is. Like four tomatoes at eight dollars versus four tomatoes at two bucks or whatever . . . it's 50 percent cheaper."

—Female, 50s, Chicago

We highlight these three examples not to poke fun at consumers' math skills—or lack thereof. Rather, we want to suggest just how much of the price difference is perceptual rather than objective. We are not suggesting that there are no price differences, merely that the perceived difference and the objective difference are likely two very different numbers. This suggests that marketers and merchandisers in the organic foods arena must contend with a widespread perceived notion of large price differentials.

Future efforts aimed at reducing barriers to participation will want to consider *perceived*, as well as *objective*, price differences. Some consumers acknowledge that the perceived additional cost is negligible given their income level, but explain they object in principle.

Availability

At the most basic level, many consumers who express an interest in organic foods also admit that they often bypass this option based on problems with availability. Many resist consistently visiting an extra store in order to obtain organic foods.

This barrier will certainly prove less significant in the future with the continued expansion of upscale retail specialty chains such as Whole Foods and Wild Oats, and as more and more conventional supermarkets add organics to their shelves.

Quality

Organic foods still suffer from the consumer *perception* that they are somehow inferior in quality to standard offerings. This perception remains a significant barrier to participation in this product world and can take several different forms, as illustrated below:

> *"Organic vegetables in general don't look as good to me as the other ones [laughs]. So I'm seldom tempted when I look at the fresh vegetables."*
>
> —Female, 20s, New York

> *"Organic, though, is different. One time a girlfriend had bought some organic broccoli and we had steamed it and were eating it and all of a sudden I looked into the broccoli and noticed all these dead bugs. Yeah, it's great that they don't use chemicals, but I don't want bugs in my vegetables. Ever since then I've never bought organic vegetables or anything like that. I'm not stupid."*
>
> —Male, 30s, Seattle

In the first example, the consumer echoes a common consumer complaint that organic foods "don't look as good." The second, however, notes a more dramatic complaint—he worries that organic foods might contain bugs, presumably from the failure to use pesticides.

Three Key Themes: Definition; Pragmatism, Place and Lifestyle; and Flavors

Definition

The world of organic food, and the organic industry in general, has historically been plagued by a lack of public consensus on the definition of "organic." In addition, consumers appear confused about the possible "wellness" benefits derived from participation in the organic foods product world. Part of this confusion stems from definition problems. Most describe organic foods as being "pesticide free," but consumers have, at best, a hazy perception of organic definitions. In our many interviews with consumers, we have found that the label organic appears to signify a broad array of meanings—everything from "pesticide-free" to "home grown" to "healthy" to "tasty," and even to "using incense(!)"

It remains clear that most consumers identify organic products as "pesticide free." Since the definition of the term "organic" is much more complex, such discrepancies must be resolved before consumers can derive any coherent meaning or message within this product world.

Definitional disputes still plague the organic industry. Many in the industry would argue that certain natural pesticides and chemicals are allowable under the organic standard. There are even organic experts who have argued that some natural pesticides may be worse for the environment than some of the synthetic ones used in conventional agriculture. Other points of serious contention relate to the use of biotechnology in the form of genetically modified organisms, and what the certification process must include in order to be legitimate.

A key implication of the organic industry's definitional debate is that if the controversy were communicated to average consumers, deep confusion and even distrust could result. In effect, the positive aura surrounding the "organic" identity in the minds of consumers could easily be put at risk if industry disputes over the definition became widely known among consumers.

Another key issue is corporate greenwashing. This occurs when a company claims that critical components of a product or service are "natural" or produced with environmentally friendly methods, when in actuality there's little that's sustainable or natural about the product or the production method.

In the natural market, and in the certification of products ranging from organic food to sustainably produced timber, this is an important issue because any company can state on packaging or elsewhere that their product is "organic," "natural" or "sustainably produced." Without an agreed-upon definition for terms such as "organic" or "sustainably produced—and without a certification system to ensure products making these claims fit the definition—the claims lose value and consumer confusion and distrust can result. Greenwashing dilutes consumer opinion and belief in products and services that actually are "green."

Co-op America, a nonprofit group in Washington, DC, works to identify corporate members of a wide variety that it views to be legitimately "green" and then helps promote these companies to consumers as environmentally sound choices. This type of effort helps consumers gain confidence in claims made by companies about their products or processes.

Pragmatism, Place and Lifestyle

As a set, three related factors—pragmatism, place and lifestyle—combine to frame much of the participation in the organic foods product world. Many consumers participate on a part-time basis out of self-interested, pragmatic concerns. While many of these consumers speak of a strong preference for organic foods, they also willingly admit their behavior doesn't always follow their beliefs. Some refer to their behavior with adjectives such as "ignorant" or "irrational," yet offer perfectly logical explanations. In the following examples, the first consumer simply doesn't like the "bruised appearance" of organic produce. In the second, the consumer refuses to buy organic potatoes and onions because they are "too heavy" to carry.

> *"The other stuff looks better. I mean most organic fruit and vegetables are bruised . . . which is a terrible reason. . . . I'm being very honest with you, I know what I'm saying is very ignorant—because I know that being bruised means nothing and they're healthy, but I'm being honest with you—when it looks good, I tend to choose that perfect piece of fruit. I'm very good at fruit picking. But I probably would be much better if I chose the organic one, even though I don't always."*
>
> —Female, 40s, New York

> *Interviewer: "Are there any vegetables that you don't buy organic?"*
>
> *Consumer: "Oh, potatoes sometimes. Potatoes and onions and stuff like that. Because they're heavy to carry and sometimes I have to go on the bus, I try to buy them someplace close [to where I live]. I know it's totally irrational, but it's just practical. And I don't eat them as much as I eat some of the others."*
>
> —Female, 30s, San Francisco

Pragmatism blends into place as a significant factor affecting regular participation in the organic foods product world, especially in terms of the location and availability of specialty grocers like Whole Foods and Wild Oats. Here place appears branded in much the same way as retail destinations in the VMHS world. In these cases, Whole Foods has practically become synonymous with the idea of organic foods, and many consumers suggest that their participation is related directly to their proximity to a Whole Foods location.

Thus, pragmatism and the retail purchase location combine to create the lifestyle that organic consumers—whether in an experimental or a dedicated manner—seek to create as they purchase and use organic products.

Flavors

A fair number of consumers report that their use of organic foods stems from larger interests in food and flavors. These individuals aren't concerned with wellness per se, but instead, appear driven mainly by personal interests in finding the best-tasting foods available. Because they consider flavor their primary motivation, consistent participation within this world cannot be ensured.

Summary and Branding Strategies

Consumers favor the *idea* of organic foods, but aren't motivated enough to purchase them consistently or to feel particularly strong connections to them. This behavior most likely results from the mixed messages they encounter regarding the meaning and characteristics of organic foods. Consumers do, however, appear a bit more consistent in their purchasing behavior of organics when they're aware that the store they frequent sells organic products. This suggests that future work on branding, product development and related issues should consider the intersection between retail experience and organic foods as a fruitful focus for research.

NATURAL HEALTH AND BEAUTY AIDS

"Tom's of Maine—this organic toothpaste—I always know people who go out and buy this Tom's of Maine, 'it's the best toothpaste'—I can't stand the stuff! It's like brushing with Vaseline."

—Male, 40s, Seattle

·◆·

"My sister-in-law—we were staying at their house and I didn't pack toothpaste, she said, 'this is all I have.' I said, 'Oh, Jill!' But I actually really liked it. It was like cinnamon, too. It was like the most bizarre flavor, but I really liked it. We couldn't get it here for a long time, so every time we'd see her, she'd bring us some toothpaste."

—Female, 30s, Chicago

·◆·

"Most of the time I'll just be looking for certain products in a place I like and I'll see a display that advertises something about eye care products or something, so I'll read the directions on it or the description and it just sounds really good. Maybe they're having a sale. That's what draws my attention. . . . So I'll go over there and take a look at it. Maybe I'll try this, especially if it's on sale. Give it a try and see if it works."

—Female, 30s, Seattle

Consumers do . . . appear a bit more consistent in their purchasing behavior of organics when they're aware that the store they frequent sells organic products.

Consumers participate in the natural health and beauty aid (HABA) product world tentatively and infrequently. Few consumers report regular, active participation in this arena and this may be due, in part, to a lack of clear definition of these products. From our sociological research it is also clear that most consumers tend to view the "natural" attributes of natural health and beauty aids secondary in importance to those of products designed for internal consumption (VMHS and organic foods) or health maintenance (alternative health care). Brand recognition and loyalty here is weak, with the notable exception of Body Shop personal care products and Tom's of Maine toothpaste. Interestingly, this is the sole product world that demonstrates clearly gendered participation—females are much more active in this world than males.

Origins, Entry and Barriers

Consumers became active in the natural HABA product world through word of mouth, store displays, general product availability or some combination thereof. For many, the decision to purchase these products often reflects a general lifestyle orientation rather than a conscious, ideologically driven decision. We stress *usually*, because this is the single product world in which ideology does play an occasional, yet none-the-less-significant, role in guiding consumer behavior. Specifically, there is a small, core group of consumers—most frequently women—who support natural HABA products because they "aren't tested on animals." The following consumers' narratives are typical of this group:

> *Interviewer: "Do you think they're [natural HABA products] better for you?"*
> *Consumer: "Well, I assume they probably are in some cases . . . also they were some of the first ones to market non-animal-tested products."*
> *Interviewer: "And that was important."*
> *Consumer: "Oh yeah, that was really important to me."*
> —Female, 40s, San Francisco

In the example above, efficacy is no more important than the status of "non-animal-tested." Others express concern with the animal-testing status, yet with a more pragmatic approach:

> *"Yeah, I try to use things that are fairly 'natural.' if I can. And I especially try to use things that are not tested on animals. So I use some products from the Body Shop, which tends to have a lot of natural stuff, and some other things I get again at the health food stores. They usually have a very good line of cosmetics and soaps."*
> —Female, 50s, San Francisco

Even in the above example, the consumer tends to use natural HABA products "when she can" and drifts between health food stores and the Body Shop. This pragmatic, practical, approach characterized the majority of participation in the HABA product world.

Finally, one of the problems confronting this sector of the natural products arena is the lack of a clear definition. Consumers often express confusion as to what qualifies as a natural health and beauty aid. For example, many struggle with the idea that Clairol's line of Herbal Essence shampoos obviously has something to do with herbs—which are supposed to be natural—but most also realize that these shampoos probably don't fit under the heading "natural products."[12] When consumers are unsure of boundaries and definitions, the experience fails to resemble that of a product world. Instead, the experience is reminiscent of merely "shopping for product." In such a scenario, all the assorted factors that combine to activate consumer interest in participation within the product world—sharing knowledge, doing research, gaining control, the search for wellness, etc.—fail to materialize, resulting in little repetitive involvement.

Consumers often express confusion as to what qualifies as a natural health and beauty aid.

Branding: Differentiation, Tom's of Maine and Beyond

Brand managers in the natural HABA segment face a particularly daunting task. In addition to the pragmatic, "pick-and-choose, here-and-there" behavior we've noted above, many consumers *consciously* change products and/or brands on a regular basis out of the belief that this promotes healthy skin and/or hair.

Lest we sound too pessimistic, there is one notable success story here: Tom's of Maine. Without a doubt, many consumers view Tom's of Maine as synonymous with natural HABA products. In fact, this is so much the case that when prompted on their use of natural health care products, many respond with questions along the lines of "Oh, you mean like Tom's of Maine?" So, what's their secret?

From our discussions with consumers it became evident that the most significant factor driving brand recognition of Tom's of Maine toothpaste is the curious taste. Some consumers are regular users, but most aren't. Yet practically *everyone* has tried Tom's of Maine and has an opinion on "the most curious toothpaste." Love it or leave it, the curious taste of Tom's of Maine has successfully built brand recognition simply through its unique characteristics—according to consumers, no other toothpaste looks, smells, feels, or tastes like Tom's of Maine.

---

[12] To be precise, we probed consumers regarding their use of "natural health, personal care products, and beauty aids" and let them define the category as they saw fit.

Differentiation—especially differentiation from traditional, "non-natural" products—will be the key driving factor behind successful branding campaigns in the natural HABA marketplace.

Another example that has, thus far, been less commercially successful is Crystal Rock deodorant. Consider the following discussion:

Consumer: "I use the Crystal Rock deodorant sometimes. I just find it fascinating [laughs], it's really funny."

Interviewer: "Is there a reason, what drew you to that?"

Consumer: "Actually I couldn't really believe it so that's why I bought it. It was just a plain crystal rock—it doesn't stop perspiration, but stopping any odor is what it provides and sometimes you can get it as shaped like a crystal or like a rock, and it lasts for a very long time. You could probably buy the stick and it would last about six months."

Interviewer: "So that's sort of a novelty that you bought that for."

Consumer: "Yes, exactly. But I mean, I've bought it again, I bought it more than once."

Interviewer: "Why did you buy it more than once?"

Consumer: "Because it worked. I was surprised that it worked and then I bought it again."

Interviewer: "Why is it better than what you were using before?"

Consumer: "I don't know if it's better. I think that it's probably a little bit better for me. Whether that's completely true, I'm not really sure."

—Female, 30s, Chicago

Note that the consumer isn't clearly convinced the product necessarily performs any better than her previous, non-natural choice, but she does recognize that it is very different—almost a novelty if you will. This is the essence of differentiation.

Hence, we suggest that *differentiation*—especially differentiation from traditional, "non-natural" products—will be the key driving factor behind successful branding campaigns in the natural HABA marketplace. The necessity to differentiate from traditional product categories is one of the unique features of the natural HABA and household products product worlds. Producers of gingko, for example, may face their own unique challenges in terms of branding strategy but they don't have to contend with a host of similar products, which have already occupied the marketplace for decades.

Increasingly, manufacturers of natural HABA products must take steps to clearly distinguish their products from those already enjoying long-term brand recognition and loyalty. This differentiation must be dramatic—simple redesign of packaging and "green values" advertising will fail to highlight distinctions in consumers' minds. Although it isn't necessary that all consumers with Natural Sensibility *like* the product, it is necessary that they be able to distinguish the product.

One HABA product line that has experienced success in terms of differentiation is Aveda. One of their most important branding techniques has been to associate their products with a **place** (such as Exotiques and Day Spas) that exclusively use Aveda products. In these day spas, customers first *experience* a wellness practice such as a massage or sauna, then associate the experience with the specific product in question. This differentiation technique serves to solidify brand recognition.

NATURAL HOUSEHOLD PRODUCTS

"I haven't used a whole lot of natural cleaners, but if I could afford to, I would. A lot of the time I use bleach and water. Soap and water."

—Female, 40s, San Francisco

·◆·

"I don't use the recycled paper ones because I think they're awfully expensive, but I always buy white and like on the Scott's, it's single ply, it's 1,000 sheets so it's more economical and as far as I'm concerned I'm doing my best."

—Female, 50s, Seattle

·◆·

"The paper towels and the toilet tissue—and it's a lot more money, but I don't care. It's not like I'm pinching pennies. I think it'd be different if I didn't have the money that I do make . . . because a dollar to me, you know, a dollar's nothing—the price of regular paper towels and this is a dollar more? Whatever, who cares? But if I was making $24,000 a year, maybe I would care. So it's definitely an economic issue."

—Female, 30s, New York

Of the five product worlds we explored, consumers appear least involved in the natural household products product world. Similar to the HABA product world, consumer involvement and participation is fragmented and sporadic, with few "fully active" constituents. Many express sympathy with the larger benefits derived from these products (healthier planet, conservation of natural resources, etc.), yet—for a variety of reasons which we will discuss below—fail to integrate these products into their daily lives. Price and availability serve as the two most significant barriers to initial involvement in the natural household products world. Finally, brand recognition and loyalty here is weak.

Ideology: The Double-Edged Sword?

One of the most intriguing observations regarding the world of natural products and services is the general lack of consistent, value-driven, ideological underpinnings to consumer involvement. As we suggested earlier, consumers frequently make vague references to values and ideologies, yet these seem to take a back seat to the pragmatic, lifestyle issues associated with daily routines. We find this especially true in the world of natural household products. Practically everyone acknowledges at least an interest in "not doing the wrong thing." Yet, they rarely demonstrate behavior consistent with these ideals. In part, this highlights a paradox that has accompanied the mainstreaming of natural products in the U.S.

As demonstrated by the widespread success of curbside recycling efforts in many U.S cities, most consumers express a desire to "do the right thing"—so long as it is convenient and priced reasonably—regardless of their values and belief structure. Thus, it is not necessary that the majority of consumers embrace "green politics," "radical environmentalism" or any other ideological movement for recycling to work. It is only necessary to make recycling convenient so that it requires minimal effort. The fact that this same logic appears to hold for natural household products should be heralded with open arms by the natural product industry. After all, moving from a small, core group with focused environmental values to the larger population with a general interest in well-being expands the potential market size indefinitely. Unfortunately, this shift comes at a cost: As environmental values diffuse to a more general, less value-driven audience, consumer behavior follows with equal parts pragmatism and ambivalence.

Consumers may have a general interest in natural household products, yet their interest isn't grounded in a strong ideological base. As a result, they feel free to limit participation based on issues of convenience, price, and availability. Consider the following exchange:

> *Consumer: "I have boughten [sic] recycled toilet paper from time to time."*
>
> *Interviewer: "Why did you buy it?"*
>
> *Consumer: "Because I recycle everything. I just think it is important and I will look at prices and sometimes I'll buy it and sometimes I won't, depends if there's something else on sale. So I can't say I'm a dedicated person, but I've picked it up probably once a month. I don't sound very dedicated! As long as it is more expensive and you're trying to save money . . . I think it really depends a lot."*
>
> —Female, 50s, Seattle

Moving from a small, core group with focused, environmental values to the larger population with a general interest in well-being expands the potential market size indefinitely. Unfortunately, this shift comes at a cost: As environmental values diffuse to a more general, less value-driven audience, consumer behavior follows with equal parts pragmatism and ambivalence.

Similarly, in the following discussion, the consumer clearly isn't hell-bent on trying to do the right thing. While he appears willing to "help out" by purchasing natural household products—in this case recycled tissue—his beliefs, values and ideologies might not sustain participation in the event of a price differential:

> *Interviewer: "And why do you use recycled tissue regularly?"*
>
> *Consumer: "It doesn't cost any more to lean toward the proper way of doing things."*
>
> *Interviewer: "It doesn't cost more and it's good for the environment?"*
>
> *Consumer: "Right."*
>
> *Interviewer: "So it's easy to be good?"*
>
> *Consumer: "Exactly. Like recycling, that's so simple, it's just a matter of which bin you throw your garbage—if you're already going to throw it away, it's not really that big of a hassle. I'm not hell-bent on trying to do the right thing, but if it's blatant I'd like to stop doing the wrong thing."*
>
> —Male, 40s, Chicago

Thus, while the natural household products marketplace has begun to enjoy mainstream acceptance within the general U.S. population, brand

Most consumers are receptive to the idea of these products, so long as they don't have to make any sacrifices in terms of convenience and price.

managers and marketers face a unique set of challenges. Values, beliefs and ideologies fade to the background as consumers attempt to integrate "doing the right thing" with the practical constraints of their modern lifestyles.

Origins and Barriers

Consumers become active in this world through product placement, product information and store displays, although few exhibit any consistent purchase and use patterns following introduction. Availability and price clearly pose the primary barriers to more active involvement in this world. As alluded to earlier, most consumers are receptive to the *idea* of these products, so long as they don't have to make any sacrifices in terms of convenience and price. Finally, even when consumers can afford the price differential without any significant sacrifices, they remain conscious of price and availability issues.

Branding and Efficacy

Brand recognition and loyalty in the world of natural household products is almost non-existent. Consumers recall only a few snippets (e.g., "green," "eco," "earth," etc.) from brand and product names and only a few appear to use a branded product on a regular basis.

Efficacy represents one final obstacle for some consumers in this category. Once past the dual barriers of cost and convenience, some feel natural household products don't perform as well as their "non-natural" alternatives:

> Consumer: "There's one—I'm awful with brand names—and I think it's called Earth's Green or something, it says it's all natural and you can almost drink it . . . I guess, it won't hurt you . . . I have boughten [sic] that. I didn't like it though, it didn't clean my clothes as well as All or Tide, but I have done it to help the earth, you know."
>
> Interviewer: "After you found out that it wasn't as effective as a detergent, did you still purchase it?"
>
> Consumer: "No."
>
> Interviewer: "So in this case would you be more willing to give it a try again if you had some reason to believe that it worked?"
>
> Interviewer: "I would."
>
> —Female, 30s, Seattle

Summary

Involvement with natural household products reflects broad consumer interest with wellness. While the general health and well-being of the planet is "on the minds" of most consumers interviewed in the *Natural Sensibility* study, their behavior within this world reflects a more self-interested, pragmatic approach to daily life. Factors such as price, availability, and efficacy rise to the forefront and contribute to their fragmented, occasional participation.

Part One Conclusion

The four chapters in this section have set out to build context around the emerging natural products industry—to construct a framework within which we can better understand consumer activity from a sociological behavioral perspective. At times, our analytical focus has been non-traditional. That is, rather than focusing on the consumer—along with associated attitudes, values, beliefs and motivations—we have directed attention to larger, societal-level processes. Even when we discussed consumer behavior with regard to product worlds, the focus was still on collective patterns and behavior.

Few would argue with the notion that the world today is a very different place than it was fifty years ago, yet for many in the market research industry, not much has changed in those fifty years. The standard tool kit for those involved in consumer research—survey research accompanied with some form of inferential statistics—saw its debut during World War II as researchers tried to better understand the effects of war on the individual. These techniques spread rapidly to commercial sectors and proved useful to manufacturers trying to shed light on a post-war, boom economy. Since then, statistical analysis techniques have become a little fancier and computer technology has made things easier, but little else has changed. When most people engage in market research today, they still head straight to their traditional survey instruments. Almost as if out of habit, the survey instrument and inferential statistics have become the hammer and nail of the market researcher's tool kit. We suggest it may be time to update the tool kit—not to throw away the hammer and nail per se, but to integrate other research methods when they appear more suited to the task at hand.

By all accounts, today's consumer lives in a very different world than the post-war consumer. Time is at a premium and the routine of daily life is more complex. Surveys—be they via phone or mail—tend to be intrusive, and customers have grown a bit cynical toward traditional marketing efforts. Thus, it only makes sense to explore alternative methodology options. As Susan Fournier suggests in *Harvard Business Review*:[13]

> *"To get inside people's heads, marketers need to turn to the tools of qualitative social science methods dedicated to richly describing and interpreting people's lives. Videotapes and photography are also good reporting tools. They can reveal what a 'day in the life of the consumer' is all about. Finally, long-term studies work better than ad hoc surveys in painting an accurate picture of how consumers react to and use products."*

In our view, the inclusion of these sorts of tools in our collective methodological tool kit is long overdue and appears especially well-suited to our task at hand. Finally, The Hartman Group has always believed in the need to utilize *all* methodologies—qualitative, quantitative, experimental or otherwise. Our approach in this book reflects that larger, fundamental belief.

---

[13] Susan Fournier, Susan Dobscha, David Glen Mick, "Preventing the Premature Death of Relationship Marketing," *Harvard Business Review*, 1/1/98.

PART II

Mapping the Consumer Segments

BACKGROUND

As demonstrated in Part I, the American social fabric is currently undergoing a dynamic and expansive cultural change apparent at almost every level of our society. In the most general sense, this change can be characterized largely by the increased value placed on "wellness" as both a state of being and a lifestyle. Such cultural changes not only provide the backdrop or playing field, but serve as the primary catalysts in the astounding growth of several wellness-oriented product worlds. In order for businesses operating in these areas to succeed in these increasingly dynamic markets, these increasingly dynamic markets, they must have access to the tools required to make informed, strategic decisions about product development, channels of distribution, retailing, branding, and promotion. Understanding the consumer is central to developing the natural products market.

Despite the tremendous opportunities for growth in burgeoning arenas, it is no secret that much room for improvement still exists. No other industry exhibits such latent potential for tremendous success. It is this discrepancy—the difference between the industry's current performance and its potential—that motivates our studies. Time and again, our research has proved one undeniable fact—product development and marketing within the natural products marketplace ignores the most basic, and also the most crucial, element: the consumer.

To rectify that situation, we embarked on a wide mix of new, innovative research to provide intimate profiles of the consumers unique to various segments of the natural products industry. These consumer segmentations open a window on the profound lifestyle changes Americans undertake as they increasingly aspire to achieve wellness, seeking physical, mental, emotional and spiritual health from an ever-widening variety of products and services. Typically, such shifts in attitudes, values and behaviors (both individually and throughout our society) are embodied in the everyday actions people take and the choices they make. This includes health treatment and maintenance methods, preventative health care options such as exercise and dietary supplementation, as well as the foods they eat and the products they adopt into their daily routines. The details can be seen in a series of detailed consumer segmentations of the natural marketplace product worlds of food and the environment; the organic industry; vitamins, minerals herbals and dietary supplements; and alternative health care.

Understanding the driving forces within the consumer segments unique to each natural product world can mean the difference between companies who ride the industry's wave to unimagined levels of success and those who get left behind. The following segmentation studies differ from the previous sociological analysis of product worlds and Natural Sensibility, and are the result of three years of nationally representative attitude and usage studies conducted using state-of-the-art survey and analysis methodologies.

CHAPTER 5

An Intimate View of "Green" Consumer Segments

"I've used Tom's of Maine toothpaste before—I do like the fact that it's all natural. But—this is going to sound really funny—the way my bathroom is set up, it's just nice to have a pump. I bought some Mentadent . . . it stands up and you don't have to squeeze it and have things gooking out the end. It's fast in the morning."

—Female, 30s, New York

◆

"I have bought some of the natural, or phosphate-free, detergents. But I don't buy a huge amount. I think about it, but I don't really buy very much. I think all chemicals are bad—I know they're bad—but they work. So, I don't really stick to my principles."

—Female, 30s, Seattle

◆

"I considered buying the biodegradable detergents, just because I am concerned about the environment. But it's just harder to get . . . you have to go to the organic store. You can't just pick it up at the drugstore. It's more expensive, it doesn't smell as nice. I don't like putting toxic things in the earth—it's important, it really is—but I don't do it even though I know it's important."

—Female, 50s, New York

INTRODUCTION

Environmental concern is not exactly uncharted territory. Slowly but surely, environmental awareness has escalated to a point of popular acceptance. In fact, some trendy environmental issues bear the banners of political correctness. You'd be hard-pressed to find many suburban areas without extensive recycling centers, or even curb-side pick-up. Before other environmental issues reach similar levels of consumer popularity, it will take considerable education efforts on the part of those who seek consumer participation.

Already, more than half of Americans express interest in or concern about environmental issues. In fact, nearly one-third of our population comprises the core target market for "green" food and agricultural products—those with earth-sustaining, environment-friendly characteristics. Yet, sales of such products account for only two percent of all U.S. food sales. What accounts for this paradox?

FOOD AND THE ENVIRONMENT STUDIES—FINDINGS

This is precisely what we set out to discover through a series of studies called *Food and The Environment: The Consumer's Perspective* (*Phases I, II* and *III*).[1] In its broadest sense, this long-term work set out to determine both what motivates and what inhibits purchase of green products.

More specifically, we realized that product development and marketing within the green marketplace lacked emphasis on the most basic, but also the most crucial, element: the consumer. The environment and the quality of our food supply have been two of the country's hottest topics over the past ten years; however, we still know virtually nothing about the consumer perspective. Unfortunately, no environmental product introduction, despite the great potential of this market, will succeed without understanding consumers and their values and wants.

Therefore, we took on the task of offering the first comprehensive definition of the "green" food marketplace from the perspective of the consumer. The *Food and the Environment* studies explore uncharted territory, intimately profiling the people who inhabit various green agricultural product worlds.

---

[1] For more information about these studies, see Appendix I.

Food and the Environment: Phase I (1996)

In Phase I, we discovered two basic insights. First, the potential green market—the number of consumers interested in earth-sustainable products—is enormous, much more significant than anyone imagined. Second, this consumer group consists of vastly diverse populations. But in our eyes, the most significant finding is the market's latent potential—the huge number of consumers who want to buy "green" but who don't.

In particular, we've broken the U.S. population into six different consumer segments based on their environmental interest and green consumer attitudes and behaviors (see figures 5-1 and 5-2). We con-

Figure 5-1. Six Segment Summary

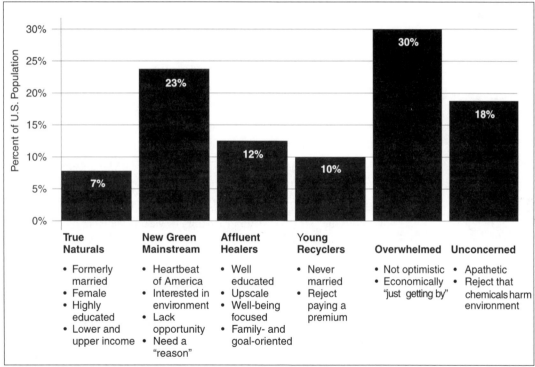

Source: *Food and the Environment: Phase I*, The Hartman Group, Summer 1996

sider the first four segments the *environmentally inclined*. These groups, comprising 52 percent of the U.S. population in 1996, represent consumers with an interest in sustainably produced or environmentally enhanced food and beverages. The **True Naturals** (7 percent) express the most deeply held environmental concerns and follow through in their

Figure 5-2. 1996 Consumer Segments (percent of U.S. population)

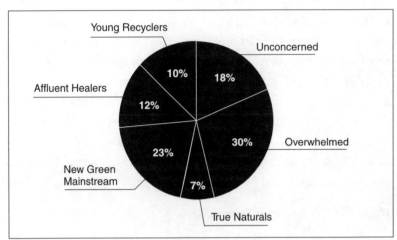

Source: *Food and the Environment, Phase I*, The Hartman Group, Summer 1996

actions and purchases. The **New Green Mainstream** (23 percent) also profess significant concerns regarding the environment, but they tend to alter their behaviors and shopping choices only when convenient to do so. They share enough environmental concerns with the True Naturals that they will most likely respond to the same green product appeals, as long as the benefits are made clear and the actions required are simple. The **Young Recyclers** (10 percent) and **Affluent Healers** (12 percent) each have a distinct, if not somewhat self-centered, slant on their environmental concerns: The Young Recyclers lean toward "trendier" solid waste issues and the Affluent Healers toward issues that have the greatest impact on their personal health. These segments are less likely than the other two to consider environmental factors in their purchase decisions. However, the right message and product attributes can appeal to their more self-oriented concerns.

The last two consumer segments, comprising 48 percent of the U.S. population, generally lack sensitivity regarding environmental matters and we don't consider them targets for environmentally oriented products or services. We call them the *environmentally disinclined*. The **Overwhelmed** (30 percent) and the **Unconcerned** (18 percent) are unlikely to engage in positive ecological behavior or favor a food product for environmental reasons; however, they would not necessarily reject an environmentally improved product if it met all their other purchase criteria. As their names suggest, the Overwhelmed tend to feel too caught up in life's demands to worry about the environment, and the Unconcerned simply do not pay much attention to the environment or do not feel it is seriously threatened.

Food and the Environment: Phase II (1997)

Phase II developed the environmentally inclined segments in greater detail, focusing on the four market segments which indicated an interest in buying earth-sustainable products. While Phase I offered the initial topography of these target groups, Phase II went directly to the heart of the matter, answering the question of why consumers do and do not purchase green products. It not only identified purchase behavior unique to each segment, but thoroughly explored the deepest factors influencing their attitudes and marketplace choices (see figure 5-3).

Figure 5-3. Family with and Importance Place on Agricultural and Environmental Issues

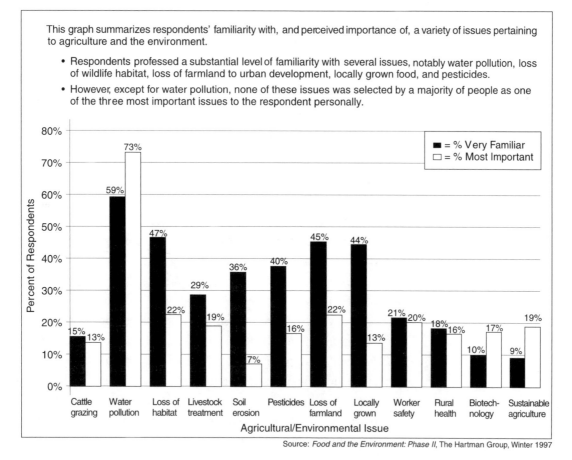

This graph summarizes respondents' familiarity with, and perceived importance of, a variety of issues pertaining to agriculture and the environment.

- Respondents professed a substantial level of familiarity with several issues, notably water pollution, loss of wildlife habitat, loss of farmland to urban development, locally grown food, and pesticides.

- However, except for water pollution, none of these issues was selected by a majority of people as one of the three most important issues to the respondent personally.

■ = % Very Familiar
□ = % Most Important

Source: *Food and the Environment: Phase II*, The Hartman Group, Winter 1997

Perhaps most important, Phase II determined that these consumers and their attitudes are dynamic and continuously evolving. They're on the move—they develop new marketplace attitudes and behaviors every day. They change on their own terms and not necessarily in the way and at the rate that environmental purists and other industry members would like.

Food and the Environment: Phase III (1998)

In the two-year period following the initial phases of the *Food and the Environment* reports, a great deal of attention has been focused on the issues of food, health and the environment. Government regulations for organic labeling that have been developing for over a decade have moved from the backwaters of bureaucratic committees out into the marketplace. A host of books critical of the impact of pesticides on health have been published. Organic and sustainably grown food products that were previously only available in specialized health food stores are now readily available in mainstream grocery stores.

While consumer attitudes and behaviors normally change slowly, the presence of these dynamic marketplace changes suggested that it would be appropriate to remeasure the market and see how things have changed.

Food and the Environment: Phase III revisits 1996 consumer segmentation to measure changes *in* and *between* the segments; to identify the forces influencing these changes; to examine the differences as part of an overall cultural shift taking place in the natural products marketplace; to provide some case histories from key retailers that point the way to the future; and to suggest how growers, manufacturers and retailers should approach this evolving green consumer to maximize their sales opportunity.

Interestingly, with the exception of the True Naturals, and consistent with findings in 1996 and 1997, most green consumers currently do not primarily base their changing marketplace decisions on environmental considerations. Rather, food and agricultural products must first satisfy other "core purchase criteria" such as convenience, price and personal value. Environmental attributes can often function as a "tie-breaker" of sorts when consumers must choose between two products that otherwise fulfill their needs. As such, environmental attributes may serve a "value-added" function.

For instance, a shopper may stand in front of the grocery store egg display and face a decision between four different types of grade AA, extra-large eggs, all at similar prices. The value added by cage-free production methods could offer they key tie-breaking difference. Similarly, packaging made from post-consumer (recycled) material could help determine a shopper's decision between two brands of raisin-bran cereal.

For this reason, consumer education is key. In many ways consumer education must meet the grade levels of those consumers in the class being taught. Are we teaching basic math or calculus—are the consumers coming to school or playing hooky? In order to achieve long-term substantive market success, natural product marketers must develop vocabularies that are understandable to mainstream consumers and must remain in dialog with consumers as their attitudes evolve to "deeper shades of green." By this, we mean that the green marketplace operates in a very technical environment filled with complex methods of growing, manufacturing and packaging all designed to benefit, or reduce harm to, the environment. Only the most dedicated consumers—those who have progressed to the deepest shades of green—understand or care about the technicalities. Communicating consistently with the less-knowledgeable, but still interested consumer groups in an easily understood manner will help those "less-green" consumers progress through the spectrum to join the ranks of the most dedicated natural product consumers.

We hope that The Hartman Group's research will help more and more businesses realize that consumers truly want earth-sustainable products. They will purchase them if they are offered the right conditions and the right information. As target consumers become better educated regarding relevant environmental issues, consumer attitudes and behaviors will prove to be the most powerful forces driving sustainable change. This can also translate into success for green manufacturers and retailers who focus on these consumer attitudes and behaviors.

Our goal, and the industry's production and marketing challenge, is to educate consumers and match earth-sustainable product attributes with the core purchase criteria of consumers who profess an interest in buying these products.

It will require significant education in fundamental environmental issues before less-familiar, specific farming techniques that primarily affect continued agricultural productivity will compel purchase on their own merit.

GREEN CONSUMPTION IN THE GROCERY MARKETPLACE

One particularly interesting contradiction remains consistent throughout our research. Despite strong indications that consumer interest in environmental issues grows stronger each year, this does not seem to translate into changes in purchasing behavior or even to consistently held concerns on a wider, societal level. Rather, we find that consumers have resisted moving along the continuum from awareness to adoption. In particular, we've noted the following consistencies in U.S. purchasing trends and consumer attitudes and concerns regarding green food and agricultural products:

- Consumers have yet to internalize environmental concerns. Their agreement with environmental principles contradicts both their stated and actual marketplace behaviors. For example, consumers state an interest in products such as bathroom tissue made from recycled material, but they fail to support their stated interest with actual purchases.
- While consumers profess a growing interest and curiosity in environmental issues, the majority of the general population does not yet take the initiative to learn more.
- In general, consumers demonstrate a limited understanding of current environmental issues and terminology related to earth-sustainable product manufacturing, growing and production methods. In fact, few have a clear definition of the term "organic" and few can distinguish between "organic" and "pesticide-free." Some consumers may even retain negative perceptions of the term "organic."
- Consumers profess a willingness to pay a higher price for a product labeled "chemical-free" than for one simply identified as "organic."
- Consumers place the greatest value on pesticide and water issues over other environmental concerns. They concern themselves primarily with issues having a direct effect on them and their families, but also about issues affecting wildlife. Therefore, pes-

ticide residue on food and water pollution through pesticide seepage and runoff remain the most important environmental considerations. Issues related to soil, such as erosion and loss of fertility consistently receive low importance rankings.

> **Once a product or shopping outlet meets the core criteria of convenience, quality, cleanliness and price, environmental attributes may serve as a tie-breaker by providing an added value.**

- Consumers most often support farming and production methods that they already have some familiarity with and that offer the most tangible, personal benefits. It will require significant education about fundamental environmental issues before less-familiar, specific farming techniques that primarily affect continued agricultural productivity will compel purchase on their own merit.

- Lack of information and concrete understanding of environmental issues inhibits consumers' interest in purchasing earth-sustainable products, especially if they must pay a premium for such products.

- On the other hand, thorough understanding of environmental issues contributes to the perceived value of such products and consumers may be willing to pay more.

- Convenience, quality, cleanliness, price and other individual benefits remain the primary considerations or "core purchase criteria" when consumers choose either a product or a shopping outlet.

- Once a product or shopping outlet meets the core criteria of convenience, quality, cleanliness and price, environmental attributes may serve as a tie-breaker by providing an added value. As of yet, earth sustainability or other environmental attributes do not by themselves offer enough value to compel purchase by consumers, with the exception of True Naturals.

UNDERSTANDING "GREEN" CONSUMER SEGMENTS

Considering the inconsistent purchasing behavior of the general population with regard to green products, it is crucial to understand the factors driving such marketplace behaviors. Until we understand green consumers' key psychographic and demographic characteristics, as well as their dispositions regarding the environmental aspects of grocery purchases, we will remain unable to meet their needs or improve the performance of earth-sustainable products within the conventional food and beverage marketplace.

On a more basic level, how much sense does it make to simply develop a product and market it to "a consumer" without taking into account the variations within consumer groups as impacted by larger, societal and institutional factors? If our consumer populations are as diverse and dynamic as our research indicates, then the products as well as the marketing and educational campaigns directed toward them must be equally diverse and dynamic.

Figure 5-4 shows the breakdown of consumer segments in 1998. Although the distribution has shifted slightly between segments since 1996 (as shown in figure 5-2), core attitudes about the environment have not changed. More than half of all consumers (53 percent) express concern about the environment and the effect that its degradation will have on their lives. This is up only 1 percent from three years ago.

Figure 5-4. 1998 Consumer Segments (percent of U.S. population)

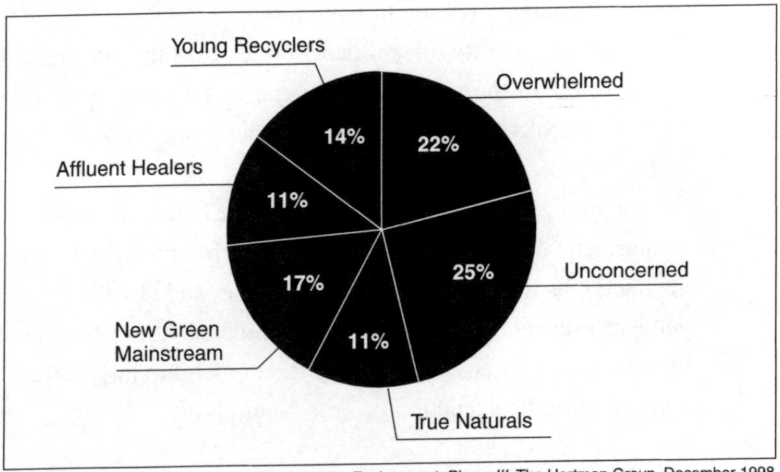

Source: *Food and the Environment, Phase III*, The Hartman Group, December 1998

The following sections offer more detail about the attitudes, behaviors and motivations of individuals in "green" consumer segments, as well as discussing how these segments are changing.

CONSUMERS LACKING CONCERN FOR THE ENVIRONMENT

Nearly half of consumers do not care about the environment relative to food. However, within this category of consumers—which includes the Overwhelmed and the Unconcerned segments—the composition has shifted significantly in the past two years. The following sections define these two segments in greater detail.

Overwhelmed

The Overwhelmed segment of the population is driven primarily by economic necessity. They express a general apathy for life, lack confidence and generally adopt a defeated, negative outlook. They take little interest in their own well-being, care little for nutrition and do not modify their diets for health reasons. They exhibit little concern with food preparation and primarily buy canned or frozen vegetables.

Not only do they lack ecological concern, they do not believe alternative farming methods can benefit the environment while maintaining current food production levels. They take a commodity approach to groceries, buying the least expensive products, and perceive no added value in earth-sustainable products. In fact, they are the least likely of the total population to pay a premium for any products.

We can, perhaps, explain their bleak outlook on life through their more downscale demographics. They have below-average incomes and are less likely than the population as a whole to have finished high school. They fall into the younger age brackets, with a disproportionate share under the age of forty.

Unconcerned

The Unconcerned do not live simple lifestyles, but seem to act in a financially responsible manner. They enjoy socializing with others, do not feel the need to have specific goals and they lack environmental and social consciousness.

The Unconcerned don't perceive a link between food production and the environment. In fact, they remain skeptical that alternatives to chemicals used in agriculture exist. They believe current farming practices, specifically fertilizers and pesticides, are necessary to ensure the food supply. They appear unconcerned about the foods they consume and express a conscious lack of concern about chemical additives, pesticide residue or nutrition. In addition, they have no interest in conservation or renewal of resources.

This group tends to be male, have somewhat above-average incomes and live in the Mountain/Pacific regions. Otherwise, their demographic profile parallels the general population.

Changes from 1996 to 1998

In 1996, nearly 30 percent of the U.S. population—the Overwhelmed segment—professed that their socioeconomic condition precluded them from actively caring about environmental issues and their food. But by 1998, the strong economy, low unemployment and the lowest interest rates in a generation have shrunk this group to only 22 percent of the population (see figure 5-5).

Interestingly though, while 8 percent of the population left the Overwhelmed segment between 1996 and 1998, nearly all migrated to the Unconcerned segment.

Figure 5-5. Consumer Migration

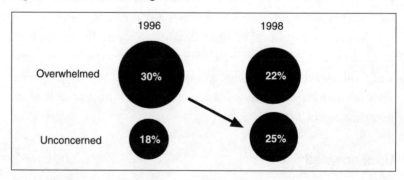

It is not clear whether this reflects a long-term negative attitude by these consumers about the environment or a temporary unwillingness to consider the effect of the environment on their health until they are confident about their improved economic status.

CONSUMERS WHO CARE ABOUT THE ENVIRONMENT

Shoppers who make a connection between the environment, their personal health and the grocery products they purchase fall into four attitudinal groups, described in the following sections.

True Naturals

The True Naturals segment consists of the smallest proportion of environmentally inclined consumers, but they represent the core of the earth-sustainable marketplace. They tend to be very strong-willed, independent, and confident people who take control of their lives. They hold unequivocal views on right and wrong behavior and follow through with their actions. While they believe all people should be self-reliant, they also possess strong social consciousness and compassion. They lean toward simplicity in their lives and surround themselves with family and friends.

These consumers hold the strongest views on environmental issues and demonstrate the greatest commitment to their ideals. As environmentalism is a driving force in their lives, True Naturals are the only segment that regularly consumes organic products, and the only segment currently willing to pay a premium for earth-sustainable products and actively doing so. This results from concern for the environment and their own and their families' nutritional health. They do not limit their dedication to food products. They care about packaging and reuse of resources and take a stand, refusing to buy over-packaged products.

Demographically, we describe this group as "graying children of the 60s." They tend to fall into somewhat higher age brackets, are highly educated, and work in managerial, professional, or executive occupations. Nevertheless, they are over-represented in the lower-income group (under $25,000) but proportionately represented among higher income groups ($55,000+). They are more likely to live in single-member households (particularly women living alone) and to be formerly married.

New Green Mainstream

The New Green Mainstream represent the greatest opportunity for market expansion of organic and earth-sustainable products. They demonstrate significant social and environmental consciousness as well as a tendency to stand up for what they believe. Their environmental attitudes fall second only to the True Naturals and they display growing curiosity about and openness to environmentalism.

They express particular concern about the impact of chemical pesticides and fertilizers on the food supply, but remain resistant to paying a premium for environmentally sound products. Although this segment is more likely than average to have purchased an earth-sustainable product or visited a health food store or supermarket in the past month, product availability and other personal purchase criteria remain barriers to increased purchasing of organic products. While they profess a growing interest in environmental issues, members of the New Green Mainstream do not consider themselves particularly knowledgeable, nor do they actively seek information.

With the exception of a slight under-representation in the younger age groups (younger than 35), their demographics don't differ from the population as a whole.

Affluent Healers

Although the Affluent Healers represent only 12 percent of our population, they have a tremendous amount of disposable income and offer a significant opportunity with regard to their purchasing power. Perhaps most important, these people represent the leaders in our society. If they begin leading the charge toward green consumption, they will bring large numbers of followers with them.

The members of this group profess satisfaction with their lives. They appear self-directed and goal-oriented. Perhaps because of this, they achieve higher levels of education, hold managerial, professional, and executive positions and fall in the higher-income brackets.

They would like to help the environment, but don't place it among their top concerns. They primarily concern themselves with personal nutrition and health. They care most for the nutritional value of the foods they buy rather than the environmental aspects of food production. They try to maintain up-to-date knowledge of the latest nutritional reports and modify their eating habits and exercise regularly. They express below-average concern regarding the potential effects of chemical pesticides and fertilizers.

The Affluent Healers express cynicism regarding the hype surrounding many environmental issues and require products to fulfill their nutritional needs before they pay a premium for environmental attributes. They do seek value and reasonable price in the products they purchase and use coupons regularly. Currently, this group is less likely than average to pay a premium for earth-sustainable products; however, they are slightly more likely than average to have shopped in a health-food store or supermarket.

This group tends to consist of women older than 35 and people who live in large urban or suburban markets in the Pacific region.

Young Recyclers

The Young Recyclers compose a secondary target for environmentally sound products. This group consists largely of young people who, perhaps because they tend to be unmarried, have fewer responsibilities and can afford the luxury to live a somewhat self-centered and carefree lifestyle. In part because of their age, they may not be entirely goal-oriented and their attitudes toward food and nutrition are still in the formation stage. They have not necessarily modified their diet and prefer convenience foods that require little preparation. They concern themselves less with issues specifically relating to the food supply and consequently have little interest in organic or earth-sustainable foods.

Although they may often act in a self-indulgent manner, they do behave with financial responsibility. They appear less likely than the average consumer to pay a premium for earth-sustainable grocery products. They focus on broad environmental issues, largely related to recycling. Although they profess an interest in environmental concerns, they display somewhat mixed behavior. They claim to seek products that are made with recycled materials and are prudently packaged. Yet, their actions do not prove steadfast. In actuality, they are no more likely than the average population either to refuse purchasing over-packaged products or to actively seek earth-sustainable products.

Purchase Motivations and Environmental Issues of Importance

While each of these four environmentally inclined segments possesses its own distinct set of motivations, preferences and purchase influences, the most green of each group also share some common purchase motivations that distinguish them from the rest of the general consumer population:

- They see a connection between the health of the environment and their own well-being. A majority of these consumers feel the environment is worse today than twenty years ago.
- They express a preference for locally grown produce and products made from recycled materials.
- They are cynical. They don't necessarily believe in a product's safety or professed environmental or nutritional attributes simply on the basis that the brand or retail outlet makes such claims.
- They try to stay informed about nutrition and food safety issues and want to learn about the production methods for food products (more so than the general population); however, few profess above-average levels of knowledge about environmental issues. Those who understand the processes behind an ecologically or nutritionally improved product tend to perceive more value in the product.
- They express concern regarding pesticides and other chemicals in food. They find products that are labeled "grown without pesticides" more compelling than those labeled "organic," despite the fact that organic production imposes stricter limits on toxic chemicals beyond the avoidance of just pesticide use.
- They feel water protection and limited use of pesticides carry more significance than other agricultural improvements.

Besides emphasizing pesticide and water issues far more than other environmental concerns, green consumers also place importance on loss of wildlife habitat, loss of farmland due to urban development and the value of choosing locally grown foods. For instance, the majority of the True Naturals—followed distantly by the Young Recyclers—report significant familiarity with the loss of wildlife habitat caused by the drainage of wetlands. In addition, all green segments (the Young Recyclers the least so) overwhelmingly report a preference for purchasing locally grown produce.

Green consumers appear more willing to buy grocery items produced with a combination of environmentally sound techniques than those produced using a single techniques alone. In addition, techniques that don't reduce pesticide use will not alone motivate purchases. For example, integrated pest management (IPM) generally does not appeal to green consumers unless it specifically reduces pesticide use.

Responses regarding the value of biotechnology in agricultural production varied widely. In general, green consumers do not seem to find fault with the practice, although the Affluent Healers seem to agree with the practice more strongly than the other segments. Rather, green consumers agree less strongly than the other segments that it *shouldn't* be used. Responses in favor of biotechnology specifically designed to reduce pesticide use were much stronger. Ironically, though, biotechnology generally serves to improve the resistance of food products to increased pesticide and fungicide use. This could represent another example of limited knowledge and understanding of environmental and agricultural processes.

As noted previously, green consumers demonstrate a growing interest in environmental concerns; however, they do not profess above-average knowledge of such matters. Phase II research showed an increased knowledge about environmental issues among green consumers and revealed that more of them actively seek such knowledge. In particular, they seem to crave information related to dairy, meat and poultry production.

In addition, consumers report a desire to purchase products that provide this type of information . . . and many of them would pay a premium. By far, environmental and nutritional information on the label is the most compelling. Flyers and 800-numbers generate the least interest. Perhaps most important, green consumers prefer environmental claims made by independent, third-party sources over those made by manufacturers or producers. Third-party verification seals are seen as fairly trustworthy information sources—especially for the True Naturals.

Green consumers' exposure to third-party information disseminated by the mass media—through reading periodicals and viewing television—often parallels that of the general population. However, some differences are worth noting. For instance, the True Naturals appear to watch less television than other segments. When they do watch television they tend to opt for programs such as *60 Minutes* or other news programs. Interestingly, *ER* outranked other television programs by far (followed by *Seinfeld*) across all segments. The True Naturals read many more food and cooking magazines than the other segments.

Personality and Character Differences

In addition to demographic differences, in our 1997 and 1998 studies we profiled six underlying personality and character traits within each segment. We identified distinct differences in 1) self-sufficiency, 2) status-consciousness, 3) work ethic, 4) insecurity, 5) thriftiness and 6) altruism.

The True Naturals scored highest on self-sufficiency and consciousness of their social status. They subscribe to the work ethic but only to a moderate degree. They express self-security and appear thrifty in the use of their financial resources. They also score high on altruism.

The New Green Mainstream segment shows some definite differences in its psychographic make-up. While they also appear self-sufficient and status-conscious, they demonstrate these characteristics to a lesser degree than the True Naturals. They don't score highly on work ethic, nor do they seem thrifty. However, like the True Naturals, they are secure and score slightly higher on altruism than other segments.

The Affluent Healers scored particularly high on work ethic and thriftiness. This likely accounts for their affluence. In addition, they profess a sense of security.

The Young Recyclers seem relatively self-sufficient and status conscious; however, they scored quite low on work ethic. Perhaps, considering their youth, this will improve with time. They demonstrate a moderate sense of insecurity, again perhaps due to age. They did score relatively high on thriftiness and altruism, but their altruism scores seem somewhat lower than average when compared with the other green segments.

Shifts between the Green Shopper Segments, 1996 to 1998

In 1996, we identified the New Green Mainstream as a group that represents nearly a quarter of U.S. households and who are beginning to emerge in terms of their environmental motivation. These shoppers were becoming active in their environmental purchases. At the same time, they were clear to point out that their continued involvement must be on terms that were convenient for them.

As we will identify in the following section on outside influences, earth-sustainable and organic products were not only more convenient and available but were supported by heavy levels of media attention.

By 1998, the New Green Mainstream segment gave up nearly 3 percent of shoppers to the True Naturals segment as shoppers began to enjoy ready availability of organic products in their local supermarket. Figure 5-6 shows the shifts in green shopper segments between 1996 and 1998.

This near doubling of the True Naturals segment with the addition of former New Green Mainstream shoppers has diminished the segment's overall strength of conviction on key attitudinal measures. Whereas former True Naturals came to organic food through a deep lifestyle conviction, the True Naturals of 1998 are now a mix of lifestyles and are far less committed to "counter-culture" values.

Figure 5-6. Shifts in Green Shopper Segments

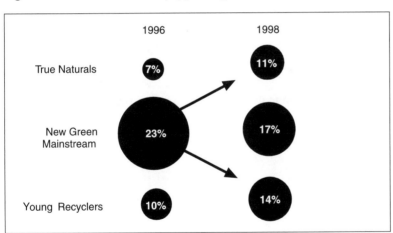

Some of the key differences between these Classic True Natural buyers and the new True Natural buyers are summarized in Table 5-1.

Table 5-1. Comparison of Classic Organic Buyers and New Organic Buyers

	Trial purchases are driven by:	Repeat purchases are driven by:	Breadth of Purchases:	Depth of Purchases:
Classic Organic Buyers	Desire to change the world	Moral commitment to protecting the environment	Consistently across many product categories	Deeply committed
New Organic Buyers	Desire to protect my family and myself	Lifestyle and fashion commitment to health and well being	Selectively among and between categories	Flexibly committed

During this same period, nearly 4 percent of New Green Mainstream moved into the Young Recyclers segment as their commitment to recycling grew stronger but their commitment to organic and sustainable food products diminished.

Changes in True Naturals and New Green Mainstream

To clearly represent the evolving attitudinal and behavioral change of shoppers we should compare and contrast the changes in beliefs and activities of True Naturals and New Green Mainstream shoppers side by side.

Importance of Organic Food to Store Shopped

From 1996 to 1998, the need for retailers to provide organic offerings for these shoppers has increased considerably. More than half of True Natural shoppers now cite the availability of organic as a key motivator for deciding which stores to shop. Figure 5-7 shows the percentage of these green shopper segments that say they shop at certain stores because they carry organic products.

Figure 5-7. "I shop at certain stores because they carry organic food and beverages."

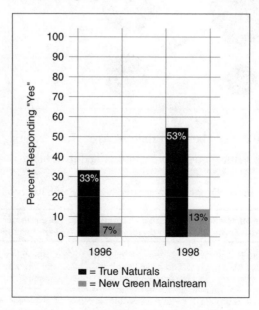

While New Green Mainstream shopper commitment is significantly less intense at only 13 percent, this measure has nearly doubled in importance over the two-year period and we expect it to continue to grow as more organic and earth-sustainable offerings are available at reasonable prices and good quality.

Consumer Recognition of the Availability of Natural and Organic Products

A key component of the True Natural lifestyle has been the willingness to seek out and actively shop at outlets that cater to natural and organic food products. Because of this targeted shopping behavior their perception of natural and organic product availability has not changed.

New Green Mainstream shoppers on the other hand have noticed the increasing availability of natural and organic foods over this period (see figure 5-8).

Figure 5-8. "Natural and organic products are not available at the grocery store where I usually shop."

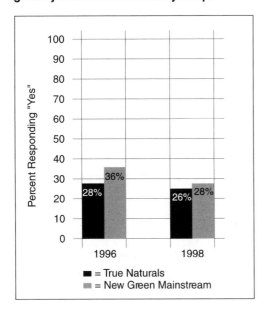

Continued Willingness to Pay a Price Premium

Both of these shopper segments continue to be willing to pay a limited price premium to purchase natural and pesticide-free products. As expected, the intensity of commitment for True Naturals is consistent and higher than that of the New Green Mainstream.

Figure 5-9. "I am willing to pay a little more for foods which are free from pesticide residues and are processed without artificial preservatives, additives or colorings."

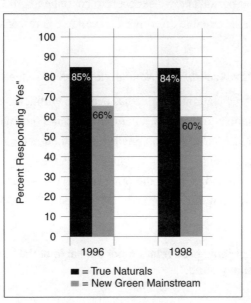

In fact, New Green Mainstream consumers' willingness to pay a price premium has decreased slightly from 1996 to 1998.

Frequency of Organic Food Purchases

Nearly four out of five True Naturals report an increase in their frequency of purchase of organic foods and beverages. This number is only slightly down from 1996 and is a clear indicator of this group's commitment to these products (see figure 5-10).

In keeping with the increased convenience and availability of organic food products over the two-year period, nearly a third of New Green Mainstream shoppers report that their frequency of organic food purchase is rising. This is a substantial gain from the 24 percent reported in 1996.

It is important to note that these are not measures of actual frequency of purchase but a reporting of change in frequency of purchase by these shoppers.

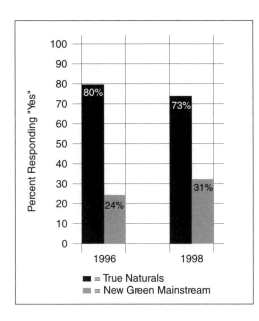

Figure 5-10. "I'm buying more organic foods and beverages than before."

Confidence of Knowledge About Environmental Issues

In 1998 compared to 1996, fewer True Naturals and New Green Mainstream consumers believe they knew more than others about environmental issues (see figure 5-11). This may come from a belief by these shoppers that the media onslaught concerning the environment and food is broadening overall awareness about these issues.

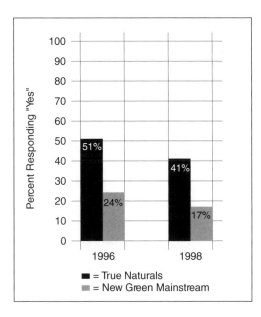

Figure 5-11. "I know more about environmental issues than most people I know."

Active Involvement in Environmental Organizations

Another clear dividing line between True Naturals and New Green Mainstream consumers is their active involvement in environmental organizations (see figure 5-12).

While nearly one in five True Naturals are actively involved in an environmental organization, less than one in twenty New Green Mainstream consumers are active in an environmental organization. Perhaps more dramatically, while the True Natural commitment has held steady, New Green Mainstream involvement has dropped by a third.

These psychographic elements may both influence and combine with other purchase motivators or inhibitors to determine actual green marketplace participation.

Figure 5-12. "I am active in environmental organizations."

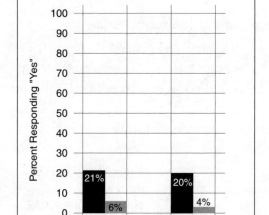

Impact of Outside Influences

Several other factors have recently had an impact on consumer attitudes toward natural and organic foods.

Regulatory Focus on Organic

In 1997 the USDA released for public comment a proposed set of standards for organic food labeling. This initial version of the proposed rules met with an overwhelmingly negative response because of key issues which flew in the face of traditional understandings of what organic has traditionally meant.

Organic farming and trade organizations, along with consumer advocacy groups, created a media furor to raise awareness about the offending components of the impending legislation. Town hall meetings with United States Department of Agriculture (USDA) and industry representatives were conducted in Boston, Seattle and Los Angeles. The resulting publicity generated over 275,000 comments to the USDA.

It is expected that a revised set of standards that do not contain the offensive issues will be released in 1999. This new version will in turn be submitted for public comment creating another opportunity for increased awareness and attention to organic.

Media Attention

Media attention to natural food and agriculture has been growing rapidly over the past decade. Between 1996 and 1998, major articles on natural food have appeared in national magazines ranging from *Time* and *Newsweek* to *Business Week* and *Women's Day*. Newspaper coverage has included major articles in the *New York Times* and the *Los Angeles Times*. Even *Consumer Reports* included an evaluation article on organic food and pesticide residues. Figures 5-13 and 5-14 show the increase in media coverage between 1988 and 1998 of topics related to natural food products as well as environmental issues related to food and agriculture.

Figure 5-13. Appearance of Topics "Environment" (with) "Food and Agriculture" in 2,591 U.S. Magazines and 70 Major U.S. Newspapers, 1988–1998

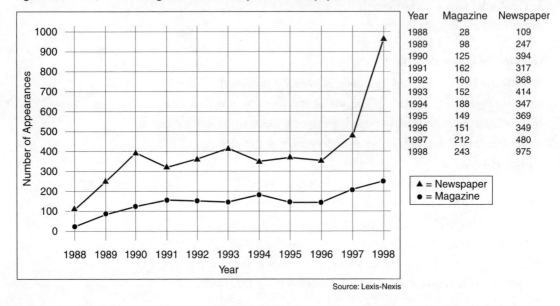

Year	Magazine	Newspaper
1988	28	109
1989	98	247
1990	125	394
1991	162	317
1992	160	368
1993	152	414
1994	188	347
1995	149	369
1996	151	349
1997	212	480
1998	243	975

▲ = Newspaper
● = Magazine

Source: Lexis-Nexis

Figure 5-14. Appearance of Topic "Natural Food" in 2,591 U.S. Magazines and 70 Major U.S. Newspapers, 1988–1998

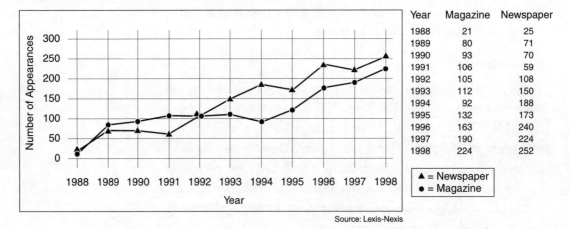

Year	Magazine	Newspaper
1988	21	25
1989	80	71
1990	93	70
1991	106	59
1992	105	108
1993	112	150
1994	92	188
1995	132	173
1996	163	240
1997	190	224
1998	224	252

▲ = Newspaper
● = Magazine

Source: Lexis-Nexis

Two notable books on the issues of food and the environment have gained notoriety during this period as well. Theo Colburn's book *Our Stolen Future: Are We Threatening our Fertility, Intelligence, and Survival?* suggests that man-made chemicals are unintentionally blocking or mimicking hormone action at critical points in fetal development.[2] Sandra Steingraber's book *Living Downstream* combines gripping personal narrative with scientific analysis to clearly present the growing body of evidence linking cancer to environmental contamination.[3]

SUMMARY

Each of these purchase motivators and inhibitors will continue to shift over time. To more fully understand the intricate web of considerations consumers rely on when making green purchases requires an even more intimate portrait of green consumers. The differences and similarities in each segment's underlying attitudes and priorities—as well as the relationship between ecological concern and actual behavior—will continue to shift over time. Thus, it is important to remember that this is a *dynamic* marketplace. Changes are bound to occur over time, whether provoked by external influences or the natural internal development of the segments themselves. Such changes may alter the characteristics within a segment or promote migration of consumers from one segment to another.

[2] Theo Colburn, *Our Stolen Future: Are we threatening our fertility, intelligence, and survival? A scientific detective story* (New York: NAL/Dutton, 1997).
[3] Sandra Steingraber, *Living Downstream: An ecologist looks at cancer and the environment* (Reading, Mass: Addison-Wesley Publishing, 1997).

CHAPTER 6

Organics . . . the New Rules of the Game

"All I think of is it must be in Santa Cruz somewhere, in some field [laughs]. But that's what brings to my mind when I think about organic, you know, that people take a little more care, they use other than pesticides, they use incense or whatever, they actually go out and pick off the bugs. My impression is that they're probably smaller farms that are doing this."

—Male, 30s, California.

•◆•

"Of course, the other stuff looks better. Most organic fruits and vegetables are bruised—because they're not [grown the same way] as the other stuff. That's a terrible reason [to not buy organically] . . . it's terrible."

—Female, 40s, New York

INTRODUCTION

While the *Food and the Environment* reports provided an invaluable, unique overview of the consumer market for sustainably and environmentally enhanced food and beverages, they also directed us to our next step. *Food and the Environment* highlighted a set of challenges faced by a sub-industry of the green marketplace that both parallel and magnify those of earth-sustainable products in general.

The organic industry has demonstrated astounding growth—the current $4 billion U.S. organic products market has doubled in size every year since 1990. Yet, Hartman Group research shows that the current 1 percent market share held by organic food products barely taps the market's potential.

Sound familiar? This paradox closely mirrors that of the general green marketplace, and the reasons for this paradox are much the same. For example, nearly one-half of our population expresses an interest in organic foods—and many of them follow through with purchases; However, as discovered in research conducted in the *Food and the Environment* reports, a significant portion of consumers don't actually understand what "organic" means, nor do they understand complex production methods.

The organic industry has historically represented one of the most significant, yet least understood segments of the food and agricultural products industries. This industry is *not* a superficial fad. While actual demand has never matched the latent desire for organic products, the industry now faces widespread, inherent changes that have the potential to put an end to this paradox.

For example, traditional consumer barriers such as limited availability, uninspiring quality, poor awareness and high pricing have begun to collapse. Awareness through media has increased dramatically (see figure 6-1). At the same time, fundamental cultural values have begun to shift as people become more concerned with personal health, community, nature, spirituality and integrity. Due to changes such as these, the prospect of strong growth in the industry is promising, but there are still many challenges posed by rival product claims, consumer confusion, mainstream market entrants and changing retail channel relationships.

At the most fundamental level, the organic industry faces an entirely new type of competition requiring novel strategies and skills to achieve success. The rules of the game have changed—dramatically.

First of all, the players have become much more diverse. The organic agricultural movement first began to make a comeback in the 1960s, spearheaded by the rise of the "counter-culture" and a "back to the earth" movement. Historically, organic growers, purveyors and consumers all shared fundamental philosophies and values based on integrity and the health of the body, the earth and the spirit.

Figure 6.1. Appearance of Topic "Organic Food" in 2,591 U.S. Magazines and 70 Major U.S. Newspapers, 1988–1998.

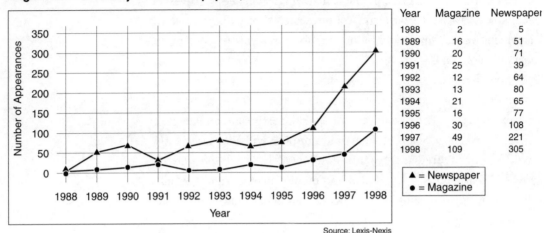

Year	Magazine	Newspaper
1988	2	5
1989	16	51
1990	20	71
1991	25	39
1992	12	64
1993	13	80
1994	21	65
1995	16	77
1996	30	108
1997	49	221
1998	109	305

▲ = Newspaper
● = Magazine

Source: Lexis-Nexis

As the organic industry now becomes big business, controversy and confusion reign. The tenacious trailblazers of the past are learning to compete in a mainstream marketplace flooded by new competition and retail outlets. The burgeoning ranks of marketers newly drawn to the industry must learn to function in a market originally founded on deeply held philosophical values. Manufacturers, retailers and consumers alike face a sometimes overwhelming re-education as science and technology advance and regulations and definitions change.

To describe these changes, The Hartman Group prepared a report called *The Evolving Organic Marketplace* to help organic industry participants understand the market dynamics and strategic requirements for competitive success in the context of the consumer. The depth of research and analysis in this report supplies a penetrating perspective on the complex, evolving organic arena and gives those looking to the future the tools to achieve significant success. As in the *Food and the Environment* reports, The Hartman Group has successfully profiled the intricacies within the various organic consumer segments as well as the motivators and inhibitors to participation in the organic market.

In *The Evolving Organic Marketplace,* we detail our expectation that developments among organic consumer segments and industry trends will both open opportunities and raise new threats to companies selling in the organic marketplace. Our research findings and the strategies we developed inform industry participants on how to achieve a sustainable market position to build their companies and care for their evolving organic consumers. This means understanding that this dynamic market, occupied by diverse consumers, requires new, more differentiated strategies and decisions formulated with long-term commitment.

These are the new rules of the organic game.

THE DEFINITIONAL CHALLENGE

There's no question—the organic industry stands as one of the fastest growing sectors in the United States. While the industry enjoys rapid growth and enduring consumer interest, consumers seem to have little concrete knowledge of what the term "organic" means or what its processes involve. At the same time, the majority of consumers have a strong sense of the concept. Approximately one-third of our respondents could state two or more criteria which they thought might be used to define organic.

This suggested that in addition to raising organic awareness, it is also important to focus on consumer education. As suggested in the *Food and the Environment* reports, the complexities of organic definitions and processes pose serious communication challenges. Consumer education is crucial, considering that consumers must first have real understanding before they can perceive real value in an organic product.

The organic industry has debated for years about organic growing and processing qualifications. The National Organic Standards Board has long held a position of authority on this issue and identifies the primary goal of the industry as attempting to optimize the health and productivity of interdependent soil, plant, animal and people communities. This means using materials and practices that enhance the ecological balance of natural systems and that integrate the parts of the farming system into an ecological whole. To do so promotes and enhances biodiversity, biological cycles and soil biological activity. It relies on minimal use of off-farm inputs and on management practices that restore, maintain and enhance ecological harmony.

While this definition seems all-inclusive, definitional disputes still plague the industry. For example, some industry members insist that organic means pesticide- and chemical-free growing and manufactur-

Consumer education is crucial, considering that consumers must first have real understanding before they can perceive real value in an organic product.

ing processes, while the most common definition prohibits the use of only *synthetic* pesticides. In addition, few consumers recognize the complex array of agricultural management techniques that are involved in organic growing. Few consumers even connect the term "organic" to manufacturing processes at all, but connect it only to growing methods. In addition, while they easily connect the term with the health of the environment, few consumers recognize the personal health benefits associated with organic food products.

An essential implication of these definitional issues is that understanding what makes a product organic requires a somewhat involved technical knowledge of agricultural and manufacturing processes. These aren't simple concepts that can be succinctly and easily communicated to consumers. Yet, communications are fundamental to stimulating demand for organic products. Most consumers want to know more about organic products and significant numbers of consumers have become actively involved in protecting the industry.

Recently, the USDA made its first attempt at regulating the organic industry by proposing a set of legislative organic standards that permitted far more leniency in organic definitions than the industry allowed through self-regulation. In fact, the new regulations approved genetically modified organisms (GMOs) or biotech foods, irradiation and the use of biosolids (municipal sewage sludge) as fertilizer. Organic purists, expecting only unadulterated foods to bear the organic label, responded with more than 200,000 letters, faxes and emails overwhelmingly objecting to these issues—the largest number of consumer responses ever received by the USDA.

U.S. Agriculture Secretary Dan Glickman responded, "[the proposed standards] neither fit current organic practices nor meet current consumer expectations about organics. Therefore, these products and practices won't be allowed to bear the organic label." Thanks largely to consumer demands, the proposed standards will undergo fundamental revisions.

Even if these issues eventually find legislative resolution, it will still fall to manufacturers and retailers to educate consumers about the technicalities of organic growing and production. However, if conflicts and definitional disputes within the industry are communicated to consumers, further confusion—and even distrust of the industry and its claims—may result.

Although we have identified a limited awareness and positive association regarding organic products within the general population, awareness of the problem is not enough. We believe many consumers, including
those genuinely well-disposed toward organic ideas, do not spend much
time thinking about organic products as concrete opportunities to improve their health or help the environment. We refer to this as a lack of
"top-of-mind" awareness. This deficiency likely results from a lack of
advertising repetition and experience-derived reinforcement.

THE ORGANIC SEGMENTS

Our organic survey segments provide the basis for a strategic blueprint of
how to steadily open the floodgates of the immense untapped reservoir
centered on America's organic products market. Expanding the purchase
of organic products across the diverse organic marketplace requires meeting the specific needs of each segment we have identified.

Figure 6-2: Organic Consumer Segments (% of the U.S. population)

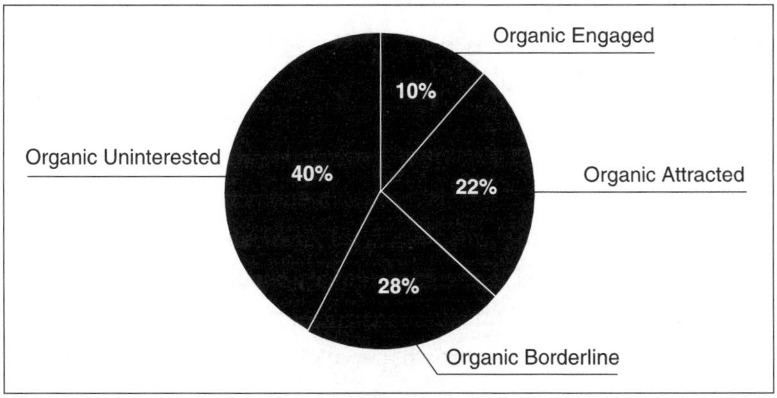

Source: *The Evolving Organic Marketplace*, The Hartman Group, Fall 1997

Organic Engaged

The Organic Engaged (10 percent) have the highest level of interest in
purchasing organic products. They each mentioned, without assistance,
at least two types of organic products they've purchased within the last
year—and 66 percent could mention three or more products. In addition, they claim to have been purchasing organic products for more than
one year. They express the most familiarity with organic definitions,

although many likely operate under a faulty or incomplete definition of what organic means (they may simply equate organic products with a lack of pesticides). They demonstrate the strongest interest in the emerging cultural trends of nutrition, environmental concern, feminine values and spirituality. The Organic Engaged are the most likely to patronize health and natural products stores, although like the general population, the majority favor conventional supermarkets.

We've divided the Organic Engaged into two subsegments based on the relative priority of different purchase criteria.

The **Organic Engaged Purists**, comprising only 2 percent of U.S. consumers, demonstrate the highest propensity to favor health or environmental friendliness over price, convenience and—to some extent—availability. They represent the most loyal organic consumers of the past, when the industry demanded more significant sacrifices. In fact, this consumer group largely forms the base that supported the growth of the organic industry and they continue to account for a disproportionate share of organic sales relative to the group's size.

If the Purists represent the organic market of the past, the **Organic Engaged Pragmatists** (approximately 8 percent of U.S. consumers) comprise the market of the future. These two groups share many of the same values and behaviors, but the Organic Engaged Pragmatists tend to balance health and environmental concerns with more practical purchase criteria such as price, appearance, taste, ease of preparation and—especially—availability. Meeting these purchase criteria first will greatly increase the likelihood of purchase for this group.

With the right education and product appeal, we expect this segment to lead the industry's growth curve. They represent the best target for leading organic companies seeking to increase sales, as this subsegment will grow significantly in size as demographic and cultural trends fuel interest in organics and as public awareness deepens and more pragmatic organic choices become available.

Within both Organic Engaged subsegments, the price premium must be commensurate with the added value offered.

Organic Attracted

As their name implies, the Organic Attracted (22 percent of the U.S. population) profess significant attraction to organic products and express moderate buying interest, but have demonstrated less organic marketplace behavior than the Organic Engaged. While their concerns about health and the environment appear high, these concerns are not as important as they are to the Organic Engaged. Organic Attracted consumers could on average mention only 1.1 organic products they had purchased compared with 2.7 products purchased by the Organic Engaged segment. They demonstrate less knowledge of organic characteristics and have a shorter history of purchasing organic products. In fact, we suspect that half of this group lacks an understanding of organic definitions. This does not mean they should be eliminated as potential consumers; rather, it simply requires generating more "top-of-mind" awareness, increasing their already positive organic associations and providing products that can compete in the mainstream marketplace.

Organic Borderline

The Organic Borderline segment (28 percent of the U.S. population) consists of two types of survey respondents—consumers who either express ambivalence toward or moderate interest in organic products, coupled with a lack of purchase behavior in the organic arena. In principle, this group is fully open to organic products, but their purchase interest remains low. They exhibit fairly high health concerns and moderate environmental concern—but will likely purchase organic products only when doing so requires no sacrifice of other purchase criteria.

Although the members of this segment have limited knowledge of organic characteristics, most have at least minimal organic awareness from which to gradually stimulate demand. They don't associate organic products with personal or environmental health. Therefore, it will require basic awareness-building to encourage this group to engage in consistent purchase behavior. We see this group as an important long-term opportunity not warranting any immediate marketing focus. We suspect they will notice and gradually respond to education and marketing efforts directed at other segments.

Organic Uninterested

As one might expect, the Organic Uninterested (40 percent of the U.S. population) express no interest in purchasing organic products and we see little value in marketing to this group. However, as with the organic borderline segment, they may also respond to education and marketing messages directed at other segments.

Table 6-1 summarizes the approaches for marketing to each organic consumer segment.

Table 6-1. Basic Approaches for Marketing to Each Organic Consumer Segment

Segment:	Strategy:
Organic Engaged	Expand product offerings and availability, and reduce prices or establish clear value-related benefits for premium pricing.
Organic Attracted	Target communications to intensify their existing organic awareness.
Organic Borderline	Take no specific action; allow communications targeted at the Engaged and Attracted segments to create basic organic awareness in Borderline consumers, who then may migrate to the Attracted segment.
Organic Uninterested	Ignore this segment. Some members with health and environmental concerns might migrate to higher segments as they encounter organic communications efforts targeted to other segments.

SEGMENTATION IMPLICATIONS

Simply separating consumers into segments is not enough. It is the specific attitudes and beliefs within each segment regarding certain issues that truly determine market participation. Understanding these attitudes and beliefs allows organic marketers to reach the right consumers in the right way. If this knowledge is used correctly, it is possible to increase consumer awareness and understanding of organic products, which may result both in a higher value placed on them and in higher numbers of purchases.

In addition, while regular supermarkets and grocery stores remain the most attractive retail outlets for all consumer segments, natural products and health foods stores tend to attract the most organically inclined, including a sizable minority (26 percent) of the Organic Engaged. While natural products stores offer an opportunity to reach the most dedicated consumers, conventional retail channels are sitting on a gold mine. Since such stores often represent the primary entry point into the organic market, these retail channels represent an ideal opportunity for both consumer education and market growth. However, those consumers who are not yet dedicated are also the hardest to educate.

The more dedicated a consumer, the longer they have likely been involved in the market. As one would guess, the length of purchase history mirrors our consumer segmentation, with the organic engaged demonstrating the longest purchase history. Interestingly, the percent of consumers claiming to have bought a non-produce organic product within the last three years stands at about half of the 60 percent claiming to have purchased organic produce during the same time period.

The organic consumer segments also demonstrate strikingly different purchase criteria. For all consumers other than the Organic Uninterested, health remains the most significant purchase requirement. Environmental considerations drop one position in importance within each succeeding segment and conventional supermarket availability hovers around the second or third position for all segments. Convenience of preparation hovers around the fourth or fifth spot. Price becomes increasingly more significant progressing from the Organic Engaged down to the Organic Uninterested.

It is important to note that we did not include taste in our survey, but it likely represents significant purchase criteria among all segments. In fact, it might be the most significant criteria besides price. Other considerations such as appearance also likely play a role in purchase decisions. In addition, we suspect that consumers tend to overstate the importance of "ideal" criteria such as health and the environment more than they do "mercenary" considerations such as price. Despite this, the topics of health and the environment remain crucial elements of consumer communication and education efforts aimed at increasing organic market participation. The most involved organic segments are much less likely than others to demonstrate significant price sensitivity. However, the Organic Engaged and Organic Attracted still profess a desire to buy a lot more organic products if the prices were more competitive.

Table 6-2 shows the relative importance each organic consumer segment places on certain key purchase criteria.

Table 6-2. Relative Importance of Key Purchase Criteria by Organic Consumer Segment

Segment	Factor Priority	Criteria	Percent of Respondents Rating "Extremely Important" [4,5]	Percent of Respondents Rating "Very Important" [4,5]	Total Percent
Organic Engaged	1	Health	52	39	91
	2	Environment	38	43	81
	3	Availability	38	35	73
	4	Price	24	27	51
	5	Convenience	18	30	48
	6	Appearance	18	22	40
Organic Attracted	1	Health	42	42	84
	2	Availability	30	46	76
	3	Environment	33	41	74
	4	Price	25	38	63
	5	Convenience	19	37	56
	6	Appearance	15	31	46
Organic Borderline	1	Health	31	42	73
	2	Price	27	42	69
	3	Availability	21	40	61
	4	Environment	19	38	57
	5	Convenience	16	35	52
	6	Appearance	14	29	43
Organic Uninterested	1	Price	29	33	61
	2	Health	27	32	59
	3	Availability	23	35	58
	4	Convenience	21	27	48
	5	Environment	20	26	46
	6	Appearance	21	21	42

Source: *The Evolving Organic Marketplace*, The Hartman Group, Fall 1997

[4] Figures represent percent of segment which considered factor important.
[5] Figures may not appear exact due to rounding differences.

CHAPTER 7

The World of Vitamins, Minerals, Herbals and Dietary Supplements

"I'm the director at work now . . . I'm at the desk more often now and I really don't have the energy I used to. I'm an early bird. I get up at six every morning and I work very hard. But by three p.m., boy, I start going downhill. So, it [taking supplements] was my way of trying to get more energy because the demands are pretty excessive out there in the workplace."
—Male, 40s, San Francisco

.•.

"I think of them [supplements] in terms of wellness as opposed to remedies. I don't think I'm taking these vitamins to fix anything. That's sort of funny, since I expect them to make me feel better, but it's not like I'm seeing them as repairing anything. I just see them as enhancing health as opposed to remedial treatment."
—Female, 30s, Chicago

.•.

"I started taking vitamins, minerals and herbal products probably thirteen or fourteen years ago for health reasons. At that time I found out I was HIV-positive and there was nothing in terms of medication. I had read some articles about vitamin and herb regimens and I figured they couldn't hurt—and maybe

they could help. So, I put together a program from a couple of
books. I would see the same herb or mineral repeated a number
of times as immune-related and thought they must be good. I've
modified the program over the years."

—Male, 40s, New York

INTRODUCTION

As growing scientific evidence validates the efficacy of nutritional supplementation and studies from abroad prove the benefits of some herbal remedies, more and more consumers are starting out the day with an extra nutritional boost. While the majority of consumers limit their supplementation to a single multivitamin, others opt for an individualized "cocktail" approach, distributing a complex combination of nutrients throughout the day in efforts to alleviate or prevent a host of specific health conditions. Whatever the approach, the world of vitamin, mineral, herbal and dietary supplementation is growing like never before, fueled by a growing acceptance within the conventional health care community.

Our studies regarding the organic industry and food and the environment provide key insights into the connection between pragmatic health concerns and social and environmental consciousness. However, our series of studies on the vitamin, mineral, herbal and dietary supplement (VMHS) product world delves more thoroughly into self-centered issues of personal health.

Our VMHS research represents a new empirical standard in understanding what drives consumer purchase and use of products in this category. As with our other consumer segmentation studies, our VMHS research scrutinizes consumer participation in this arena. By focusing on the connection between consumer segments, brands and product types, it examines key factors regarding how and why consumers begin using VMHS products. It explores the sources from which consumers seek VMHS information. It also addresses which health benefits they seek and the specific symptoms they attempt to treat with specific products.

Our study titled *U.S. Consumer Use of Vitamins, Minerals, Herbals and Dietary Supplements: Phase I*[6] (*VMHS: Phase I*) surveyed 60,000

---

[6] See Appendix I for more detailed information on this study.

U.S. households to offer insight regarding consumer use not only of twenty-five commonly used vitamins and minerals, but also seventy-two other dietary supplements including herbal and botanical therapies. Among our most important findings is that approximately 20 percent of U.S. households have used seven or more VMHS products within a recent six-month period. It is important to note that once households cross the threshold of using four to six supplements, average use jumps to nearly thirteen supplements. This clearly demonstrates consumers' profound and growing interest in and acceptance of VMHS products. Tables 7-1 and 7-2 show the percent of the U.S. population taking vitamins, minerals, herbals and other dietary supplements.

Table 7-1. Percent of the U.S. Population Taking Vitamins and Minerals

Vitamin/Mineral	Percent of Total U.S. Population Using
Multi-vitamins	51.1
Vitamin C	28.7
Vitamin E	27.0
Calcium	24.6
Zinc	10.8
Children's Vitamins	10.4
Vitamin B Complex	9.7
Iron	8.3
Potassium	8.1
Vitamin B12	6.6
Chromium Compounds	6.3
Vitamin A	5.0
Folic Acid	4.9
Selenium	4.6
Lecithin	4.4
Vitamin B6	4.3
Vitamin D	4.0
Vitamin B	3.5
Niacin	3.4
Vitamin C with Bioflavonoids	3.0
Trace Minerals	2.7
Vitamin B1	1.8
Biotin	1.6
Vitamin B2	1.3
Pantothenic Acid	1.1

Source: *VMHS: Phase I*, The Hartman Group, March 1998
Respondent Sample: 43,442

Table 7-2. Percent of the U.S. Population Taking Herbals and Other Supplements

Herbal or Supplement	Percent of Total U.S. Population Using
Garlic	12.0
Ginseng	9.6
Ginkgo/*Ginkgo Biloba*	8.8
Echinacea	7.4
Anti-oxidants (blend or formula)	7.3
Beta Carotene	5.9
Chamomile	5.7
Alpha Hydroxy Acids	5.4
St. John's Wort	5.2
Diet Supplements	5.0
Cayenne	4.6
Energy Supplements	4.6
Melatonin	4.4
Acidopholus	4.3
Ginger Root	3.9
DHEA	3.4
Bee Pollen	3.3
Fish Oil	3.0
Goldenseal	3.0
Meal Replacement Products	2.6
Amino Acids	2.5
Glucosamine	2.5
Alfalfa	2.5
Saw Palmetto	2.4
Cranberry Extract	2.3
Valerian Root	2.1
Green Tea Extract	1.9
Sports Nutrition Supplements	1.8
Evening Primrose Oil/Primrose	1.7
Enzymes	1.7
Grapeseed Extract	1.5
Kelp	1.5
Bilberry	1.4
Chondroitin	1.2
Feverfew	1.2
Royal Jelly	1.2
Licorice Root	1.1
Dong Quai	1.0
Flax Oil	1.0
Ephedra/Ma Huang	0.9
L-Carnitine	0.9
Spirulina	0.9
Essential Oil Blends (EFA)	0.8
Barley Grass	0.7
Milk Thistle	0.8
Yohimbe	0.8
Creatine	0.7
Eyebright	0.7
Guarana	0.7

Continued on next page

Herbal or Supplement	Percent of Total U.S. Population Using
Wheat Germ Oil	0.7
Kava Kava	0.6
Black Cohosh	0.5
Pine Bark Extract	0.5
Red Clover	0.5
Hawthorn	0.5
Yucca	0.4
Cholestin	0.3
Inositol	0.3
Borage Oil	0.3
Carotenids	0.3
Soy Isoflavones	0.3
Alpha Lipoic Acid	0.2
DHA	0.2
Pygeum	0.2
Glutathione	0.1
Hemp Oil	0.1
Lutein	0.1
N-acetyl Cysteine (NAC)	0.1
Vitex/Chaste Berry	0.1
Beta Sitosterol	0.1
Horse Chestnut	0.1
Lycopene	0.1

Source: *VMHS: Phase I*, The Hartman Group, March 1998, Respondent Sample: 43,442

We will more fully explore *VMHS: Phase I* data and other findings, as well as what this means within specific consumer segments, later. First, in order to understand the foundation supporting such explosive growth, we feel it is crucial to understand the key catalyst responsible for many of our wider social and cultural changes: the pursuit of wellness.

EVOLVING MOTIVATIONS

We see a variety of demographic, health-care-related and marketplace changes influencing the adoption of a more complex approach to health and wellness. We've broadly classified these into the categories described in the following sections.

Aging of the Baby Boomer Population

As the "baby-boomers" turn fifty, this growing consumer group drives changes throughout the health care marketplace. These consumers are better-educated, more comfortable with technology and more individualistic than previous generations. They have an intense interest in living longer and improving the quality of their later years.

Entry of the Second Baby Boomer Wave into the Adult Population

Many second-generation Boomers grew up familiar with concepts associated with environmental protection and preventive health care. The incorporation of dietary supplementation into their daily lives comes more easily to this group. In addition, the more affluent among them use herbal supplements in much greater proportions than the general population.

More Widely Disseminated Information on Preventive Medicine and Alternative Health Care

Through the explosion of health-information media, health promotion campaigns and the dramatic growth of Internet use, consumers have access to a much wider variety of health-related information than ever before.

A computer search of the Lexis-Nexis database covering 2,591 U.S magazines and 70 major U.S. newspapers uncovered a total of 75 references to the words "herb" or "herbal" in 1988, more than 1,200 references in 1997, and an estimated 1,300 or more in 1998 (see figure 7-1).

Figure 7-1. Appearance of Topics "(Herbs or Herbal and Dietary) and (Supplements or Medicine)" in 2,591 U.S. Magazines and 70 Major U.S. Newspapers, 1988–1998

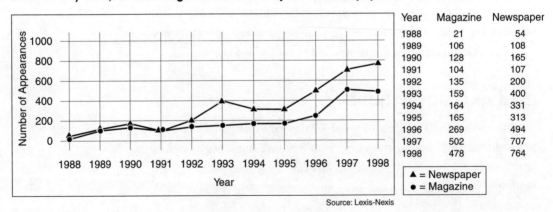

Year	Magazine	Newspaper
1988	21	54
1989	106	108
1990	128	165
1991	104	107
1992	135	200
1993	159	400
1994	164	331
1995	165	313
1996	269	494
1997	502	707
1998	478	764

▲ = Newspaper
● = Magazine

Source: Lexis-Nexis

Consumers can now conduct their own research online and communicate with other VMHS users, sharing experiences and recommendations, within a matter of minutes. Health-related magazines and newsletters have proliferated and specialized health information has filtered down into general-interest publications that require a much lower reading level. Thus, we see a growing interest in supplementation at all age levels and even within lower-income groups.

Limits Imposed by the U.S. Health Care System

Ironically, while preventive medicine gains more acceptance in conventional health circles, limits imposed by the structure of U.S. health care systems may push some to take more responsibility for personal health. As such, the U.S. population has begun to rely much more heavily on methods of self-care, including dietary supplementation.

This results in part from the rise of Health Maintenance Organizations (HMOs) as key features of the U.S. medical system. In some cases, HMOs may make it unprofitable for medical practitioners to thoroughly evaluate and respond to patients on an individual basis. Heath professionals who belong to HMOs typically receive the same payment per patient whether or not an office visit takes place, resulting in diminished doctor-patient contact and relationships. While a family doctor used to treat all members of a family over several decades, becoming acquainted with both the genetic and cultural environment of family members, this is no longer the case. Office visits now may occur between a doctor and patient who have never previously met. When corporations change their HMO providers frequently, individuals and their family members may be forced to continuously change practitioners as well. As a result, some patients have become dissatisfied with their quality of care and choose to treat their health conditions themselves.

Insurance Coverage Of Alternative Therapies

Health insurance and managed care companies have begun offering coverage for alternative medical practices such as acupuncture, chiropractic and naturopathic medicine. While this change likely relates to lowering treatment costs associated with chronic disease, it also increases potential access to alternative therapies. Once consumers begin thinking outside the "proverbial box" of conventional medicine, it is only a matter of time before individual responsibility for health becomes the norm rather than the exception.

Increased Availability of VMHS Products

Dietary supplement brands and product lines have become prevalent in grocery stores, club stores and all types of discount outlets and superstores.

Many supplements, particularly herbals, which were once found only in health food stores, have become available in stores such as K-Mart and Target. Additionally, the proliferation of direct-mail catalogs and advertising has made the purchase of VMHS products both convenient and more affordable, even to those with restricted mobility.

Increased Acceptance of Preventive Medicine in Conventional Health Care Circles

Practitioners in a variety of medical professions have begun to recognize the benefits of VMHS supplement, especially with basic nutrients such as vitamin C, Vitamin E and calcium. Forty-four schools throughout the United States have implemented alternative medicine courses, including those covering dietary supplementation. In addition, Harvard University has begun hosting an annual conference on alternative medicine.

Increased Scientific Proof of the Efficacy of VMHS Products

Research and access to information that uncovers the health value of supplementation is a very important factor in the escalating consumer purchase and use of dietary supplements. Supplement research is also likely a significant factor in the growing acceptance of alternative therapies, including dietary supplementation, in conventional health care circles. Not so long ago, the picture was entirely different.

As recently as the late 1970s, the concept of preventive medicine was nearly nonexistent. In fact, the U.S. Department of Health, Education and Welfare first acknowledged the power of a preventive approach to health when it established the Office of Disease Prevention and Health Promotion in 1976. In 1979, this department produced *Healthy People: The Surgeon General's Report of Health Promotion and Disease Prevention*, which was at that time a revolutionary step in managing the nation's health. It represented "an emerging consensus among scientists and the health community that the nation's health strategy must be dramatically recast to emphasize the prevention of disease." In 1980, the U.S. Department of Health and Human Services published *Promoting Health/Preventing Disease: Objectives for the Nation*, which, for the first time, officially emphasized the importance of decreasing smoking and improving nutrition, physical fitness and stress management as methods for promoting health.

In 1990, the Secretary of Health and Human Services, Dr. Louis Sullivan, presented *Healthy People 2000: National Health Promotion and Disease Prevention Objectives*. This program expanded on the initial health objectives and emphasized managing the risk factors associated with cardiovascular disease, cancer, diabetes and other chronic and/or disabling diseases. The development of *Healthy People 2010* has already begun as our nation's health organizations continue to address the importance of managing economic burdens and threats to quality of life as we enter the next millennium. These new objectives will focus even more on "emerging issues such as changing demographics, advances in preventive therapies and new technologies," factors that have played central roles in the adoption of a broader approach to health.

Two decades after the initial *Healthy People* report, acceptance of preventive medicine continues to grow, especially in the realm of nutrition management and therapy. For example, in April and August, 1997, the National Academy of Sciences released the first two in a series of seven reports which will restructure the Recommended Daily Allowance (RDA), the standard by which we have judged our nutritional status for the past fifty years. First developed in the 1940s to prevent acute deficiency diseases such as scurvy and rickets, the RDAs are being updated and improved by new measurements called Dietary Reference Intakes (DRIs). The DRIs will reflect scientific studies that prove the efficacy of nutrition not only in alleviating deficiency diseases, but also in promoting and maintaining optimal health.

The first set of DRIs nearly doubles the recommended intake of calcium for some populations such as teenage girls. The most recent report on folic acid and the B-complex vitamins verifies long-held theories that folic acid not only prevents neural tube birth defects, but effectively protects against cardiovascular disease. Such claims are supported by a recent meta-analysis that concluded that 56,000 deaths from heart disease could be prevented annually if Americans consumed protective amounts of folic acid. Reports to follow include those on antioxidants (such as vitamins C and E and selenium), macronutrients (such as protein, fat and carbohydrates), trace elements (such as zinc and iron), other food components (such as fiber and phytoestrogens) and electrolytes and water.

The conventional medical community long resisted claims that nutritional therapy could prevent chronic diseases such as cardiovascular disease and cancer, relying instead on conventional, technical means for treating disease, but that is rapidly changing. "Our understanding of the relationship between nutrition and chronic disease has progressed to the point where we can now begin to recommend intakes that are thought to help people achieve measurable physical indicators of good health," says Vernon Young, chair of the Institute of Medicine's (IOM) standing committee on DRIs. "The new DRIs represent a major leap forward in nutrition science—from a primary concern for the prevention of deficiency to an emphasis on beneficial effects of healthy eating."

Similarly, prior to the restructuring of the RDA, Congress passed groundbreaking legislation that not only improved the public's access to nutritional products such as vitamins and minerals, but also included herbal remedies (such as St. John's wort, garlic and gingko) in the category of dietary supplements. The Dietary Supplement Health and Education Act of 1994 (DSHEA) also mandated increased consumer access to information and education about such products. DSHEA called for the establishment of the Office of Dietary Supplements, which has developed a set of guidelines to improve the education of conventional medical practitioners, pharmacists and retailers regarding the safe use of these products.[7]

All of these factors interact to positively affect the VMHS industry. Dietary supplements may be essential to slowing the aging process, increasing immune system responses and minimizing the effects of a stressful lifestyle. Additionally, they may treat colds and flues, two common causes of office visits. They may even moderate the effects of lifestage changes such as menopause. For women in their childbearing years, VMHS products may contribute to the health of their babies, even preventing some common birth defects. Once individuals begin using supplements, they almost undoubtedly see an improvement in their health or well-being. As a result, they consider the use of additional supplements. As mentioned earlier, once users cross that four- to six-supplement threshold, they jump using on average more than thirteen supplements.

---

[7] Dietary Supplement Health and Education Act, Public Law 103-417, October 24, 1994.

More than three out of ten VMHS product users (9,167 respondents) fell into our multi-product category, meaning that they used more than seven supplements in a recent six-month period, far exceeding average use. In fact, many vitamins and minerals enjoy a usage rate by these consumers that is ten times higher than average. The multi-product users constitute a distinct, highly supplementation-oriented group warranting a much closer examination, which we performed in the second part of our VMHS series, *U.S. Consumer Use of Vitamins, Minerals, Herbals and Dietary Supplements: Multi-Product Users.*[8]

MULTI-PRODUCT USERS

For clarity, the term "average use" in this section refers to average use among the multi-product users, who make up 20 percent of the U.S. population.

Consider the medicine cabinets in multi-product user households. More than four out of five will contain a multivitamin and fully two-thirds will contain vitamins C and E. More than half of multi-product users will stock their cabinets with calcium and garlic supplements. One-third of these users will stock up on zinc, B-complex vitamins, ginseng and other herbals.

Even though dietary supplementation has increased dramatically in recent years across all segments of our population, the rate of usage among multi-product users is astounding. So, who are these people and what products do they use most often and for what purpose? What accounts for their penchant for pill popping—what motivates their purchases and what keeps them coming back for more? Perhaps more importantly, what can we do to influence the rest of the population to join the ranks of the multi-product users?

We answered these as well as other questions in our cluster analysis of the multi-product users and came up with five clusters: the Auntie Oxidants, Herbalvores, Flavorites, Basic Care users and High-Energy Parents. The size and characteristics of each segments are summarized in Figure 7-2.

---

[8] See Appendix I for more detailed information about this report.

Figure 7-2. Multi-Product Users: Relative Cluster Sizes, Usage Patterns and Signature Supplements

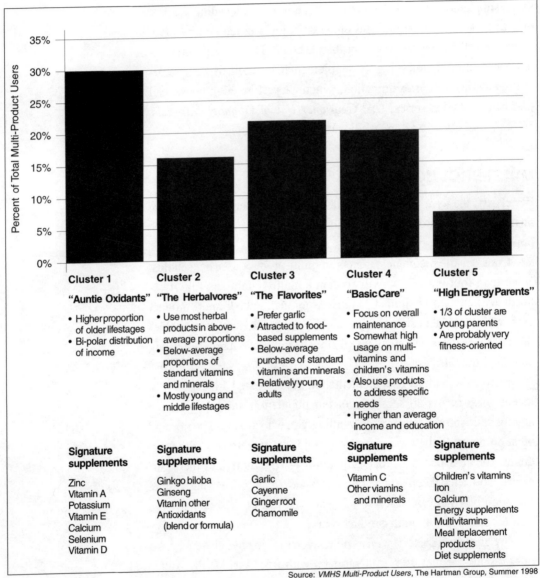

Source: *VMHS Multi-Product Users*, The Hartman Group, Summer 1998

Cluster One: The Auntie Oxidants

So-named because this group contains nearly half of the females in the thirty-five-years-and-older age group, the members of this cluster use supplements—such as antioxidants and a variety of other vitamins and minerals—to strengthen their immune systems and resist chronic disease. This cluster contains an over-representation of pre-baby boomers and for the most part remains loyal to "doctor-recommended" supplements. Their supplement use mirrors the supplementation profile of the older age groups in general. Auntie Oxidants demonstrate above-average purchase of zinc, vitamin A, potassium, vitamin E, calcium, selenium, vitamin D and the B vitamins, as well as a host of other supplements. They don not appear interested in herbals, although some members have begun to venture into the herbal arena.

The Auntie Oxidants form our largest cluster: More than three in ten multi-product users fell into this classification. This cluster's predominant lifestages include older singles (14 percent of the cluster), working older couples (17 percent), retired older couples (17 percent) and older parents (17 percent). Half of retired older couples, as well as nearly three out of five older singles fell into this cluster. Correspondingly, this group contains a below-average proportion of young singles, young couples and young parents. As with the majority of the older population, incomes within this group range across a broad spectrum. Two out of five in this cluster have yearly incomes less than $25,000 and they demonstrate below-average representation in the income groups above $25,000. Nevertheless, more than one-quarter earn more than $60,000 yearly.

Females in this cluster have a slightly higher representation at the lower end of the educational spectrum and are generally below average in their level of formal education. However, this may partly result from the fact that higher education wasn't considered appropriate for these women forty or more years ago. Auntie Oxidant males have an above-average representation at the lower end of the educational spectrum. Nearly half of those with only a grade school education fall into this category; however, nearly one-third of males with post-graduate degrees fall into this cluster as well.

Thus, this segment cannot easily be categorized with the exception of its over-representation by the older lifestages. The term "savvy seniors" probably most accurately describes this cluster. Whatever their marital status or educational level, they promote health through supplementation and appear knowledgeable in their choices.

Cluster Two: The Herbalvores

Herbalvores limit their VMHS use almost entirely to botanical, herbal and related products. In particular, a much greater proportion of Herbalvores use ginkgo/*ginkgo biloba* and ginseng compared to the average multi-product user. They use most herbal products at least as much as the average multi-product user. These users are also partial to antioxidant blends (25 percent above average). When looking at the range of products used in above-average proportions by this group, one gets the impression that these are "experimenters" who may try out various herbal and dietary supplements. Compared to the majority of multi-product users, this group has a low level of standard vitamin and mineral use, particularly vitamin C, calcium and vitamin E. This group definitely does not follow "doctor's orders" to use commonly preferred supplements.

The Herbalvores' incomes skew toward the higher end of the scale— nearly one-third (32 percent) have yearly household incomes above $60,000. Females in this group are much more likely to have earned associate's degrees and are somewhat more likely to have earned postgraduate degrees. The males in this segment are more likely to hold an associate or bachelor's degree.

With respect to lifestage, Herbalvores have a higher percentage of young singles, middle singles, young couples, middle parents and older parents than the multi-product group as a whole. Compared to other older groups, working older couples are more likely to fall into this segment.

Cluster Three: The Flavorites

Overall, Flavorites are relatively young, near average across most demographic variables and united by a strong preference for food-related herbals. They have a strong preference for garlic; in fact, nearly everyone in the cluster has used this supplement in the past six months. These cluster members share an attraction for any supplement that relates to a familiar food or tea, including cayenne, ginger-root, chamomile, ginseng, green tea extract, royal jelly, cranberry extract, and licorice root. In general, they purchase supplements that have a distinctly "non-food" sound, such as "inositol" in below-average quantities. Like Herbalvores, Flavorites have below-average use of standard vitamins and minerals, particularly zinc, calcium and other nutrients.

The Flavorites more likely fall into the young couple, young parent or middle parent lifestages. As with Auntie Oxidants, Flavorites are more likely to occupy the lower ends of the income scale, but also have a fair representation in the above $60,000 range. Male members of Cluster Three fall near the multi-product-user average in educational level, but are slightly less likely to have a bachelor's degree or post-graduate degree. Females in this group follow a similar pattern.

Cluster Four: Basic Care Users

Unlike the Herbalvores, members of the Basic Care segment are more focused and appear to select only products that fulfill distinct needs. They limit their supplementation to basic requirements for general maintenance (vitamin C, multivitamins and children's vitamins) as well as other products such as chondroitin, glucosamine and St. John's wort, to address specific health needs. Members of this group shy away from garlic, zinc, potassium, ginseng, iron and ginkgo/*ginkgo biloba*. They also generally have below-average purchase rates of other "food-related" herbal products. Looking at the highly represented products of this cluster, one gets the impression that this is a "no-nonsense" group, composed of members who probably neither buy products on impulse nor randomly try various herbs to achieve a desired level of health.

Relative to multi-product users as a whole, Basic Care Users are more likely to be young couples, young parents, middle parents or older parents. Possibly as a function of having two working household heads, Basic Care Users are more likely to occupy the upper range of the income scale. More than one-third have household incomes above $60,000. This group has the best-educated female heads of households. More than one quarter of the females with post-graduate degrees are found in this group. For males, this forms the most highly educated cluster (second to Cluster One).

Cluster Five: High-Energy Parents

Picture this group as your typical, modern, frantic young family. Looking at the highly represented supplements for Cluster Five, one gets the impression that the High-Energy Parents typically rush through their day and make up for a lack of nutritious meals with vitamins for the children as well as other dietary supplements, energy supplements and meal replacement products for themselves. Like the Auntie Oxidants, High-Energy Parents make sure they get their iron and calcium, but they prefer multivitamins to individual vitamin supplements. They most likely have above-average physical fitness levels and use sports nutritional supplements to replace important dietary elements. This active cluster seeks supplements such as ephedra/ma huang and L-carnitine to improve performance.

One-third of this group consists of young parents, even though young parents make up only 12 percent of the multi-product users. Young singles have a slightly above-average representation, while all older lifestages are under-represented. Females in the High-Energy Parent segment are more likely than average to have an associate or bachelor's degree. Incomes of High-Energy Parents mirror the multi-product group as a whole.

SUMMARY

Overall, the market for VMHS products is gigantic. The Hartman Group continues to lead nationally in research on consumer purchase and use of dietary supplements. Our ongoing national purchase and usage study, *Supplement Report*, tracks weekly purchase and use of over 150 supplement products, by 140 brands, through 13 different purchase channels. *Supplement Report* projects the total U.S. market for dietary supplements at more than $10 billion for the July 1998–July 1999 year. *Supplement Report* is described more fully in Appendix I.

CHAPTER 8

U.S. Consumer Attitudes Toward and Use of Vitamins, Minerals, Herbals and Dietary Supplements

Whereas *VMHS: Phase I* focused on defining the broad strokes of consumers using supplement products, *U.S. Consumer Use of Vitamins, Minerals, Herbals and Dietary Supplements: Phase II*, conducted in August 1998, focused in depth on consumer attitudes, history of use, reasons for use, and a vast array of perceptual factors aimed at getting into the *why's* of consumer supplement use. *VMHS: Phase II* respondents were identified through the 29,000 supplement users researched in *VMHS: Phase I*. Thus, information in Chapter 8 reflects the attitudes and opinions of current U.S. supplement users. Over 2,000 supplement users were questioned on VMHS subjects, including the following:

- Duration and frequency of VMHS use
- Average doses of VMHS consumed per week
- Expected time to see results from using VMHS
- Forms of VMHS preferred
- Reasons why specific VMHS are used
- Importance of characteristics of VMHS
- How VMHS rate on key characteristics
- Attitudes toward VMHS

- Sources used to learn about VMHS and the trustworthiness of these sources
- Importance of VMHS brands
- VMHS purchasing behavior

DURATION AND FREQUENCY OF VMHS USE

Among current supplement users, vitamins have been taken for a longer period of time than either minerals or herbal supplements. Close to half of vitamin users have been taking vitamins for over ten years, compared to less than 40 percent of mineral users and about 15 percent of herbal supplement users. Figure 8-1 shows the mean number of years that vitamins, minerals and herbal supplements have been taken by current VMHS users. Consistent with *VMHS: Phase I* findings, supplement usage tends to increase with age. Older VMHS users are more likely than younger users to have been using supplements for a longer period of time, to use supplements daily, and to take seven or more doses of supplements per week. Figure 8-2 shows the percent of VMHS users who take supplements daily.

Figure 8-1. Mean Number of Years Using VMHS

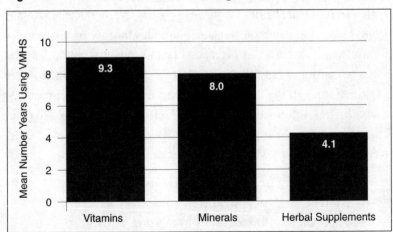

Figure 8-2. VMHS Users: Percent Who Take Supplements Daily

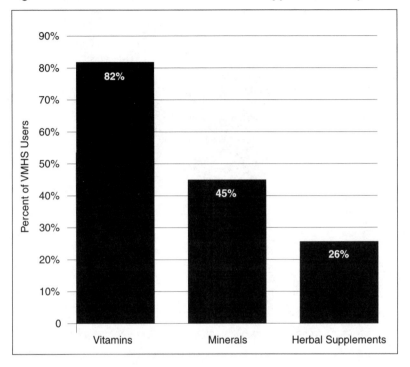

About 35 percent to 40 percent of current supplement users would increase their usage if they knew more about the products they take. For all types of supplements, younger users (under 50 years of age) would benefit more from VMHS knowledge than older users. As of 1998, most VMHS users (66 percent) have maintained their use of VMHS in the past year (see figure 8-3). However, about 30 percent of users had increased their supplement use, mainly they claim because:

- they want to improve or maintain their overall health
- they have become better informed about VMHS
- they are getting older.

VMHS usage is growing most among users under the age of 50, with 38 percent of this group increasing usage vs. a year ago.

Figure 8-3. Current VMHS Usage Compared to One Year Ago

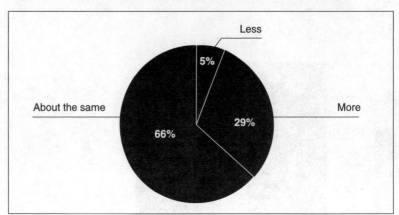

On average, VMHS users take about three different types of vitamins in a typical week and about two different types of minerals and herbal supplements. Consistent with the other usage behavior, users over the age of 50 take more different types of VMHS in a typical week than younger users.

Most *vitamins* and *minerals* are used for the general purpose of promoting health and wellness (see figure 8-4). The few vitamins and minerals that are used by most respondents for specific purposes include Vitamin C and Zinc (for colds, flu, fever), Calcium (for osteoporosis/bone weakness), Iron (for anemia), and Chromium Compounds (for weight control).

Figure 8-4. Reasons for VMHS Use

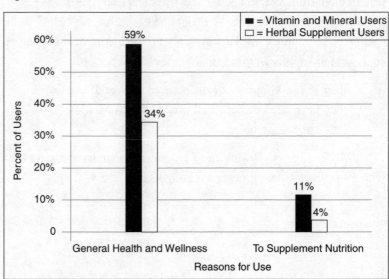

In general, *herbals* and other *dietary supplements* tend to be used for more specific purposes than vitamins and minerals. Some of the most frequently used herbal supplements and their reasons for use include Echinacea (for colds, flu, fever), Ginkgo (for memory loss), Ginseng (to increase energy levels), and St. John's Wort (for depression).

Close to 95 percent of VMHS users consider it extremely important or very important to take supplements to maintain or enhance their overall health, while about 85 percent consider it important to take them to prevent specific health problems.

One major reason why older consumers tend to take more supplements than younger consumers is because the majority (56 percent) of VMHS Users agree that the benefits from taking VMHS increase as you age. This belief is most strongly held by those users over the age of sixty.

> In general, *herbals and other dietary supplements* tend to be used for more specific purposes than vitamins and minerals.

INFORMATION SOURCES AND CONSUMER KNOWLEDGE

The most common sources of information consumers use to learn about VMHS include physicians and friends or relatives, with over one-half of users utilizing these sources (see table 8-1). In addition, physicians and pharmacists are considered the most trusted VMHS information sources, with over 90 percent of users rating these sources as extremely or very trustworthy (see table 8-2). Supplement users do not put much faith in VMHS advertising, as is shown by the fact that they consider some of the least trustworthy information sources infomercials (14.5 percent), TV commercials (18 percent), and print ads (19.1 percent) (see table 8-2).

Table 8-1. Sources of Information Used to Find Out About VMHS

Source	Percent VMHS Users Using
High Use Sources	
Physician	56.1
Friend/relative (other than mother)	49.7
Books	30.7
Magazines (not natural products)	29.5
Pharmacist	28.1
My mother	27.8
Magazines (natural products)	27.0
Advertisement (print)	24.6
Catalog/direct mail	20.4
Newspaper	19.1

Continued on next page

Medium Use Sources

Store display	17.2
TV commercial	16.2
Other health care practitioner	14.7
Store clerk/salesperson	13.7
Manufacturer's brochure	13.6
Nutritionist	13.0
Product sample(s)	12.8
Natural products company	12.2
TV program (not a commercial)	11.5

Low Use Sources

Chiropractor	10.7
Drug or pharmaceutical company	8.4
Herbalist	8.3
Internet	5.7
Government	5.4
Infomercial	5.1
Homeopath	4.6
Acupuncturist	4.2
Other	3.9
Naturopath	3.5

Total Sample, n=2,305

Table 8-2. Trustworthiness Ratings of Dietary Supplement Information Sources

Source	Percent of Users Who Found Source Trustworthy
Sources with High Trust	
Physician	95.0
Pharmacist	90.7
Nutritionist	85.4
Mother	84.5
Other health care practitioner	81.2
Friend/relative	80.1
Chiropractor	78.8
Other	76.8
Herbalist	72.1
Sources with Medium Trust	
Books	63.2
Homeopath	54.4
Acupuncturist	52.6
Product sample(s)	51.4
Natural products company	49.5
Natural products magazine	48.8
Drug or pharmaceutical company	47.1
Naturopath	43.0
Sources with Low Trust	
All other magazines	33.0
Store clerk/salesperson	32.9
Manufacturer's brochure	32.2

Continued on next page

TV program	31.8
Government	30.9
Catalog/direct mail	29.9
Newspaper	27.7
Store display	24.7
Internet	24.6
Advertisement (print)	19.1
TV commercial	18.0
Infomercial	14.5

Total Sample, n=2,274

Of all the attitudes about VMHS that were researched in *VMHS: Phase II*, the one that is held by the most respondents is the desire to know more about VMHS.

Not surprisingly given VMHS users' high trust in their physicians, close to 60 percent of users wish that their primary care physician could tell them more about dietary supplements.

Of all the attitudes about VMHS that were researched in *VMHS: Phase II*, the one that is held by the most respondents is the desire to know more about VMHS. Two-thirds of VMHS users wish they were more knowledgeable about VMHS, while only about one-quarter consider themselves more knowledgeable about VMHS than most people. Not surprisingly given their higher usage, older respondents feel more comfortable with their knowledge of VMHS than younger respondents. Many respondents claim that they would use more vitamins, minerals or herbal supplements if they knew more about them (see figure 8-5)

Figure 8-5. "If I knew more about VMHS, I would use more . . ."

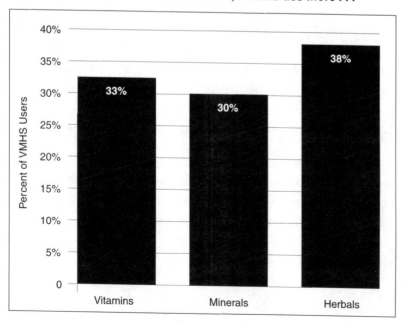

About 40 percent of VMHS users own books about VMHS, while about 35 percent regularly read publications about VMHS (see figure 8-6). The most popular publication for VMHS information is *Prevention*, with close to 60 percent of VMHS users who read VMHS publications reading this magazine. Other publications that are read by over 15 percent of these respondents include *Health* (31 percent), *Fitness* (18 percent), and *Natural Health* (16 percent).

Figure 8-6. VMHS Users. "Do you regularly read publications which cover VMHS?"

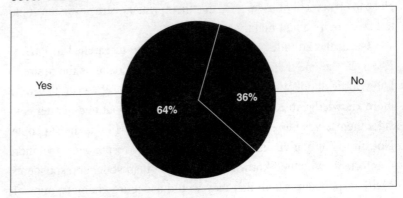

VALUE OF TRADITION

Tradition does not appear to be a significant factor behind respondents' use of herbal supplements. Only around 20 percent of VMHS users agree that VMHS are safe because of their long-term use in Europe and China, while less than 10 percent have a family history of using herbal supplements.

CONCERNS ABOUT USE OF DIETARY SUPPLEMENTS

Many supplement users (46 percent) are concerned about using supplements in combination with prescription medications. Although older consumers are more likely to take VMHS, they are also more concerned about using supplements in combination with prescription medications, possibly because their likelihood of taking prescription medication is much higher.

PRODUCT FORMATS AND EXPECTATIONS ABOUT EFFICACY

Preference about the format of supplements is fairly similar for vitamins and minerals, but very different for herbal supplements. About one-half of vitamin and mineral users prefer tablets, approximately one-third prefer capsules, and about 15 percent prefer gel-caps. Comparatively, the most-preferred forms for herbal supplements are capsules (41 percent), tablets (22 percent), gel-caps (18 percent), and teas (13 percent).

Most VMHS users expect to see results from taking supplements fairly quickly, with about one-third expecting results within one week, and 60 percent expecting results within one month.

BRAND ALLEGIANCE, LOYALTY AND MERCHANDISING

Consumers exhibit almost non-existent brand loyalty in the supplement category. Figure 8-7 shows brand switching among users of vitamins, minerals and herbal supplements. Only about 40 percent of VMHS users consider brand name to be important for vitamins and minerals, and only 32 percent consider it important for herbal supplements. Only about 20 percent of VMHS users believe that it is important to buy only nationally known brands of herbal supplements.

Figure 8-7. Brand Switching Among Supplement Users

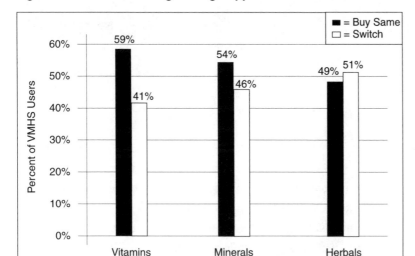

Consumers exhibit even less brand recognition and trust of various supplement brands. Figure 8-8 shows unaided responses to "best, most trusted supplement brands." The extremely low percentages of respondents citing specific brands indicates the fragmented nature of the market and the lack of importance consumers place on buying particular brands.

Figure 8-8. Best, Most Trusted Vitamin, Mineral, Herbal and Supplement Manufacturers (unaided responses)

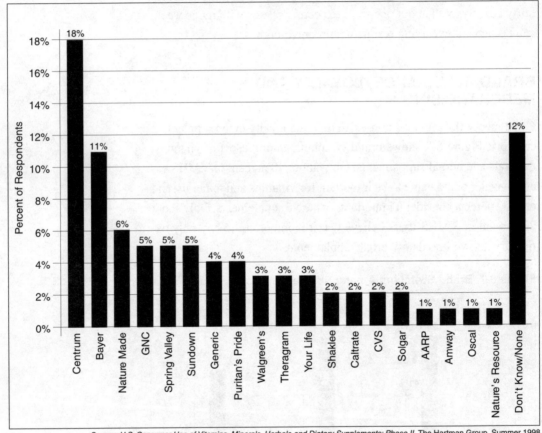

Source: *U.S. Consumer Use of Vitamins, Minerals, Herbals and Dietary Supplements: Phase II*, The Hartman Group, Summer 1998

Although having a well-known brand name is not particularly important, most VMHS users do believe there is a difference between VMHS brands. Only about one-quarter of VMHS users agree that all brands of vitamins and minerals are the same- so that they buy what is least expensive.

VMHS merchandising and store displays do not appear to be particularly important, as only about 7 percent of users rate them important for vitamins, minerals, or herbal supplements.

Herbal supplement manufacturers are well positioned to capitalize on cross-marketing opportunities. Because most herbal supplements tend to be used to treat specific conditions, herbal supplement manufacturers should consider packaging together several supplements that are used by consumers to treat the same condition. The package could be marketed as the best "natural" way to treat or prevent that particular condition.

CONCLUSIONS AND IMPLICATIONS FROM *VMHS: PHASE II*

Based on results from *VMHS: Phase II,* vitamin, mineral, herbal and dietary supplement manufacturers will benefit from helping to increase consumer knowledge, as consumers indicate that they would likely increase their purchasing of VMHS if they were more knowledgeable in this area. Current VMHS users want to learn more about dietary supplements; more users agreed with this statement than any other included in the study.

One possible way to increase consumer knowledge of dietary supplement is to focus on increasing physicians' knowledge and comfort with the category, perhaps following on the traditional pharmaceutical marketing model. Physicians are a key source for dietary supplement information and are considered by consumers to be the most trustworthy information source.

Branding implications as they relate to the supplement market and as raised in *VMHS: Phase II* are addressed in Chapter 13.

CHAPTER 9

When Alternative Medicine Stops Being Alternative

"I think the alternative practitioners have a much more wellness-oriented approach—but I couldn't have said that before my trip to California. The alternative theory is that you go to a chiropractor not because something hurts, but to see that things don't hurt . . . you don't necessarily wait until something's broken to go see them. Western medicine, other than annual physicals, has to do with fixing something rather than maintaining something."

—Female, 40s, Chicago

"You have to look upon your body, your personality and your soul more or less as a total picture. I think when you take care of your body, you have to realize that things you do to one part of your body can affect others. That's why I like the natural approach to health. Alternative medicine does look upon the body as a whole rather than just compartmentalizing it, looking at individual things. Natural products have a tendency to treat the whole self. They help you look at the overall health of your body and well-being."

—Female, 30s, Chicago

"It seems as if the doctors always just want you to take a pill. I think there's just too much dependency on [conventional/ synthetic] medicines in Western medicine culture. It's too much for me . . . I won't do it. I just don't see the point. If I have a headache in the middle of the night I take an aspirin. I'm not going to try to create a potion for myself. But, at the same time, I just don't think it's necessary to go to the doctors for something I can take care of myself."

—Female, 30s, New York

BACKGROUND

Just as recycling moved from the fringe to the mainstream, the organic industry and large segments of the alternative health care industry are now doing the same. Massage has become much more than an indulgence and acupuncture is often viewed more as a line of first defense rather than a last resort in cases of chronic pain. In the 1980s, talk therapy became the trend of choice; now that distinction belongs to chiropractic care, massage and nutritional counseling. Media attention on alternative medicine topics is rapidly on the rise (see figure 9-1).

Figure 9-1. Appearance of Topic "Alternative Medicine" in 2,591 U.S. Magazines and 70 Major U.S. Newspapers, 1988–1998

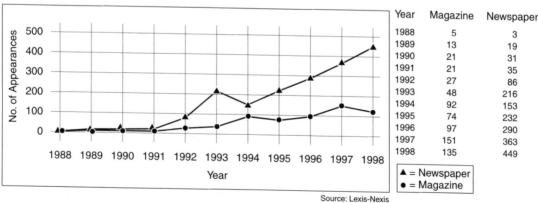

Year	Magazine	Newspaper
1988	5	3
1989	13	19
1990	21	31
1991	21	35
1992	27	86
1993	48	216
1994	92	153
1995	74	232
1996	97	290
1997	151	363
1998	135	449

▲ = Newspaper
● = Magazine

Source: Lexis-Nexis

Alternative and conventional health care practitioners often work side-by-side and many conventional health care facilities have incorporated a variety of so-called "alternative therapies," including massage and nutritional counseling, into their offered services. Where the medical community once viewed such practices as no more than "voodoo"—or, at the least, indulgent, futile and nonsensical—members of that community have begun to recognize the validity of some alternative healing practices, or at the very least, recognized the escalating consumer interest. More than forty-four U.S. medical schools have incorporated alternative healing courses into their primary coursework and one prominent medical school hosts an annual conference on alternative medicine.

Such developments represent an important cultural shift in the United States. More than the professed desire for "wellness" discussed in Part I, many Americans express an increased appreciation for nature, tradition, community, spirituality and personal responsibility. While this changing paradigm reverberates throughout many aspects of our society, its effects on the health care system are especially apparent. It has manifested itself in the emergence of holistic medical therapies such as acupuncture, herbal supplements, hypnosis and chiropractic into popular health care culture. These therapies, once outside the status quo, have become mainstream.

Physicians, insurance companies and health maintenance organizations, educational institutions, the government, pharmaceutical companies and the natural products industry have begun to turn their attention to these broad fields of healing often referred to as alternative, complementary alternative or unconventional medicine.

One of The Hartman Group's most recent studies, *Integrated Health Care: Consumer Use and Attitudes*, explores these issues by exploring consumer use of and perspectives toward various alternative healing practices. The one consistent finding that weaves throughout the study highlights the fact that the majority of the public views alternative medicine as a complement to conventional medicine rather than entirely separate from it. In fact, large numbers of respondents express an unprecedented interest in exploring the potential synergy between alternative and conventional medicine.

The Integrated Health Care study also found that only 13 percent of respondents would resist telling their medical doctor if they used an alternative practitioner. This is especially significant considering a finding reported in the *New England Journal of Medicine* in 1993 by David Eisenburg, M.D. of Harvard Medical School.[9] In his 1990 study,

[9] Eisenburg, David et al, "Unconventional Medicine in the United States: Prevalence, Costs and Patterns of Use," *New England Journal of Medicine* 328 (1993); 246–52.

Eisenburg found that 72 percent of Americans failed to tell their medical doctors about their use of alternative medicine. While there are differences in methodology between the two studies that cannot substantiate exact comparison, our results do suggest that communication between the public and their medical doctors may have improved. It may also signal the mainstreaming of alternative medicine and growth of integrated health care.

Considering the relative "newness" of some alternative practices in the mainstream health care industry, it is not surprising that perceptions regarding which modalities fall under the moniker "alternative" differ widely. For example, 60 percent of respondents view herbal supplements as alternative, but only 30 percent categorize vitamin and mineral supplements in the same way.

Despite such discrepancies, use of certain alternative modalities has become commonplace. For example, 69 percent of Americans supplement their diets with vitamin and mineral products, 34 percent use chiropractic, 24 percent use herbal supplements, 23 percent practice relaxation therapy and 22 percent opt for midwifery care. Most striking is the fact that people use alternative medicine to treat and prevent specific health conditions rather than to promote general well-being. In fact, respondents cite more than fifty health conditions treated by alternative medicine. Ten percent or more of the population uses alternative medicine to treat conditions such as backaches, colds/flues/fever, weight control, headaches, arthritis, stress, constipation, diarrhea, osteoporosis, sinus problems, fatigue, decreased energy level and sore throats.

Consumers opt for alternative medicine for a variety of reasons; however, our respondents cite the efficacy of alternative medicine most frequently as a reason, reflecting a history of satisfactory experiences with such modalities. In addition, many turn to alternative medicine due to dissatisfaction with the efficacy of conventional practices in ameliorating their health conditions. They also choose alternative medicine because they prefer natural substances to synthetic drugs.

While people may have an affinity for natural, "drug-free" treatments, they also remain cautious about their inherent safety. They cite similar concerns regarding the safety and side effects of alternative treatments as they do for conventional treatments. In addition, they have concerns regarding the potential drug interactions between alternative and conventional medicines. Interestingly, the perceived lack of scientific testing and validation remains one of the largest barriers to the adoption of alternative medicine. Many consumers consider scientific validation of safety and efficacy much more reliable than evidence based on traditional or historical use.

Scientific or not, the public is hungry for consistent, quality information about alternative healing practices. They routinely and actively seek information from a variety of sources, especially medical doctors, pharmacists, books, mass media, personal recommendations and health care insurance provides. While the majority of the population cites medical doctors as their primary health care information source, 45 percent rely on a variety of sources other than medical doctors.

Despite their interest in gathering information, most respondents don't consider themselves particularly knowledgeable regarding health topics. This may reflect a lack of quality, consistency and clarity in the presently available health care information. Lack of effective communication about existing scientific research may significantly impede alternative medicine's adoption potential. This discrepancy also suggests a primary opportunity for the emergence of a more trusted information source to address integrated health care topics.

ALTERNATIVE HEALTH CARE MARKET SEGMENTS

As with the rest of our consumer segmentations, the nine alternative health care segments that resulted from a cluster analysis provide insights regarding key barriers to participation in the alternative medicine industry. We've separated the segments into four groups based on level of participation: Heavy Usage, Moderate Usage, Light Usage, and Minimal Usage. The sub-segments within each group demonstrate unique considerations regarding adoption of alternative medicine.

High Usage

Our high usage group includes the Natural Lifestylers (9 percent) and Natural Therapeutics (7 percent), which are not surprisingly our smallest segments. The **Natural Lifestylers** segment consists of young respondents falling into the 18- to 39-year-old brackets. At the same time, this group is represented by a large number of older parents. These highly educated professionals have the highest incomes and live in New England and Pacific cities. They take responsibility for their own health, assign lower importance to scientific evidence regarding the efficacy of alternative medicine, have high interest in health and nutrition information, enjoy a tradition of family usage in alternative medicine and respond to the motivation of health insurance coverage of alternative medicine. In particular, they have above-average participation in relaxation therapy, stress management, nutrition and diet, regular exercise, acupuncture, midwifery, hypnosis and imagery.

Our youngest segment, the **Natural Therapeutics**, tend to hold technical or sales positions. They take responsibility for their own health, have a high interest in using alternative practitioners, feel that prescription and over-the-counter medications have side-effects while alternative medicines are safe, and attribute high efficacy to herbal supplements. They respond to the motivation of health insurance coverage of alternative medicine, have high self-assessed health and nutrition knowledge levels, have high environmental concern and have a family tradition of using herbs and alternative medicine.

Moderate Usage

The Herbal Allies (7 percent) and the Aligned Plus (12 percent) make up our moderate usage group. As the name implies, the **Herbal Allies** demonstrate above-average use of herbal supplements as well as vitamins, minerals and other natural remedies. Herbal Allies are more likely than average to be fifty to sixty years of age or older and live in lower-income households in smaller towns in the East South Central region.[10] Nearly half (48 percent) of Herbal Allies stated that expanded insurance coverage of alternative medicine would probably motivate them to use more of these therapies. Members of this segment take responsibility for their own health, attribute high efficacy to herbal supplements, have high self-assessed knowledge about herbal supplements and believe that diet and exercise are key determinants of good health.

---

[10] This is a region classified by the U.S. Census. See Appendix III for region descriptions.

The **Aligned Plus** contain a higher percentage of the lower age groups, primarily consisting of consumers 18 to 49 years of age. These young singles are highly educated and live in middle- and higher-income households. They take responsibility for their own health and have a high concern for the benefits of diet and exercise. They demonstrate above-average participation in chiropractic, nutrition and diet, regular exercise, vitamin and mineral supplements and midwifery. The Aligned Plus are the group least likely to believe that alternative medicine is safe, and scientific research proving its safety and efficacy may be important to their future adoption of alternative medicine modalities.

Light Usage

Our light usage group consists of the Healthy Traditionalists (10 percent), the Self-Reliants (13 percent) and the Aligned (11 percent). More likely to consist of respondents in the middle age brackets (30 to 49 years old), the **Healthy Traditionalists** have above-average incomes and live in the South Atlantic regions.[11] Though they have a higher self-assessed nutrition knowledge levels, they feel health maintenance falls more under their physician's responsibility than their own and they have a low interest in using alternative medicine. They assign high importance to scientific evidence regarding the safety and efficacy of alternative health care practitioners and modalities. They profess above-average participation in midwifery, nutrition, regular exercise and stress management practices.

Although **Self-Reliants** likely fall in the same age groups as Healthy Traditionalists, members of this segment express an openness to alternative health care practitioners and modalities if provided with scientific evidence. As professional, highly educated, married young parents, they believe that diet and exercise are key determinants of good health. They demonstrate above-average participation in and use of self-help practices, stress management, relaxation therapy, nutrition and diet, regular exercise, and vitamin and mineral supplements.

The **Aligned** include all demographic characteristics. Considering their wide population representation, it is interesting to note that they report above-average participation in chiropractic, but below-average

---

[11] This is a region classified by the U.S. Census. See Appendix III for region descriptions.

participation in all other health care methods. They have a lower interest in health and nutrition information and low interest in alternative health care practitioners and modalities.

Minimal Usage

In the minimal usage group, we find the Uninvolved (13 percent) and the Fitness Fans (18 percent).

Members of the **Uninvolved** segment are more likely to be seniors, particularly retired older singles. They tend to have only a high school education and live in lower-income households. This group consists of an above-average percentage of West South Central residents.[12]

Members of this group aren't jumping through any hoops in the pursuit of health. They feel the responsibility for personal health lies mainly with their physician rather than with themselves; they view themselves as patients rather than active participants in their own health care regimen. In fact, they aren't likely even to have a health care regimen—we could easily refer to them as Passive Patients rather than simply Uninvolved. They demonstrate low concern for the benefits of diet and exercise, have low interest in health and nutrition information and are not motivated by insurance coverage to use alternative health care practitioners and therapies.

Although the **Fitness Fans** group also consists largely of seniors or older, retired singles, they demonstrate an entirely different action profile than do the Uninvolved. Although they have below-average interest and participation in alternative medicine, they demonstrate above-average participation in regular exercise. They also have low self-assessed knowledge levels of health and nutrition.

Figure 9-2 shows the breakdown of the population into these alternative health care user segments and Figure 9-3 summarized the characteristics of each segment.

---

[12] This is a region classified by the U.S. Census. See Appendix III for region descriptions.

Figure 9-2. Alternative Health Care User Segments (percent of U.S. population)

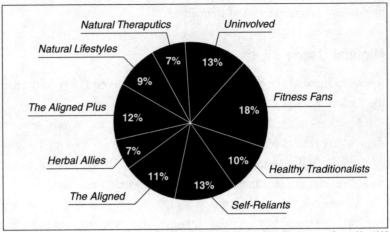

Source: *Integrated Health Care*, The Hartman Group, Nov 1998

Figure 9-3. Summary Alternative Health Care Cluster Descriptions

	NATURAL LIFESTYLES 9%	NATURAL THERAPEUTICS 7%
Heavy Usage	Above-average participation in alternative medicine, especially relaxation therapy, nutrition/diet, stress management, regular exercise, acupuncture, midwifery, hypnosis, practitioners, imagery	Above-average participation in alternative medicine, especially natural remedies, vitamin/mineral supplements, treatments by alternative health care very high herbal supplement usage
	More likely to be: 18–39 years old, Older Parents, Professionals, Highly Educated, Highest Average Income households, New England and Pacific Residents, City Dwellers	*More likely to be:* 18–29 years old, Technical and Sales Occupation

	HERBAL ALLIES 7%	THE ALIGNED PLUS 12%
Moderate Usage	Above-average participation in vitamin/mineral supplements, natural remedies and especially herbal supplements	Above-average participation in chiropractic, nutrition/diet, regular exercise, vitamin/mineral supplements, midwifery
	More likely to be: 50–60+ years old, Lower Income, East South Central Residents, <100,000 Population Area Residents	*More likely to be:* 18–49 years old, Young Singles, Highly Educated, Middle and Higher Income Households

	HEALTHY TRADITIONALISTS 10%	SELF-RELIANTS 13%	THE ALIGNED 11%
Light Usage	Above-average participation in nutrition/diet, regular exercise, stress management, midwifery	Above-average participation in self-help, nutrition/diet, regular exercise, relaxation therapy, vitamin/mineral supplements	Above-average participation in chiropractic with below-average participation in all other health care modalities
	More likely to be: 30–49 years old, Higher Income Household, South Atlantic Residents	*More likely to be:* 30–49 years old, Married, Middle and Higher Income Households, Highly Educated, Young Parents, Professionals	*More likely to be:* Average representation of demographic characteristics

	UNINVOLVED 13%	FITNESS FANS 18%
Minimal Usage	No participation or below-average participation in health care modalities	Above-average participation in regular exercise with below-average participation in alternative medicine
	More likely to be: Seniors, Older Singles, Retired, High School Educated, Lower Income	*More likely to be:* Seniors, Older Singles, Retired

Exploring America's Changing Culture and Lifestyle

BACKGROUND

Consumers are individuals with goals, preferences, and attitudes, but consumers are also real people responding to a host of pressures, influences, and constraints, many of which emanate from larger societal forces. These forces include culture, institutions (e.g., economy, family, religion, work) and trends (e.g., fads and fashions), all of which have the power to modify and direct consumer behavior.

Researchers often target the individual consumer with a well-honed collection of research strategies and methods. These approaches are most often derived from an individual perspective on human behavior. Traditional accounts of consumer behavior in economic and business literature focus on the individual consumer, often neglecting the role that societal-level forces play in patterning consumer behavior.

Economists typically model consumer behavior in a starkly individualistic, utilitarian world of costs and benefits, as if consumer behavior takes place in a vacuum without influence from the outside world. Similarly, much business literature—applied as well as academic—relies heavily on psychology and related studies of the individual to better explain consumer behavior.

The Hartman Group, working in conjunction with NFO Worldwide,[1] has fielded and analyzed the results of a series of major studies designed specifically to measure the effects and impacts of social and cultural trends on individual consumers—the people who actually purchase natural and organic products; vitamins, minerals, herbals and dietary supplements; and natural household, health and beauty products—as well as consumers who seek out alternative healing practices and services.

Part III describes The Hartman Group's innovative approach to learning why consumers act as they do, with the goal of providing insights, strategies, and tactics for both natural and conventional marketers of consumer products and services.

---

[1] Most major consumer studies conducted by The Hartman Group are fielded in partnership with National Family Opinion (NFO) Worldwide, the ninth largest market research company in the world. NFO's panel membership is the largest in the United States and consists, in total, of some 525,000 U.S. households. NFO panels are balanced and controlled to be representative of the forty-eight contiguous states, based on U.S. Bureau of Census data nationally and within each of nine Census divisions. Demographic information on each panel member is available from over 133 selected variables representing eleven major categories.

CHAPTER 10

Analyzing the Changing Consumer

BACKGROUND

Health-related products and services are some of the most turbulently changing product categories in business today. Key segments of the American population are veering away from the trusted medical and nutritional approaches of the past. Where once there were a few, prescribed methods, suddenly there are dozens of alternatives. Traditional health product and service providers are being challenged by alternative providers who in many cases do not play by the same rules in garnering and servicing customers. Understanding attitudes, use and behaviors is central to marketing to a changing consumer.

HOW WE ANALYZE

The Hartman Group utilizes all classic market research methodologies in tandem with applied sociological and anthropologic research methods. Much of our work focuses on three types of research:

1. Consumer response to new natural product and service introductions and concepts
2. Identification of consumer segments and percentages of the population using natural products and services

3. Sociological examination of underlying behaviors and drivers of consumer behavior in the natural products and services category

Table 10-1 presents some of The Hartman Group's major research studies and areas of focus.

Table 10-1. Research Studies and Work Areas of The Hartman Group
Client Needs: Assess consumer segments and identify new product offerings and potential new categories for natural product promotion and placement

Product Category	Hartman Group Products and Services
Natural and Organic Food and Beverage	• *Food and the Environment* Studies • Proprietary Organic • Proprietary Natural Food Research and Functional Food Ingredients • *Natural Sensibility 2*
Supplements	• *Supplement Report* • *Natural Sensibility 2* • *VMHS* Studies
Personal Care	• Proprietary Research • *Natural Sensibility 2*
Natural Household **Products**	• Proprietary Research • *Natural Sensibility 2*
Functional Foods	• *Supplement Report* • Proprietary Research • *Natural Sensibility 2* • New Research
Integrated Medicine	• *Integrated Health Care* studies
Wellness Category Management	• Proprietary Research • *N / sight* cultural analysis

Typically, new product introduction and concept development focuses on identifying the consumer perception of values placed on a product or service. From these findings, which typically involve focus group work, personal interviews and/or in-store observation, a working language is assembled around a product or service. Once this language is understood, we can undertake nationally representative studies using classic mail, telephone and interview methods.

Figure 10-1. Segmentation Methodology: Hypothetical Process for a Study Analyzing Consumer Attitudes and Use of Natural Health and Beauty Aids

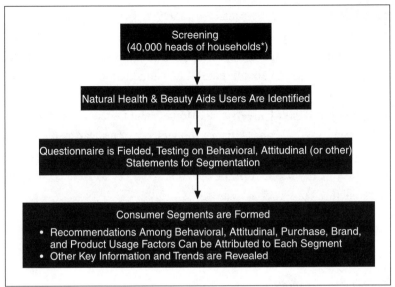

*National Family Opinion to be used for fielding and tabbing

The Hartman Group uses segmentation analyses and segmentation statistical methods performed on data derived from national studies to determine percentages of consumers open to or currently using natural products and services. Especially when there is low use of newly offered products (such as many dietary supplements), very large screening studies are needed simply to achieve accurate and projectable figures to identify user groups.

The Hartman Group's first supplement study (*VMHS: Phase I*) conducted in January of 1998 was sent to 60,000 U.S. households to determine if they had used any of 110 vitamins, minerals, herbals or dietary supplements in the past six months. Some 29,000 respondents reported that they had used one or more products, allowing for analyses of even very low-incidence use products such as black cohosh (used by approximately one-tenth of 1 percent of U.S. consumers). This screening study also allowed us to identify a list of supplement consumers from which we could recruit panel members for our continuous study on supplement users, the Natural Products Census *Supplement Report*.

The Hartman Group also undertakes corporate interviews and analyzes trade events in the natural products marketplace. This includes analysis of thirteen channels of distribution (see Figure 10-2), the natural products distributors themselves, the 9,761 natural products retailers, and the thousands of raw material providers, formulators, manufacturers and marketing companies that produce and sell the full range of currently available natural consumer products. In addition, analyses and partnership work with nonprofit institutions and groups, ranging from Bastyr University to Mothers and Others for a More Livable Planet to The Food Alliance, underscores The Hartman Group's commitment to understanding the impact that nonprofit organizations have historically had in forming the natural market, as well as their role in predicting consumer activities.

Figure 10-2. Natural Product Distribution Channels

Pharmacy/Drug Store
Mass Market Store
Grocery Store/Supermarket
Direct Mail/Catalog
MLM/Sales Representative
Health Food Store
Vitamin/Supplement Store
Club Store
Health Care Practitioner
Natural Health Food Supermarket
Insurance Company/HMO
Internet
TV Infomercial

SAMPLE PROPOSAL

The following sample proposal outlines The Hartman Group's methodology for uncovering market opportunities based on environmental enhancements. We are providing this sample proposal to show The Hartman Group's approach when working with companies to develop strategic plans.

Turning Environmental Achievements into Market Opportunities

For the last several years, the environment has emerged as an important issue for a significant majority of consumers. While only 11 percent of consumers are "True Naturals" who make purchasing decisions strictly on the basis of environmental attributes, another 42 percent of consumers have shades of green and will choose a product with favorable environmental attributes over another product of similar price and quality. Companies who have incorporated environmental attributes into their products and communicated the benefits of these attributes to consumers have enjoyed considerable sales growth.

Many companies have made considerable efforts to incorporate environmental programs into the food category, yet few companies have leveraged these commitments in the marketplace in a coordinated manner. The companies that have used these environmental commitments to their marketing advantage have been able to gain additional market share or carve out profitable new niche markets.

The Hartman Group's approach to helping a company advance its ability to earn a return on its environmental investment combines proper technical, stewardship, manufacturing, consumer and competitive research with top-level orchestration and cross-functional coordination, to help companies preempt the competition in offering integrated environmental improvements in ways that truly make a difference to consumers. Moving forward requires an accurate assessment of the current environmental situation and market opportunities. The Hartman Group assists companies in identifying new market niches and determining the "green market" potential for specific products.

Research Components and Methodology

The Hartman methodology involves seven separate elements that are integrated to provide a company with data regarding its environmental achievements and opportunities, baseline consumer reactions to initial product ideas, and recommendations regarding specific market opportunities. Most important, this methodology provides a company with a tool to leverage its current efforts into incremental revenue opportunities.

Market Assessment—Identify Unique "Green Market" Niches

Many issues and their interrelationships must be understood in order to develop a "green market" assessment and identify unique market niches for a company. The Hartman Group incorporates research and analysis to:

- Gain a qualitative understanding of consumers and an initial market assessment through secondary research sources
- Understand past, current, and future environmental product, process and stewardship improvements
- Understand the environmental needs, key buying factors, and priorities of a company's target market
- Assess channel acceptance and the competitive situation, and analyze the key factors driving successes and failures of past environmental product initiatives

The following list outlines The Hartman Group's process and methodology for estimating green market potential, uncovering incremental opportunities and identifying unique green market niches for a company.

1. **Estimate the size of the "green market" for an organization's products/brands.**
   Utilize The Hartman Group's analysis of survey research along with The Hartman Group's or client's macroeconomic research:
   - Estimate market size for key brands, product lines, and products
   - Estimate market size for potential new products

2. **Determine demographic and psychographic attributes of consumers and influence groups identified for an organization's markets.**
   Develop a preliminary profile based on existing client's or Hartman Group's consumer research, and/or interviews with the organization's personnel.

3. **Tabulate environmental improvements to date, proposed improvements and potential for "greening" opportunities of products and processes.**
   Conduct interviews with client's personnel, including marketing, public relations, market research, manufacturing and design, environmental, technical, research and development, and financial personnel

4. **Determine key buying factors (KBFs) and environmental concerns of identified consumer groups/influence groups.**
   Key buying factors include:
   - Physical product attributes
   - Preferred channels
   - Optimal communications
   - Green attributes

5. **Utilizing interviews, The Hartman Group's research, focus groups, and survey questions, we determine:**
   - Environmental product attributes
   - Environmental manufacturing and processing impacts
   - Preferred channels
   - Optimal communication approach
   - Cannibalization risk
   - Incremental revenues, product switching and product loyalty

6. **Analyze distribution channel acceptance of product categories identified.**
   Utilizing interviews, The Hartman Group's research, and survey questions, we determine:
   - What the preferred channels and communication vehicles are for environmental initiatives
   - What the key success factors and failures are in educating specific channels
   - How a company can leverage existing distribution capabilities and current marketing programs

7. **Analyze the competitive situation given identified product categories. Utilizing literature searches, interviews with client personnel and trade associations, and The Hartman Group's existing data, we determine:**
   - What competitors are doing with regard to their environmental performance improvements
   - What initiatives competitors are taking to proactively market their product's environmental features
   - What the key success factors and failures have been in the "green market" arena
   - What advantages (and disadvantages) an organization faces compared to its competitors with regard to its environmental options

8. **Assess the overall market and identify incremental revenue opportunities and unique "green market" niches for client's products.**

The Hartman Groups synthesizes focus group data, literature searches, secondary research, market surveys, and distribution channel acceptance and competitive information studies to discover unfilled consumer product needs. The Hartman Group prepares listings of product opportunities, including such details as description, target market rationale, and estimated sales.

Research Responsibilities

The Hartman Group's Responsibilities

The responsibilities of The Hartman Group include:

- Analyzing all secondary research
- Conducting all relevant interviews
- Preparing top-line analysis of environmental and technical product and process improvement options
- Designing focus group questions and preparing and presenting analysis (optional focus group moderation)
- Designing market research questions, coordinating market surveys and performing consumer analysis
- Assisting in internal data gathering
- Conducting literature and database searches
- Analyzing strategic opportunities and issues
- Preparing a final presentation including an overall market assessment and identifying incremental revenue opportunities
- Identifying unique "green market" niches for our client's products

Client Responsibilities

The responsibilities of the client include:

- Providing secondary research, environmental market research (if available), and other market data
- Providing resources for focus groups, including logistics, participants, video, and premiums
- Providing access to relevant company personnel, including marketing, market research, manufacturing and design, environmental, technical, public relations, research and development, and financial personnel
- Assisting in gathering internal data where necessary
- Providing industry and competitive data where required (and if available)

Joint Responsibilities

Responsibilities that are shared by The Hartman Group and its clients include:

- Developing market research methodologies
- Formulating specific project work plans and timetables

Example of Work Plan

The work plan activities shown in the following table include the top-line market assessment and qualitative analysis necessary for future environmental marketing decisions concerning client products and brands.

Example of Work Tasks

Lead	Start Date	Finish Date	Task Description
			Estimate Size of Green Market • Conduct survey and macroeconomic research • Estimate size of overall client green market • Estimate size of key product lines/product • Estimate size for potential new products
			Determine Demographic/Psychographic Attributes • Develop preliminary profile based on existing consumer research and interviews with client personnel • Design questions for focus group and/or survey • Conduct research and analyze findings
			Analyze Competitive Situation • Investigate existing and planned green products from client's competitors • Categorize competitor offerings by segment or product
			Determine Key Buying Factors (KBFs) of Customers • Physical product attributes • Preferred channels • Optimal communications/advertising/media approach • Green attributes: packaging, materials, environmental impact
			Estimate Willingness to Pay Green Price Premium • Analyze existing survey and focus group data • Interview client personnel, retailers, and producers of other products for similar segments • Explore sales history through focus groups and surveys (consumer or trade)
			Determine New Product Opportunities and Estimate New Market Growth • Synthesize focus groups, literature research, surveys, competitive information to discover unfilled consumer product needs • Prepare listing of product opportunities: description, target market, rationale, total market sales over time, etc.
			Analyze Existing Environmental Impacts and Greening Opportunities • Conduct interviews with client personnel • Review compliance history, pollution permits, etc.

Continued on next page

Lead	Start Date	Finish Date	Task Description
			Investigate Other Technical/Economic Issues; Estimate Manufacturing Capabilities Incremental Costs, and System Changes Required for Revised Green Products • Interview manufacturing personnel, obtain top-line number on production economics, determine key factors to assess for each potential green product addition • As product options are developed, assess manufacturing impacts/requirements through interviews and quantitative analysis
			Compile Estimates of Total Incremental Costs • Manufacturing, supplies, distribution, advertising, etc. • Differentiate between standard new product costs and specific costs of green attributes
			Perform Initial Top-Line Analysis on Issues of New product Versus Product Line Extension • Obtain information from interviews with client and other contacts • Consider focus group/survey to address this issue
			Estimate Public Relations Risk for "Go," launch, create or promote the product/service or "No Go" Decision • Interview client personnel • Analyze existing Hartman Group knowledge and resources • Create charts defining sources and magnitude of risk
			Characterize Cannibalization Risk Given a "Go" Decision • Estimate amount of cannibalized sales vs. new sales • Compare profit margins of green and cannibalized goods
			Analyze Suppliers' Existing Environmental Impacts • Conduct interviews with supplier personnel • Review environmental history of supplier • Compare environmental performance with suppliers' competition
			Identify Product Opportunities • Predict the likely competitor responses to client's green product releases • Assess the risks of each competitive product: lost sales, price erosion, supply or channel lock-up, etc.

Continued on next page

Lead	Start Date	Finish Date	Task Description
			Analyze Channel Acceptance and Price Impacts • Interview client personnel to understand channel behaviors • Interview distributors, retailers, etc. both of existing and potential new channels • Conduct analyses to form estimates
			Investigate Risk of List Sales/Market Position Deterioration Due to "No Go" Decision • Forecast development, timing, and impact of green purchasing behaviors and competitor's offerings
			Develop Basic Financial Impact Forecast • NPV, ROI, Break-even, etc. (rough estimates) • Model results
			Prepare Cost/Benefit/Risk Summary of "Go" and "No Go" Decisions
			Create Feasibility Document
			Assess Resources Necessary to Proceed with Phase II
			Complete and Present Final Feasibility Document

SAMPLE PROPOSAL: RESEARCHING WELLNESS LIFESTYLES

Whereas the previous sample proposal would result in a client determining the consumer potential for an environmentally enhanced product, the next sample proposal summarizes The Hartman Group's learnings to the potential client in the context of wellness. Learnings derived from the wellness study as outlined address the underlying motivators and inhibitors as well as the foundation beliefs and knowledge that drive consumer participation in the wellness category.

Viewing Today's Consumer
Through the Lens of Natural Sensibility

Following our first cultural study undertaken in 1998[2], it became clear that consumers enter and exit natural product worlds through a variety of different gateways: some consumers are very involved with supplements, while others are very involved with fitness and or alternative health

---

[2] *Natural Sensibility: A Study of America's Changing Culture and Lifestyle*, The Hartman Group, Fall 1998. See Appendix I for more details.

practices. Some consumers are involved in many of these products and services. The Hartman Group is now conducting further research and attempting to model and quantitatively measure the process by which consumers enter and exit natural product worlds.

To better understand this dynamically changing consumer landscape, The Hartman Group's research employs sociological and social psychological methodologies to identify:

- How consumers learn about products in the context of a network, or "product world."
- How these consumers construct their own individual patterns of use of natural products and services in the form of "wellness regimes."

In addition to giving a detailed picture of what makes up "Natural Sensibility," our research provides important insights on shopping behavior and the feelings, perceptions and lifestyles currently surrounding specific types of natural products and health-care services. These insights can be used to develop new brands or, by restructuring the marketing approach of existing brands, to better target this emerging market.

Product Worlds

A product world is a specific product category—such as VMHS, recreational equipment, or organic food—that consumers come to differentially associate themselves with based on a lifestyle experience.[3] In order to study a product world, one gathers information about:

- The social networks consumers associate themselves with
- The knowledge they seek out about a product
- The meanings they construct around products and services
- The place a product comes from and where it is purchased
- How, where, and why consumers interact with (use or purchase) a product or service

By analyzing this information, we gain a clear view of the facilitators and barriers to adoption and the diffusion of specific products and services within the broader natural products and services marketplace.

Wellness Regimes

A wellness regime is the collection of specific products, services, and actions a consumer chooses to participate in to achieve their definition

---

[3] *Natural Sensibility: A Study of America's Changing Culture and Lifestyle*, The Hartman Group, Fall 1998. See Appendix I for more details.

of wellness.[4] The general patterns of behavior that define initial frameworks of different wellness regimes emerged from initial exploratory research on culture and lifestyle change. In the next phase of our research, we will flesh out the ways consumers pick and choose among natural product worlds in order to construct different wellness regimes. The Hartman Group uses innovative quantitative and qualitative research methodologies to explore patterns of behavior that will provide insights into *how* consumers think and feel about their own particular versions of wellness. We gather information on where consumers shop in order to construct their wellness regime and the specific types of products they include in their repertoire.

The following table provides an illustration of the dynamics of cultural change within the natural products arena.

Model of Cultural Change—Factors that Influence Individual Wellness Regimes

First Step of Exploration

In March 1998, The Hartman Group fielded the first stage of a nationwide research project that examined the connection between larger cultural change and consumer behavior with regard to natural products. The study proposed to: 1) gain an initial view of *how* consumers come to be involved in some sectors of the natural product marketplace and not others; 2) examine the linkages between lifestyle and purchasing behavior in the natural products marketplace; and 3) explore the role of branding from a cultural and lifestyle perspective.

---

[4] *Natural Sensibility: A Study of America's Changing Culture and Lifestyle*, The Hartman Group, Fall 1998. See Appendix I for more details.

The data were gathered in the form of 500 hours of in-depth, one-on-one interviews with consumers in major metropolitan markets. The initial research questions included topics such as:

- How consumers first come to use VMHS, alternative health care services, organic products, natural health and beauty aids, and/or natural household products
- Where and why consumers shop for natural products in the places they do
- What kind of brand awareness exists for natural products
- How consumers talk about their use of natural products
- How consumers have begun integrating natural products into their daily lives
- What information sources consumers have been more inclined to trust

Examples of some of the narratives our respondents used to talk about their use of natural products follow:

One woman describes her first experience using omega-3 fish oil:

"Well, you know, I started taking that—actually a friend of mine and I both started taking that because we both read some of the research about that and breast cancer. And since I've had breast cancer and my friend has, I thought, well, it's certainly not going to hurt me so I started taking it."
—Female, 50s, San Francisco

And this woman explains her experience with shopping for natural products at Whole Foods:

"Yeah, I've always dabbled in that, you know. But I just made a more concerted effort now to be more organized and just buy all that stuff at one place as opposed to running all around and trying to buy this stuff. If I didn't have that grocery store, that big grocery store, I think I'd be a bit more hard pressed to buy all this stuff (VMHS, organic foods, household products) and buy as much of it, because I can go there and blow a hundred to two hundred bucks on two weeks worth of stuff. And so it's all right there. You have a cart and you just do your thing. It's like a regular grocery store experience."
—Female, 40s, New York

Expansion Stage

The next phase of research into changing culture and lifestyle will map: 1) the boundaries and textures of natural product worlds; 2) how consumers creatively combine them to construct their own individual wellness regimes; 3) how many people potentially fall into each wellness regime type; 4) the overlaps between wellness regimes and the demographics associated with each; and 5) the patterns of product adoption within natural product worlds and wellness regimes.

We will use theoretical concepts from Everett M. Rogers' *Diffusion of Innovations*,[5] to define the role that social networks play in defining the meanings, place and knowledge about specific product worlds and how consumers actually construct their wellness regimes: how many might exist, what their focal motivations might be (aging, kids, onset of health issues), how they overlap, and what combinations of products and services (product worlds) are included in each.

An important part of this research focuses on the differences in meaning of *authenticity* for different groups. What is "authentically natural" for one segment of the population may not be authentic—or important—to another segment of the population. We explore the role mass media and opinion leaders play in constructing regimes as well as how retailers and manufacturers earn or lose the right in the minds of consumers to be credible and trustworthy providers of natural products. We investigate the role of specific brands in the product worlds, how uncertainties toward a specific natural product or service can be reduced for consumers, and how to lead consumers to actually purchase and use that product or service. Lastly, we investigate what products and services could be linked together in a retail environment in order to appeal to specific segments of the population based on the attributes of specific wellness regimes.

Field Research—Social Network Observation and Interviews

Because we believe that natural products are adopted and diffused through social networks, The Hartman Group uses network studies to flesh out our quantitative efforts. Instead of recruiting random groups of strangers to participate in this research, we gather data by observing the conversations that occur within a social network of people who are familiar with each other, for example, a running club, a dance troupe or a cancer support group. This methodology provides more realistic information about how consumers perceive and talk about wellness.

The Hartman Group uses individual, one-on-one interviews to better understand the specific usage and purchase criteria of natural products and services. These interviews explore the areas in which group dynamics may inhibit exploration of certain issues, such as personal health issues. This component of the study centers around an in-depth, phone survey-interview that probes consumers on their awareness, use of, and/or interest in natural products and services. We utilize an innovative research tool that probes respondents for information that can then be used to develop "mind maps" to see how consumers perceive and talk about their use, or potential use, of natural products and services.

---

[5] Everett M. Rogers, *Diffusion of Innovations*, 4th ed. (New York: Free Press, 1995).

We draw on a stratified random sample that is broken into three segments: 1) consumers who already use a wide variety of natural products and services, 2) consumers who are aware of natural products and services but use few or none, and 3) non-users. Including respondents from all of these groups yields information about how different types of users are integrating natural products into their daily lives and how potential users may be encouraged to start acting with Natural Sensibility. Having this complete picture provides important information about different types of consumers and their needs and wishes.

Quantifying the Dimensions of Wellness Regimes

The quantitative phase of this study measures the size and texture of the wellness landscape among the American population. We do this in two parts:

1. Screening Stage—identifies incidence rates of specific product worlds, product use within those worlds and the demographic composition of those users.

2. Segmentation Stage—explores consumer perceptions and behavior within purchase, branding, and attitudinal categories. A series of statistical techniques, including factor analysis, hierarchical clustering, and iterative partitioning are then used to identify underlying attitudinal patterns and assign individuals to groups. This analysis results in identifiable segments with which various behavioral, purchase, brand, and product use patterns can be associated.

Results

The information that results from these studies is both qualitative and quantitative. We hear and see how consumers talk about natural products in their own words. These "soft" findings are also quantitatively reliable because the studies are designed to yield inferential statistics.

Pragmatic language analysis permits the creation of concept maps around people's belief systems. For example, how members of a running club talk about wellness may indeed be very different than how a cancer support group talks about wellness. In this way, we can articulate how and why groups and individuals construct wellness regimes in the ways that they do and what products they seek out and use as part of their regimes.

Because this research uncovers important insights into the culture and lifestyles surrounding natural products, we gain crucial information about how to develop and effectively market brands within this arena.

PART IV

How to Communicate

CHAPTER 11

Promotion of Environmental, Natural and Wellness Attributes

BACKGROUND

Whether in their attitudes and perceptions toward food and the environment or in actual purchase and use of vitamins, minerals, herbals, and dietary supplements, U.S. consumers have shown that they have strong inclinations to buy earth-sustainable, natural, and nutritious products. As with any emerging market, purchase behavior and commitment to individual natural brands is still fragmented. However, at least half of the population has an orientation to sustainably produced food and beverage products, and our recent integrated health care study shows that over 86 percent of Americans are now using one or more of twenty-six alternative health practices to maintain and improve their health. Currently, 68 percent of the U.S. population takes vitamins and minerals, while some 30 percent takes herbals or dietary supplements. Such numbers imply that the market for natural products and services is vast. Yet, with a total market size of over $33 billion ($15 billion food, beverage, supplements and $18 billion alternative health), these food, beverage, supplement and health products and services currently represent only a small percentage of total sales in food, beverage, over-the-counter, and health care product and service categories.

The conventional market for food and beverages tops $500 billion per year and health care now costs over $1 trillion a year in the United States. The immense gap between the current natural products and services market and the conventional market can be reduced by turning the marketer's traditional focus from *supply* (providing an endless stream of new product introductions or services) to *demand* (meeting the needs of the consumer).

Simply placing "new" natural products on shelves that have never carried such products—or placing a symbol that certifies that the product is environmentally superior to similar products—are not innovations that conventional manufacturers will ignore or that consumers will commit to in the long term. To the average consumer, the product must meet their core purchase criteria, including cost, availability and convenience, in order to foster long-term product commitment and trust in the brand. As used by conventional consumer products producers, careful brand management, use of consumer market research and understanding the underlying reasons behind consumers' purchases will lead to long-term market leadership and sustainable growth for natural product brands.

DEVELOPING THE NATURAL AND WELLNESS MARKET

Developing the market for natural and wellness products and services will require understanding the consumer and dispelling several myths that continue to pervade the marketplace.

Myths and Realities

There are five myths in the marketplace that must be addressed in order to better identify and market to the new natural consumer.

Myth #1: *There is a small niche market of consumers who will be influenced by environmental product improvements, the inclusion of natural or organic ingredients in products, or use of the term "wellness" in product promotion.*

Reality: *The wellness market is made up of a diverse majority of consumers who buy earth-friendly, natural, organic, and wellness products for different reasons.*

Traditionally, products produced with earth-sustainable or organic methods have been viewed as appealing only to those who make environmentalism a driving force in their lives. Although this group makes up a good portion of the present market for earth-sustainable *food* products, they are by no means the only consumers showing a strong willingness to buy wellness products and services. In fact, Americans are very eager to purchase wellness products and services on their own terms but with partial participation. For most consumers, purchase terms do not necessarily have to relate to the environment, to "natural" or "organic." Therefore, simply increasing the volume of health and wellness products will not result in increased sales.

A more thorough understanding of how Americans come to purchase and use earth-friendly, natural, or wellness products and services is needed. As we've noted, consumers are constructing new personal wellness regimes by incorporating a wide range of natural products and services into their daily lives. Whereas in 1996, the core component of the natural market was the half of the population with interests in purchasing earth sustainable food products, The Hartman Group's recent integrated health care and supplement studies show that as much as 86 percent of the population uses one or more natural or alternative health products or services. These findings have profound implications for marketers of conventional consumer products and services.

For example, the conventional shopper—who may demonstrate every type of conventional behavior and belief and rarely express an interest in purchasing organic or natural-market products—may today, because of a chronic backache, end up in the care of a chiropractor. This chiropractor might also market a private-label line of vitamins, minerals, herbals, and dietary supplements. This conventional consumer realizes that she has never taken a multivitamin and decides to start bolstering her general health and wellness by starting to take them. The chiropractor's prices are too high, so the next time the consumer is in the grocery store, she picks out a multivitamin in the supplement section that meets her price criteria, at the same time checking out the other products in the vicinity.

This consumer has entered the supplement category through an alternative health gateway. Depending on her health interests, she may or may not become more and more interested in vitamins and minerals. She might develop an interest in herbal and dietary supplements, or she might try the

Tropicana orange juice with calcium and magnesium because she has seen through mass media that these are important minerals for a healthy diet.

The key to developing the market for natural and wellness products is not to treat it as a niche market inhabited only by strident environmental activists. Marketers also cannot rely on a presumed widespread concern for the environment or a deep-rooted trust of the term "natural" as a means to increase sales of wellness products. The market for natural and wellness products and services does not exist as a separate world. Many of these goods are produced, distributed, and sold alongside conventional products. Therefore, they must be marketed with the mainstream consumer in mind.

As evidenced by the many consumer segmentations performed in various natural product worlds, The Hartman Group has shown that by focusing on the consumer as the missing link, companies can take substantive steps to capture consumer purchase, hence closing the gap between attitudes and behavior.

Myth #2: *Spreading health, nutrition and environmental awareness will lead to increased environmental, natural, and wellness concerns, behaviors, and purchases.*

Reality: *Consumers appreciate environmental, health, and nutrition issues, but do not necessarily translate them into specific purchasing behaviors.*

Research conducted by The Hartman Group[1] strongly indicates that consumer attitudes and concern regarding the protection of the environment, nutrition, health, and wellness are growing stronger with each passing year. Media coverage tracking charts in earlier chapters (see figures 5–13, 5–14, 6–1, 7–1 and 9–1) show that the public certainly is exposed to a lot of information on these topics, which translates into awareness and potential experimentation with products.

However, we do not necessarily see attitudes or awareness translated into behavioral changes with an increase in purchases of organic and other natural food and beverages. If this were true, then conven-

---

[1] *Food and the Environment: The Consumer Perspective* (Phases I, II and III), 1996–1998; *The Evolving Organic Marketplace*, Winter 1997; *U.S. Consumer Use of Vitamins, Minerals, Herbals and Dietary Supplements* (Phase I, Phase II, and Multi-Product Users Special Report); and *Integrated Health Care: Consumer Use and Attitudes*, November 1998. See Appendix I for more information on these and other studies by The Hartman Group.

tional grocery stores would be stocking huge volumes of organic and natural products. These apparent contradictions show that, in general, consumers are still in the early stages of moving along the continuum from awareness to adoption. This reflects the nature of the emerging natural products and services market overall.

Myth #3: *The consumer will purchase natural or wellness products and services primarily because of "earth-friendly" or "natural" product attributes.*

Reality: *Earth sustainable and natural products do not drive purchases—it is the consumer's pursuit of wellness and the natural lifestyle.*

The *lifestyles* in which consumers are participating, including their actual purchase experience, their Natural Sensibility, and their perception of a brand's authenticity, are critical to the purchase of the product. Simply labeling a product with a seal of authenticity—such as an ecolabel certifying it as organic—may not influence the consumer to regularly purchase the product. He or she is experimenting with a lifestyle that covers many different areas of personal behavior, only one of which involves understanding what an ecolabel signifies.

Simply putting a product on the shelf and calling it "natural" is not sufficient inducement for most consumers to purchase it. People are much more likely to buy a product if they perceive some sort of added value in that product. Added value—actual or perceived—comes in many forms and relates to what consumers consider their core purchase criteria. Authenticity of ingredients, the brand, the lifestyle experience, and the actual retail purchase experience (where and how they purchase) all lend enormous importance to the actual purchase of a natural product or service.

Finally, perceptions, attitudes, and motivations vary from consumer to consumer. For some, the added value of organic food will come in the form of its perceived enhanced nutritional benefits. For others, it is a matter of better quality, taste, packaging, availability, or convenience.

The relative unimportance to conventional consumers of environmental enhancements made to products is exhibited in the reasons given for choosing outlets. Our *Food and the Environment* studies[2] show that

---

[2] See Appendix I for more information.

low incidence of shopping in health food stores is not surprising because the availability of organic or environmentally friendly products is
not a prime consideration in where a *conventional* shopper chooses to
shop for groceries. Rather, the main considerations are convenience,
quality, cleanliness, and price. Earth-friendly or natural attributes of
products cannot stand alone as a means of influencing the conventional
consumer: Combined with the chronic shortage of time facing most
consumers today, natural products must be easily accessible, priced
appropriately, and taste as good or better than conventional products.

Myth #4: *The consumer will pay a premium for a product depending on environmental, health, or natural improvements to the product.*

Reality: *Price premiums can be a barrier to purchase, especially
to the conventional shopper.*

Throughout multiple studies conducted by The Hartman Group,
green shoppers have clearly expressed their willingness, and in fact their
expectation, to pay a slight premium for earth sustainable and organic
products (see figure 5–9 in chapter 5). Until the early 1990s, organic
products sold through co-ops and boutique health food stores commanded
100 percent price premiums over their conventional
counterparts. The current growth and mainstream penetration of natural
and organic products can only continue; however, price premiums will
increasingly fall, depending upon product categories.

Price resistance will occur in the common ground—the supermarket—where conventional shoppers who are interested in healthier
products but refuse to pay premiums demand alternatives to higher-priced
health products. While the classic "True Natural" consumer of 1996
was formerly relied on as the consumer segment which would pay a
premium for organics and other sustainably-produced foods,
the largest potential market for natural and sustainably-produced
products, the New Green Mainstream, has donated consumers to the
True Natural segment, diluting their willingness to pay a premium (see
Chapter 5).

As little as two years ago, natural manufacturers and retailers could
count on True Naturals' behavior to be consistent; however, the old rules
no longer apply. The original base of True Naturals identified in 1996
predominantly shared a common lifestyle that was the result of a com-

mon set of counter-cultural beliefs. This depth of conviction drove the intensity with which True Natural shoppers would seek out natural and organic products and pay a premium price for them. Further, the frequency of their purchase flowed from an overall lifestyle commitment about the environment, food choices and their standing up for a better way. Therefore, if organic products were not available in the store where they were currently shopping, they would seek another store where these products were available. If the quality of an organic product was below that of its conventionally grown counterpart, True Naturals would still purchase organic because it was more important to buy from their conscience than based on quality.

Today, the former New Green Mainstream shoppers who have migrated to the True Natural segment have not bought into the same lifestyle commitment as their predecessors. They joined the True Naturals in the context of easy availability and the high quality of natural and organic products. If organic products are not available, they purchase conventional products. If organic product quality is too low or price to high, they choose the conventional product. Their less intense commitment generates a lower frequency of repeat purchases.

However, there are exceptions to Myth #4. The Hartman Group has found that specific categories exist within the natural products and services market for which even conventional consumers will pay a premium. The best example is the vitamins, minerals, herbals and dietary supplements (VMHS) category.

This category provides fascinating insights into other wellness product categories in terms of motivations for use and purchase. Since 1997, The Hartman Group has researched consumer attitudes, product use and behavior in the $10 billion VMHS market. The Hartman Group's *Supplement Report* tracks a wide variety of purchase and usage factors.[3] Of great interest is not only the prices paid through thirteen purchase channels (with "direct from sales representative" being the highest average price paid), but also the health conditions most commonly treated based on analysis of 150 different products used to treat over 50 health conditions.

---

[3] See Appendix I for more information.

Of fifty health conditions tracked, Americans state that "general health and wellness" is the leading health condition they treat with supplement products. While consumers will list specific health conditions treated with specific products—such as using chondroition to treat arthritis—they use the majority of VMHS products to maintain general health and wellness.

Such information provides insight into the natural market itself: As an emerging market with many new products, consumers have little specific knowledge about products they use, but they purchase such products as part of a desire for a healthier lifestyle. In order to link VMHS purchases to the larger context of the natural market, it is important to understand the pursuit of general health and wellness, and how the activity of "taking a pill" makes consumers feel that they are actively taking a part in personal wellness.

The specific health benefits of foods and beverages can be more difficult to market than the benefits of supplements promoted to the end consumer. Supplements and the reasons they are purchased—including general health and wellness—can be capitalized on in a wide variety of communications. Producers of organic and environmentally-enhanced food products face a larger, more complex challenge: Our *Food and the Environment* studies show that of various agricultural initiatives to enhance food products that are posed to consumers, the most leveragable ones are those that most directly relate to controlling pollution of the water supply and pesticide residues on food. These components of production may not be as easy to equate to consumer health and nutrition goals as those found in the supplement category.

As a part of analyzing the supplement market, a key issue lies in understanding why consumers, who make up general demographic profiles, will pay premiums for VMHS products bought through a direct sales representative rather than just purchasing the same product at a pharmacy or grocery store. The Hartman Group feels strongly that such price premiums reflect an important aspect of the natural products market as a whole: As part of a healthy lifestyle, consumers communicate about and purchase health and wellness products in the context of social networks, learning about products from friends and relatives. Purchase decisions activated through sales representatives (in the case of VMHS products, through Amway, Shaklee, NuSkin, etc.) are a way of participating in a healthy lifestyle. The purchase price becomes less of an issue when buying a product from a friend or acquaintance who knows, ostensibly, what the product is good for.

Myth #5: *Consumers rank all environmental issues as being equally important.*

Reality: *Consumers relate best to the most tangible and personally relevant health issues.*

Given the average consumer's lack of sophistication regarding earth-sustainability, organic production and accompanying farming techniques (and the terminology that goes with them), or to the complexities of RDAs and DRIs, it is not surprising that there are big differences among consumers' rankings of environmental and nutritional issues. These rankings have been discovered through our *Food and the Environment* studies, which show that although the vast majority of Americans may rank "environmental protection" as very important, far fewer give the same ranking to various initiatives—such as protecting against soil erosion and loss of soil fertility—that will achieve this end.

In our *Food and the Environment* studies, water pollution issues (pesticide seepage and pesticide runoff) are consistently ranked most important by respondents. In contrast, only half as many respondents rank one of three soil-related issues (soil erosion, soil destruction, or loss of soil fertility) as the most important agriculture concern. This is not surprising in that consumers are still in the initial phases of discovering and internalizing environmentalism and lack the knowledge base to link ideas such as maintenance of soil productivity to personal benefit or added value in a product. Secondarily, issues relating to ingestion of pesticides are important. These concerns include the implications of pesticide residues on food for human consumption, as well as the potential for pesticides to poison wildlife.

Finally, consumers relate to simple things with which they are already familiar. There is only so much available mind share to market to. Farming methods with benefits that are most tangible to the consumer have the greatest potential to impact grocery selection. Water protection and eliminating pesticide residues on food are food-related issues of great concern to consumers. Other farming issues that have benefits to the consumer that are less direct are not as important in influencing grocery purchases.

Given consumers' limited knowledge about environmental issues, it is difficult for them to make the linkage between various farming techniques and a personal benefit. This suggests that considerable education in fundamental environmental issues will be necessary before specific farming techniques that benefit agricultural productivity and water and soil health will be compelling inducements to purchase.

PROMOTING WITH ECOLABELS

The use of ecolabels and seals certifying various product attributes, especially in food and beverages, has seen a widespread increase in the United States and internationally. Development of such seals and symbols has become increasingly important to regional, national, and international organizations interested in promoting products and services with environmental enhancements. The Hartman Group has analyzed consumer perceptions of ecolabels in the United States and determined that currently, regional programs structured around promoting labeled products are perhaps the most immediately applicable. Part of this rationale focuses on the fact that regionally produced fruits and vegetables, as well as other food and beverage categories such as dairy, already are associated with and purchased within a region, and can thus be branded and promoted by regional grower and processor organizations at lower brand-building costs.

What are Ecolabels?

Voluntary environmental labeling programs first began in the 1970s when public concern for environmental issues was on the rise. These labels were designed to help consumers differentiate between products. The use of voluntary labels on durable and consumable goods increased substantially in the late 1980s in response to a growth in green consumerism. The use of these green labels was initially limited to several product types, primarily non-consumable goods such as household appliances. Only recently have ecolabels been applied to fresh and processed food products, as well as a broad array of other consumer goods such as appliances and forest products.

For public health and safety reasons, the food industry has had many years of experience with labeling. For decades, government inspectors have certified the quality of agricultural products, and food processors and retailers have had to label their products with nutritional information. Because law mandates these certificates and labels, they are found on all food products. Many consumers use these labels to select the products they buy.

However, most consumers in the United States have not until recently had broad experience with environmental labels on fresh or processed food products. With the mainstream placement of organic and natural foods, exposure to label claims has broadened.

While some people are overwhelmed and not interested in environmental issues, green consumers are everywhere—in every mall, shopping center and corner store. In the marketplace, customers look at packaging as they pace store aisles in search of products to satisfy their personal needs and the needs of their families. As they scan the shelves, they see a variety of shapes, colors, symbols, pictures and words, and somehow they decide to buy a particular product—"Product X." Consumer research helps us understand why they choose "Product X" over "Product Y."

Consumers have a variety of different criteria to help them choose between products. Some people choose products based on brands they're familiar with—such as Nabisco or Coca-Cola—while others focus on price alone. For some goods, the presence of an ecolabel has become an additional variable that consumers use in making their purchasing choices. Consumers in dozens of countries have experience with third-party ecolabeling programs, managed either by a government agency or by a quasi-governmental or non-governmental organization. In 1993, the U.S. EPA conducted a study of over thirty programs, ranging from the Blue Angel in Germany to the product labeling under the Toxic Substances Control Act (TSCA) in the United States. Consumers also have experience with self-declaration claims, which are those made by manufacturers who say their product is somehow superior to the competition's. Figure 11-1 lists types of third-party environmental labeling programs.

Internationally, governments have established regulations and standards for self-declaration claims and environmental labeling programs. The U.S. government, for example, has set legal definitions for use of the terms "healthy" and "natural." In most cases, government-sanctioned labeling programs provide for voluntary use of ecolabels, although mandatory labels have been established for some products.

Figure 11-1. Types of Third-Party Environmental Labeling Programs.

Mandatory

- Hazard or Warning (e.g. pesticide labels)
- Information Disclosure (e.g. fuel economy labels)

Voluntary (Environmental certification programs)

- Seal of approval (most labels are in this category)
- Single attribute certification (e.g. energy use)
- Report Card

Source: *Status Report on the Use of Environmental Labels Worldwide,* U.S. EPA, 1993

Mandatory environmental labels may be warning labels or simply neutral labels that provide information to consumers. The effectiveness of warning labels in informing consumers has been described as "moderate at best." Warning labels and other public information campaigns about industrial hazards have, however, had an impact on the behavior of manufacturers and producers by getting them to reformulate their products and use less hazardous materials when possible. Energy guides and fuel economy labels are neutral labels (they simply provide information), but they can still have an impact on manufacturers and consumers. The labels provide a fairly simple way to compare the cost of operating products such as washing machines and furnaces, a variable which may be important in locations where the cost of energy is high.

Among the voluntary labels, the seal of approval is the most common type. Many governments see the seal-of-approval label model as being comprehensive and practical. It does not take a lot of space on the packaging (like a report card does), and it can be based on a variety of attributes or environmental impacts. When controlled by a government agency, these seals will also evolve with changes in government policy. The potential for political tampering, however, can be one of the drawbacks for government-sponsored programs, even if political goals are one of the main functions for ecolabels.

These five types of labeling initiatives serve three functions in the marketplace:

1. As an independent evaluation and endorsement of a product
2. As a consumer protection tool
3. As a method of achieving specific policy goals

The mandatory labels serve as a means of consumer and environmental protection. Voluntary labels have been used by manufacturers and producers as an added means of building brands and new markets by having an external endorsement. For example, environmental groups have helped create niche markets for tropical products by providing third-party certification to growers who use environmentally friendly farming practices. Through this arrangement, all of the stakeholders—whether government, business or nonprofit—are partners in this process. For government-sponsored programs, an ecolabel jury typically sets the standards and awards the seals; in many cases this jury is composed of diverse stakeholders, including industry, environmental associations, trade unions and public authorities.

Ecolabels are typically given to a product or service that is made or offered in a way that improves energy efficiency, reduces hazardous by-products or uses recycled materials, or because the project itself can be reused. By displaying the symbol on products that reduce the environmental impact of everyday activities, manufacturers and consumers can contribute to environmental protection. These products sell because of the motivation and willingness of individual consumers to make a deliberate choice to favor earth-sustainable alternatives. While the products may have a lower environmental impact, they do not necessarily lead to an environmentally sound society, nor do they ensure that the products are used in an environmentally sound manner or protect consumers through improved quality or safety.

International Experiences with Ecolabels

The success of certification programs is based on the interest and willingness of consumers to change or modify their purchasing habits. This is true in all societies. The first government-sponsored ecolabeling program was Germany's "Blue Angel," created in 1977 to promote environmentally sound products. Today, over 80 percent of the German public recognizes the seal, which is on over 4,000 products in 71 categories. Other international ecolabeling programs are more limited in scope and focus on a single issue or attribute, such as energy-saving computers or sustainably harvested timber.

These and other labeling programs have been effective and have had an influence on manufacturers and consumers in terms of acceptance and behavior change. For example, mandatory hazard and warning labels have caused some manufacturers to change their products, dropping certain ingredients or components in order to avoid placing a potentially negative label on their product. Retailers' behavior also can influence manufacturers: In Scandinavia, many retailers will only sell laundry detergents that carry the Nordic Swan label. Labels also have been successful in increasing both consumer awareness and sales of certain types of labeled products.

Internationally, many ecolabeling programs are affiliated with government agencies. This gives the public a sense of accountability: Someone is watching the shop and guaranteeing the integrity of the program. Government agencies play this role easily because they typically are given the task of protecting the public interest in terms of environment, health and safety.

The ideal labeling program determines product categories in such a way as to ensure the greatest improvement to the environment. Criteria are set by using comprehensive life-cycle analysis, taking into consideration the impacts at each stage of a product's manufacturing or processing. The product selection criteria are reviewed on a regular basis to ensure that advances in science and technology are incorporated, encouraging continual innovation and improvement in performance.

Consumer education is a particularly important component of a labeling program. Consumers will not believe a green product is good for the environment (and therefore will not buy it over competing products) without knowing how it impacts the environment. Education is especially important for labels that refer to a special manufacturing process. If consumers are not concerned with the process issue, such as dioxin in the pulp and paper industry, they will not be inclined to select one product (chlorine-free paper) over another, especially if the products are otherwise equal in terms of their inherent characteristics.

Nutrition labels and other information on food products generally focus on the content and use of the product, rather than how it was produced. Similarly, most environmental labels focus on the impacts associated with consumption or use of the product, not the production.

Ecolabels for home appliances, for example, may advertise energy or water conservation features. In contrast, the environmental labels for food and other agricultural products, including textiles and wood products, focus on the process of production. This creates a problem: Do customers care about production methods or do they only care about the inherent qualities of the final product? See "Consumer Response to Ecolabels and Seals" later in this chapter for insights on U.S. consumer perceptions toward food ecolabels.

Content versus process is not an insignificant question because there are international trade and market-share implications. One well-known example is the tuna-dolphin case. "Dolphin-safe" labels were created by nonprofit groups and businesses to help consumers differentiate between fish caught under two different fishing regimes. Some fishermen used methods for catching tuna that invariably killed dolphins, while others did not. The inherent qualities of the tuna, however, are identical in both cases. Because governments are only allowed to look at the inherent qualities of the product when they set trade regulations, third-party labels played an important role by shifting the demand through a change in consumer purchasing habits.

There are other examples of consumer labels that play a role in increasing the market share of certain products by helping manufacturers differentiate their products from those of the competition. The Body Shop, a British cosmetics company, had strong sales growth based on their premise of producing products without harm to animals—although the company stumbled upon entering the U.S. market. Here in the United States, Tom's of Maine sells toothpaste that won FDA approval without having to brush the teeth of lab rats. Chlorine-free paper is sold worldwide and the World Bank Group has funded the construction of a chlorine-free paper mill in Brazil.

Global enterprises are producing goods, such as paper products, that carry ecolabels. Because of the growing market for ecolabeled goods in industrialized countries, exporters in developing countries have started to take steps to meet market demands. Colombia is in the process of developing an ecolabeling program for the textile industry with the goal of promoting local conservation while also penetrating foreign markets where green consumerism is prevalent. The government of Czechoslovakia is creating a seal of approval for environmentally friendly products. In Turkey, twenty-four different crops, including fruit, vegetables, cereals and legumes, are grown on certified organic farms for export to the European market.

Food Ecolabels

One purpose of ecolabels found on food products is to attract purchasers based on the assumption that they will be attracted by the process that was enhanced to merit the symbol. Critical in understanding the effect of an ecolabel is understanding that while consumers care about the food they eat, they also care about the price, the brand and the location of the product. The high volume of sales for prepared foods suggests that many consumers are concerned primarily with convenience. Other segments of the public focus on price. Food ingredients are an issue for the millions of people who have special diets, such as those who keep track of calories, salt or cholesterol, or people with allergies to nuts or dairy products. Food safety, and even issues about where a product originates, have become increasing concerns to many shoppers.

Nutrition labels and ingredient lists are read by a significant number of consumers who use this information in their purchasing. Ecolabels add an additional variable for consumers to consider in their purchasing choices: How the food was grown. The basis for the successful introduction of an ecolabel for food products is similar to that for ecolabels on other products: education, program affiliation, manufacturer self-interest and consumer self-interest.

In the United States, the scientific community has been very involved in research on the production aspect of a food ecolabel. This led to labeling programs for organic food and, more recently, for food produced using integrated pest management (IPM) techniques. While national organic standards are under review, few corporate farms grow organic produce.

Some attribute the delay in applying comprehensive food ecolabels to the difficulty in delineating production requirements. Defining environmentally sustainable food production processes is a task typically carried out by governments and other certifying bodies, although self-declaration claims are an option used by some producers. An ecolabel or organic label must be trustworthy, and consumers have differing views of whom they trust to carry out programs and provide the certification.

Experiences with Food Labels

Food labeling initiatives can thrive only where there is an infrastructure for selling the goods and assuring product integrity and accountability. Being especially concerned with convenience, American consumers do most of their food shopping at one store (while perhaps cross-shopping less regularly at specialty stores such as supplement retailers or pharmacies), while many Europeans still follow the tradition of buying at a variety of separate stores—the baker, the butcher, the farmer's market, etc. Within Europe, the Belgian, Dutch and German consumers are more likely to go to specialized stores, while the French like buying directly from the farmer. As a result, some European consumers may also be more willing to add a "green" grocer to their shopping rounds if ecolabeled goods are not available at their traditional markets.

Studies of European consumers found differences within and among countries. One study found that German consumers of "bio-products" are more often moderate-income families with children and have only recently been buying these products, while Belgian and Dutch consumers often have higher incomes, smaller families, and a longer history of buying this type of product. The Belgian, Dutch, English and French consumers are typically younger consumers under forty-five years old, while in Germany they are found in all age classes.

To serve the local market for organic food, a Dutch label for organic foods was created in 1993. Organic products carry the EKO label alongside other brand information. In the marketplace, these products were 50–100 percent more expensive than conventional foods, so the stakeholders in the process decided to create an intermediate seal. Since 1995, the Agro-Milieukeur label has been used on potatoes, onions, wheat and greenhouse-grown sweet peppers, apples and pears to indicate that the produce was grown using earth-sustainable practices. While it does not indicate that products are organic, the Agro-Milieukeur has broad support, in part because the retail price of the products on which it appears may be comparable to conventional produce. The increase in sales of ecolabeled produce is drawing more consumers and producers toward the earth-sustainable process, yielding better economies of scale and a program that is more effective, yielding greater benefits to the environment. This middle-ground label caused some tension in the

Netherlands among the farming community. The farmers using non-conventional agricultural practices recognized, however, that it was to their advantage to cooperate in developing positive messages and advertising to increase consumer knowledge about their way of growing food for the betterment of both labels.

Examples of activities centered around ecolabels and food production are abundant regionally in the United States. The Food Alliance of Portland, Oregon, which co-sponsored The Hartman Group's *Food and the Environment* studies (Phases I and II) as well as a small consumer ecolabel study, has been very active in the Pacific Northwest in assembling a large number of growers, processors and cooperatives under an environmentally enhanced regional ecolabel. The Wisconsin Potato and Vegetable Growers' Association has entered into a unique agreement with World Wildlife Fund in a program that will encourage environmentally conscious growing practices, promote safe food for consumers and enhance habitat quality for wildlife such as the Sandhill crane and the Karner blue butterfly. The project links a program for reduction and phase-out of certain pesticides with a third-party certification system and packaging label that rewards farmers for their good practices and educates consumers about such accomplishments.

Specialty brands have also been developed to pique consumer interest. Brands that are linked with environmental issues have had some success in the marketplace by placing earth-friendly products in the places where most people regularly shop. Ben and Jerry's ice cream used sustainably harvested Brazil nuts as part of the marketing strategy for their Rainforest Crunch Ice Cream. The Rainforest Alliance created and manages the ECO-OK seal that is used on coffee, bananas, and several other products grown by Latin American farmers. When specialty brands are carried in conventional supermarkets, consumers have easy access to earth-sustainable food products.

Consumer Response to Ecolabels and Seals

During the past twenty years, there has been significant experimentation with ecolabels, including how to define product categories labeled, how to determine the more environmentally friendly processes, how to get consumers interested in buying these products, and determining what types of labels are best. Unfortunately little public information is available about U.S. consumer perceptions of ecolabels, especially as pertaining to sustainably produced foods. The Hartman Group conducted a national study on consumer response to food and beverage ecolabels, and the results of the study are summarized in the following tables.[4]

Pesticides, herbicides and food safety are important for ecolabels to communicate. Table 11-1 shows the relative importance respondents placed on various issues when asked *what* an ecolabel should communicate.

Table 11-1. What Should an Ecolabel Communicate About a Product?

Product Characteristic	Respondents Rating "Extremely Important" (%)
Ingredients grown without synthetic pesticides	77
Ingredients grown without synthetic herbicides	77
Ingredients contain no E-coli or other harmful bacteria	75
Contains no artificial ingredients or preservatives	61
Ingredients grown without synthetic fertilizers	59
Facility is in compliance with its environmental permits	58
Ingredients grown using only earth-sustainable techniques	57
Made using techniques that protect water resources	56

When asked *who* should certify products, respondents were most trusting of an independent testing laboratory, as shown in Table 11-2.

Table 11-2. Who Should Certify Products?

Certification	Respondents Rating "Extremely Important" (%)
Certified by an independent testing laboratory	36
Certified by a nonprofit organization	25
Certified by a manufacturer using standards established by a nonprofit organization	15

When asked which food categories should be labeled, respondents were unanimous in ranking fresh vegetables and fruit as the food categories most in need of a seal: Over 60 percent of all respondents ranked an ecolabel for this category as "extremely important." Table 11-3 shows other food categories listed in order of importance for needing ecolabels (as ranked by respondents).

---

[4] *Ecolabels: The Key to Consumer Support*, The Hartman Group/The Food Alliance, 1997

Table 11-3. What Food Categories Should Have Ecolabels?

Food Category	Respondents Rating "Extremely Important" (%)
Fresh Fruit and Vegetables	60
Meat	25
Poultry	24
Dairy Products	23
Packaged Foods	18
Frozen Foods	13
eafoods	12
Fruit Juice	10

The vast majority of respondents noted that they would buy a product with an ecolabel over a product with no seal even if the labeled product cost more (see figure 11-2). Of course, how such attitudes will actually translate into purchase behavior is yet to be seen.

Figure 11-2. Amount Respondents Say They Would Pay for a Product With an Ecolabel.

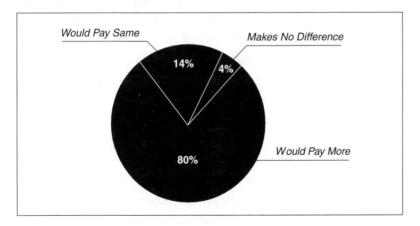

Conclusions

In the end, the consumer will determine which ecolabels and promotional vehicles are important through purchase behavior and product selection. Ecolabels are an attractive marketing strategy for food and beverage marketers because they give tangible reasons for why the shopper should choose an environmentally progressive product. Unfortunately, by their very nature, an ecolabel can "niche" a product, sometimes relegating it beyond the products considered by the conventional shopper. In order for products to diffuse broadly into large markets, niche attributes should be broadly recognized and not require a deep knowledge of complex growing principles or production methods. Finally, ecolabel "brand" recognition requires heavy promotion and education campaigns.

While the national debate on organic standards currently implies that an organic certification symbol will eventually be created, such an undertaking is formidable. From a private industry (as opposed to regulatory) perspective, the development of a *national* seal certifying environmentally-enhanced food and agriculture products will be expensive and akin to the development of a nationally recognized brand: Such campaigns cost millions of dollars. As noted previously, regional seals are anticipated to have a greater impact and more meaning to consumers, as well as lower brand building costs. On a regional scale, collaborations between growers, processors, and manufacturers using ecolabels seem to be meeting with some success.

Large conventional manufacturers and processors are not necessarily interested in the costs of promoting a nationally-placed seal or ecolabel. A number of major corporations do not want to have their food brands even associated with terminology relating to pesticides or herbicides.

There has been substantial investment made in both nonprofit and for-profit arenas to develop umbrella stewardship programs. On a national basis, to build such a system across food and agricultural product categories is an enormous task—and from the producer and consumer perspective, the added value of such programs is not entirely clear. Here again, developing umbrella stewardship systems on a regional basis is perhaps more realistic than developing a national program.

The actual ecolabels themselves should be designed keeping the following suggestions in mind:

- An ecolabel image should be visible and recognizable even when reduced to a very small size or when reproduced in black and white. (These labels are applied to individual fruits and produce in many cases.)
- The color version of the ecolabel might have green and blue highlights—helping to communicate key consumer concerns over water and agriculture.

- Simple wording, either in the label itself or more likely surrounding the image, can communicate the geographic origin of the product as well as the key concepts it is promoting.

As noted throughout this book, there are a broad array of factors influencing consumers' purchase and use of natural products and services. Ecolabels and the underlying organizations and principles they communicate are only one small component of why a natural or environmentally enhanced product might be purchased. More consumers will be attracted to environmentally-friendly and sustainable products if they can see the connection to their own health and wellness and the lifestyle they are living. Consumers are pragmatic, and before responding to an ecolabel they need to be convinced that the labeled products work as well as, if not better than, other products, especially with organics, personal care, and household products. As noted earlier, cost, availability and convenience are also some of the most significant factors in the adoption of natural and environmentally enhanced products.

PART V

Marketing Implications:

Building Natural Brands in the Wellness Category

INTRODUCTION

We have so far discussed a wide variety of factors driving the growth of the natural products marketplace. However, nothing can be considered more important than understanding that the entire spectrum of natural products available to the consumer is a new product category to be managed, just as other product categories need to be managed. While traditional category management skills are needed to manage products in the wellness category, a variety of specific concepts are centrally involved in influencing why consumers purchase natural products and services. Building natural brands that consumers trust and buy regularly is the significant task facing manufacturers, marketers, and retailers alike. The concepts of authenticity, naturalization, place, experience, originality and tradition—and how these factors influence consumer participation in the wellness category—are discussed in Part V.

CHAPTER 12

Authenticity, Naturalization and Experience

Building natural brands requires a willingness to evolve with a changing consumer and recognizing that there are profound activators that lead to natural product purchase and use. Marketers can often learn a lot simply by listening to consumers, as shown in the following exchange taken from focus group tapes of natural product users:

> *Respondent 1: "I was on asthma medicine and hormones and I took myself off every medication the doctor gave me, and I feel better on the natural stuff because it's the real thing—the synthetic stuff just doesn't do your body any good. . . . You know, that's the way God intended things—to be natural."*
> *Respondent 2: "It's true."*
> *Respondent 3: "I agree."*
> *Respondent 4: "That's very true."*
> *Respondent 5: "Absolutely."*
> *Moderator: "Wow . . . I see lots of nodding heads here."*

The Hartman Group was struck by the virtual unanimity of opinion among this group of consumers, who viewed natural products as "the real thing" and "the way God intended things to be." Of course, the next logical step for researchers, analysts, and marketers is to determine how natural products and services became sublimely ordained for this group of consumers and what can be done to convince other consumers to see natural products in the same way. The answers to these questions yield significant insight into merchandising, marketing and branding efforts.

AUTHENTICITY: THE REAL THING

As discussed in Chapter 3, understanding authenticity and its impact on the purchase and use criteria of consumers is a critical component of building natural brands. Conventional consumers are increasingly purchasing and using natural products and services because of a perception that those products and services are considered closer to the "real thing" or the "authentic" product. Examples of this include the favorable perceptions of herbal supplements compared to pharmaceutical compounds, or the satisfaction derived from the more personalized, less bureaucratic nature of alternative health care services. Whatever the case, consumers are looking for authenticity, and they can find it in natural products and services.

Such behavior raises a fundamental question: Who decides what is authentic and how is it decided? While there is no perfect answer or magic bullet, a useful approach to understanding why consumers participate in the wellness category is emerging from The Hartman Group's work.

Fabricating Authenticity

Rather than considering authenticity as an inherent, objective property of an object or event, authenticity can be best viewed as a *status* or *designation* bestowed upon the object. This status or designation indicates a shared belief that this version is, indeed, the *truest expression* of the object or event in question. (For example, some Americans view country music as the authentic American music, while others choose jazz.)

This status is negotiated and maintained by social networks of consumers, fans, experts, writers, journalists, historians and other interested parties—including marketing or financial-related groups. In the case of country music, its "authentic" status would be influenced by fans, record producers, industry executives, music critics and journalists.

The negotiation and maintenance that supports authenticity claims requires effort. This "work" can be in the form of discussion, word-of-mouth testimonials, expert recommendations, critical commentary, informational articles, interactions, advertisements or experiences. From this perspective, we can view authenticity as created—or literally fabricated.

Sociologist Richard Peterson applies this perspective to the world of popular music, demonstrating that much of the success and long-term popularity of country music can be attributed to the collective efforts to fabricate authenticity—in this case to create and maintain a history that portrays country music as the authentic product of naive country folk with all the trappings of an indigenous, grounded spirit.[1]

Naturalization of authenticity refers to efforts by all interested parties—conscious or otherwise—to construct their version of authenticity so that it appears as part of the "natural order of things."

To use a more familiar example, consider soft drinks and Coca Cola's "most authentic" cola. In this case, "the real thing" is not found in the can itself, but in the brand, the logo, the brand image, the closely-guarded "secret formula," T-shirts, merchandise, sporting events, and other items created to reinforce Coca Cola's image.

The claim to authenticity is literally fabricated through the collective work of consumers, brand managers, pop-culture historians, merchandisers, placement deals, and sponsorship of major events.

Naturalization of Authenticity

As brand managers in crowded markets realize, there is a constant struggle between competing authenticity claims (e.g., Coke versus Pepsi, Gap versus Levi's). One of the most effective strategies in such a scenario is to attempt to naturalize a particular version of authenticity. By naturalization, we are referring to efforts by all interested parties—conscious or otherwise—to construct their version of authenticity so that it appears as part of the "natural order of things." In this scenario, the fabricated, "authentic" version is seen as emanating from the natural—not social—world, where larger, "otherworldly powers" govern.

Once naturalized, the authenticity claim is extremely difficult to challenge. People accept it tacitly as the "way things are in the world." Levi Strauss, for example, has invested a lot of money and time trying to convince the world that Levi's jeans are part of the "natural order" of authentic youth culture.

[1] Professor Richard A. Peterson, Department of Sociology, Vanderbilt University, and as discussed in his *Country Music: Fabricating Authenticity* (Chicago: University of Chicago Press, 1997).

Turning to an example from the natural products arena, Prozac, Zoloft, and St. John's Wort are all thought to elevate one's mood by modifying serotonin levels in the brain. While product ingredients may be very different, and come from very different places, the battle over authenticity takes place outside the capsule. Scientists, drug company sales representatives, physicians, pharmacists, professional organizations (AMA, APA, etc.), retailers, integrated health care specialists, consumers, and journalists all play a part in fabricating the authenticity claims of these various products.

Further, many of these parties—specifically, professional organizations, pharmaceutical companies and herbal supplement manufacturers—have a vested interest in this process, lending a distinctly political character to the contest as they attempt to naturalize one version over another. For many years, the AMA and pharmaceutical companies were quite successful in this regard, since for most consumers, antidepressants prescribed by a physician or psychiatrist were the naturalized, authentic option; that was the way things were. Recently, fierce battles are being waged between professional organizations as St. John's Wort begins to challenge the "natural order of things." As we saw in the original quote above, some consumers consider natural products to be the "real thing,"—the way "God intended things to be."

Marketing Implications

Marketers and brand managers familiar with the business literature might react skeptically. After all, the idea that what is "inside the package" is often less important than the "image" is nothing particularly new. Yet as noted previously, there is a great deal more going on than the traditional branding literature themes of image, identity, association, awareness, and so on.

When we include consumers, fans, writers, journalists, and historians in the pool of laborers necessary to fabricate authenticity, the task becomes more complicated, requiring specialized approaches tailored to specific industries. While nobody would be naive enough to suggest a formula for controlling larger social processes (consumer tastes, preferences, collective discourse, trends, etc.), we can offer insight into strategies that appear particularly well-suited to fostering authenticity in the natural products industry. These strategies take into account more of the work and more of the laborers involved in fabricating authenticity. Finally, because the marketplace for natural products is still emerging and has a largely unexplored branding terrain, we find branding strategies based on authenticity are particularly crucial.

Place, Experience, Originality and Tradition

The Hartman Group's qualitative and quantitative analyses of natural product consumers isolate several themes driving authenticity in the natural products arena. These include place, experience, originality, and tradition. We offer summary explanations of all four themes and then discuss place and experience in more depth.

Place

The ability to associate a given product or service with a geographic point of origin significantly enhances authenticity claims. For manufacturers and producers, place figures most prominently both in the source of components and ingredients (where ingredients come from as well as the source of production) and the source of purchase. For retailers—especially chains—the place of origin (i.e. the location of the first store) can be used to bolster authenticity claims.

Experience

Consumers increasingly desire experiences, and these experiences are intimately linked with authenticity. Authenticity maintains the credibility of the experience and, likewise, experience enhances the authenticity claim.

Originality

To be viewed as authentic, goods and services should have some claim to originality. This originality can derive from historic connections (e.g., the first producer of echinacea as an herbal supplement) as well as differentiation processes (e.g., the "rock" deodorant released by Crystal Rock). In many ways, organic and natural brands intrinsically build on the power of the originality of the product itself: Presumably, while natural products represent innovations in and of themselves, they also usually have fewer additives and ingredients than conventional products, and are therefore closer to the original product or ingredient.

Tradition

The ability to place a product or service in context within a larger, established tradition enhances authenticity claims. Long-standing, nationally recognized brands tend to emphasize the connections between their product and an indigenous history. Some natural product consumers and alternative health practitioners, for example, promote the use of St. John's Wort by pointing out the fact that it has had "a place in German medicine for centuries."

The Importance of Place

For natural product consumers, authentic goods and services come from somewhere, and that where that somewhere is makes a difference. Emphasizing the point of origin for assorted goods and services in the natural products industry will positively enhance authenticity claims. This can be obvious—as in the case of Tom's of Maine—or subtle.

The fact that some of the herbal supplements under the Nature's Way label are produced from herbs grown organically on Trout Lake Farm in the state of Washington, for example, has not gone unnoticed by some consumers. In the context of alternative health care, knowledge regarding the geographic origins of a given practitioner's training (e.g., "my herbalist was trained in China," "My naturopath came from Bastyr.") lends significant credibility to authenticity claims.

Memorializing a specific location, often in the form of an interactive experience, is yet another way of establishing authenticity. REI's flagship store in Seattle and the Kellogg's Cereal City museum in Battle Creek Michigan are two examples from outside the natural products industry. It is much easier to associate a place with a product or experience once one has visited the place. And, as some forward-thinking companies have realized, the best way to attract visitors is to create a themed, destination experience.

The Importance of Experience

One of the ironies of the modern condition is the degree to which consumers desire authentic experiences. As depicted in the film City Slickers, people are willing to pay top dollar for the chance to engage in what most would consider grueling physical labor because the experience is seen as authentic. Compared to the perceived artificiality of the modern existence—where successes and failures are measured by tiny bits of electronic information—cattle drives, archeological digs, wine making and gold mining all represent authentic experiences—offering people the opportunity to show "who they really are."

Often, authenticity and experience interact as mutually reinforcing processes. Thus, experience figures most prominently in the fabrication of authenticity for natural product consumers.

Within the natural products market, we see examples of experience everywhere. Specialty retailers such as Whole Foods, Trader Joe's and Wild Oats routinely offer experiences such as cooking demonstrations, wellness clinics, libraries, nutrition clinics, and massage workshops. Here, experience operates on two levels. First, simply experiencing a demonstration or interaction with a product or service lends credibility to the authenticity claim. However, higher-order processes are also involved. The sum total of these experiences contributes significantly to the credibility and authenticity of the retail location (Trader Joe's, Whole Foods, etc.) so that merely locating a demonstration or informational seminar within one of these destinations brings a "value-added" benefit in terms of enhanced authenticity. Put another way, an informational seminar on kava kava seems more authentic at Wild Oats than it does at Rite Aid.

Finally, it is useful to think about experience as an innovation in the brand manager's tool kit. As suggested above, most of the branding literature deals implicitly with how to influence and relate to consumers. It does not have much to say about influencing larger social processes— fads, tastes, preferences, and the like. *Experience* is one way to steer such processes. Whole Foods and Wild Oats have admirably demonstrated that once they have a consumer in their store, the total experience can influence a substantial market-based purchase.

As Starbucks demonstrates, while a single company—even with the help of brand managers and advertising agencies—cannot force a coffee culture on the American people, what it can do is set the stage for an authentic experience. Starbucks set the stage and scenery for an authentic experience and then waited for consumers to create the coffee culture. The company has been rewarded with tremendous growth.

CONSTRUCTING THE FUTURE IN THE IMAGE OF THE PAST

Authenticity, place, tradition, and experience all play an increasingly important role in driving purchase and behavioral trends. While collectively, American skills, technology and scientific knowledge have produced many of the miracles of the modern age, they have also squeezed a lot of the mystery out of life. Indeed, this is so much the case that a modern existence is often marked by a distinctly ironic—often cynical—edge. Nostalgia—the consumer love of all things cherished and old—tops the charts as society casts a collective wink at previous generations' "true expression of the self."

Nostalgia and the drive for the past have produced a trend whereby retailers, marketers and consumers themselves consciously construct the present in the image of the past. As a result, comfort food, khaki pants, swing dance and cigars are back in fashion.

Similarly, try naming a city in America that has not either undertaken or considered the revitalization of its downtown core so that things would "be like they used to be" in the "good old days." Youth culture—devoid of any sense of self-discovery and self-conscious of the possibility for exploitation—recycles fashion trends from the past, recasting them in the spirit of a distinctly post-modern image. Indeed, as several cultural theorists have noted, youth culture today appears much more concerned with recreating the past than merely "letting the present happen."

With regard to natural products and services and the important connections consumers make between these products and originality, an important question would center on how marketers can go about constructing the present in the image of the past.

The answer lies in the domain of *experience*. Not content to sit back and let the present or future merely "happen," modern consumers create and seek out *experiences*. Likewise, these are not just any experiences, but carefully constructed *authentic* experiences. Of course, authentic experiences don't simply happen—they are consciously crafted and managed, with nothing left to chance.

At the end of the work week, consumers don't wander out into the woods, content to explore nature the way their ancestors did. Instead, they contract the services of mountaineering guides, invest a lot of time and money in intricate outdoor gear and travel into nature to engage in an "authentic wilderness experience." Similarly, whereas cattle drives, fruit harvests and archeological digs were once considered sheer drudgery—grunt work delegated to the low-skilled among us—consumers are now willing to pay top dollar for the chance to engage in these carefully managed, "authentic" experiences.

WELCOME TO THE EXPERIENCE ECONOMY

The desire for authentic experiences has not gone unnoticed by commercial interests. In fact, theme and experiential retail environments—stages for the enactment of authentic experiences—are just beginning to populate the retail landscape. While most of us have some familiarity with the early precursors—Nike town, Planet Hollywood or the Hard Rock Cafe—perhaps the best illustration of this idea put into practice is REI's flagship store in Seattle, Washington.

Opened in September of 1996, the store's featured attractions include the world's tallest indoor climbing structure, an outdoor, mountain-bike test trail, a boot-test trail with "non-trivial" steepness, water filter testing stations and an indoor rain room (for testing water-resistant gear under inclement conditions). Under one roof, the "outdoor" consumer can now engage in a collection of carefully managed authentic experiences. Such a retail setting implies that forward-thinking retailers must also create, manage and sell experience in addition to the typical offering of products that consumers expect in a store.

While many marketers and consumers have an intuitive sense that experience is starting to be an important influence, the topic remains largely unaddressed in business literature. Joseph Pine and James Gilmore are among the first to consider this subject with their recent article in *Harvard Business Review* titled "Welcome to the Experience Economy."[2] Pine and Gilmore distinguish *experiences* from *services* and in doing so, set experience up to be the next evolutionary phase of the world economy, following in the footsteps of its predecessors—the agrarian, industrial, and service economies (see figure 12-1). As they contend, "From now on, leading-edge companies—whether they sell to

---

[2] Pine, Joseph and James Gilmore, "Welcome to the Experience Economy," *Harvard Business Review* 76, no. 4 (7–8/98): 97–105, and Joseph Pine and James Gilmore, *The Experience Economy* (Boston: Harvard Business School Press, 1999).

consumers or businesses—will find that the next competitive battle-ground lies in staging experiences." In this world, companies that are able to present the most compelling experiences will command price premiums and brand equity.

Figure 12-1. The Progression of Economic Value

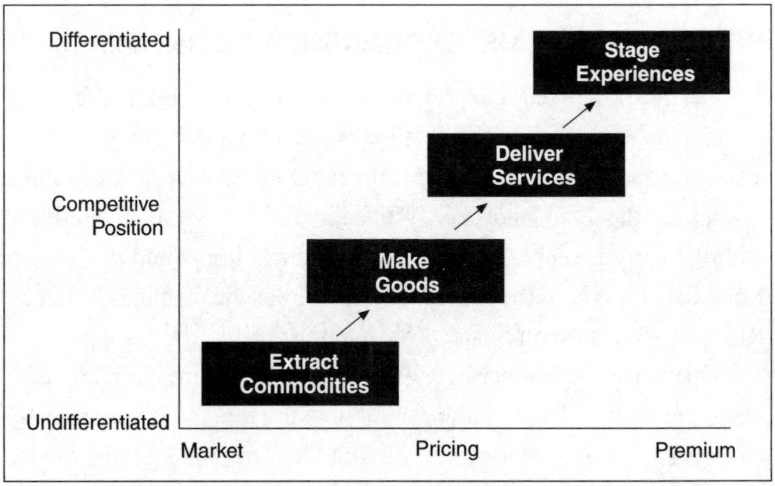

Source: Pine & Gilmore, *Harvard Business Review*, 7–8, 1998.

While Pine and Gilmore's conclusions are tentative and should be treated with caution (after all, predicting the evolutionary trajectory of the world economy can be pretty tricky stuff) their work does provide some useful insights into how the commercial world is beginning to conceptualize experience. The Hartman Group has also been exploring these ideas with specific regard to the natural products industry. Over the past two years, we have conducted a number of one-on-one interviews and consumer focus groups that addressed these issues in some detail. Results allow us to offer some insights regarding the role of experience in the natural products industry.

EXPERIENCE AND NATURAL PRODUCTS

Ironically, the natural products industry—a relative newcomer to the history of American commerce—is an ideal match for the experience economy. After all, one of the hallmarks of the authentic experience is a direct reference—literal or symbolic—to a pre-modern, less industrialized era. By simple virtue of being categorized as "natural," these products stand in direct opposition to the "less authentic" products of an advanced, industrialized economy.

As The Hartman Group's research demonstrates, many consumers view natural products and services as "less modern," "less fabricated," "traditional" and "more authentic." Thus, according to consumers, St. John's Wort is more authentic than Prozac because it is "less manufactured and less chemical," "it comes from the ground" and "Europeans have been using it for centuries." Likewise, organic produce appears more authentic than its non-organic competition because, according to consumers, it is evocative of an "old fashioned, less mechanized approach to agriculture." In short, a lot of the hard work—time spent figuring out how natural marketers are going to construct notions of authenticity—is already out of the way. The tricky part, then, is deciding how to foster and stage experiences.

Retail

One way to start thinking about how to incorporate experience in the natural products arena is to look at already existing examples. As it happens, leading grocers in the natural products arena have been tinkering with the role of experience—albeit on a smaller scale—for quite some time. The now ubiquitous "massage while you shop," forever a fixture of health food stores and food co-ops, has played a prominent role in developing Whole Foods' retail experience.

At Whole Foods, the act of receiving, or even watching, a massage reinforces the notion that this is no average retail experience. Make no mistake, this is an authentic wellness experience, and other key design features of leading natural grocers reinforce this distinction. Many are probably also familiar with the small, intimate reading rooms often located near vitamin, mineral and herbal supplement displays. Here, customers are invited to read and study, at their leisure, the latest information regarding the wellness benefits of such products. Similarly, we often find open display kitchens for public demonstrations and lectures offered by visiting chefs and nutritionists. Some retailers even organize community outreach programs, such as neighborhood cleanup days and watershed restoration programs, and invite consumers to participate.

More subtle design touches—such as strategically located skylights, wood floors, and hanging plants—serve to further enhance the overall legitimacy of the wellness experience.

The sum total of all of these individual experiences, however seemingly insignificant, contributes to a larger wellness experience. It is important to realize that the wellness experience here is not necessarily related to the products themselves. Rather, the wellness experience arises from all of the associated experiences involved in shopping and purchasing the products. For example, the simple act of purchasing a bottle of Echinacea at Fred Meyer does not constitute an authentic wellness experience in the same manner as purchasing the same bottle during a visit to the local Whole Foods Market.

Such retailing embodies the construction of an experience economy. Further developments in retail will continue. First, expect to find an engaging dialogue at all levels of the retail experience. Here, the goal is to engage the customer in a dialogue regarding some aspect of a highly differentiated product or service category. It will no longer be enough to simply place multivitamins on a shelf and expect them to sell well. Instead, customers will be responding to thoughtful education and recommendations from trained experts and knowledgeable professionals. We should add here that the phrase "trained experts and knowledgeable professionals" means just that. We are not talking about well-intentioned, interested employees, but rather certified nutritionists and pharmacists that can provide concise, authoritative information. Similarly, wine will no longer be sold with shelf tags or recommendations from the produce department. Instead, a trained sommelier will provide that service.

Next, expect to see the traditional boundaries of the retail environment extended to encompass experiences physically distinct from the retail store. Outdoor recreational equipment retailers already sponsor white-water rafting and mountain climbing expeditions. One wonders why forward-thinking retailers couldn't sponsor similar trips to organic farms, harvests, or wineries, or host wine tasting or other events.

Manufacturing

The preceding discussion considers the power of retail establishments to foster, create and manage experience. This raises an important question: How do manufacturers who are not traditionally involved in the retail sector play a role in the furthering of experience? While the answers here are not as clear, there is some early evidence that they do exist. Odwalla, a California-based beverage manufacturer, has subtly fashioned experience, perhaps unwittingly, into the consumption of fresh juices. By locating their unique, stand alone refrigerators in coffee shops, cafes, bistros, student food courts, and diners—as well as more traditional retail environments such as grocery stores—consumers come to experience the product as an authentic part of "everyday life." The simple act of grabbing a bottle of fresh juice from the Odwalla refrigerator at one's neighborhood coffee shop transforms an ordinary retail transaction into a "life experience," not dissimilar from "grabbing juice from mom's refrigerator."

CONCLUSIONS

The natural marketers who control access to authentic experiences will be best positioned to command brand equity and price premiums. In such a world, economic power—and profits—won't likely emanate from economies of scale, production efficiencies, or manufacturing concerns. Instead, retailers, merchandisers and designers will likely drive the successful branding campaigns—and revenue streams—of the experience economy. Among other things, this suggests that manufacturers lacking the means or power to shape and control experience may increasingly find themselves delegated to the production of private label brands for third parties.

Starbucks underscores notions about the power of brand building in the context of authenticity and experience. Starbucks didn't create a global branding empire by paying a lot of attention to the production and distribution of coffee and related products (although certainly the company pays close attention to the roasting of its beans). After all, issues of vertical integration and production, if necessary, can be outsourced. Starbucks also did not engage in massive, high-concept advertising campaigns. Instead, the company focused on creating and managing the coffee experience, one store at a time. Their retail "coffee shops" are living, breathing shrines to the authentic *coffee experience.* Consumers are invited to step on up to the counter and watch as a trained barista (no mere employee) builds the perfect coffee drink before their very eyes. The authentic aromas of recently roasted coffee abound. Next, proceed on over to the lounge where one can relax next to a fireplace and converse with friends from the neighborhood. The genius of Starbucks was the vision to build thousands of stages on which the theater of coffee experience is played out daily. Following in this vision, Starbucks only recently began offering their signature coffees in retail grocers. Only now, once most customers have had some exposure to the authentic coffee experience, has Starbucks even bothered with the mainstream retail grocery arena. At the same time, the company is building off the strength of having created a coffee culture and is now moving into food.

The lesson to be learned: Don't be afraid to build the authentic experience first and worry about the manufacturing and branding later. If Pine and Gilmore are correct, there will be plenty of displaced manufacturers vying for the contract-production business of the visionaries with the foresight to enter the experience economy. The ability of marketing companies (including manufacturers) to connect rapidly and directly to the changing consumer will impact who wins and loses in the long-term as the natural market consolidates. The ability of such companies to partner with powerful retail outlets (whether physical or virtual) will also impact whether or not the company sells a consumer brand or merely produces them for other members of the value chain.

CHAPTER 13

Manufactured by Nature: Building Supplement Brands

INTRODUCTION

The explosively growing vitamin, mineral, herbal and dietary supplement category is an excellent category of products by which to examine principles of building natural brands. How can authenticity, retail experience, and brand equity be developed in a $10 billion category within which hundreds of little understood products have proliferated and are sold through over thirteen different channels?

Let's start with the big picture. The American consumer is purchasing more and more supplements. The Hartman Group's *Supplement Report,*[3] which tracks weekly consumer purchase and use of over 150 major supplements, projects the size of the U.S. vitamin, mineral, herbal, and miscellaneous dietary supplement market at over $10 billion, and it is growing steadily at double-digit rates. Nearly 30 percent of consumers—60 million Americans—are currently purchasing and using one or more herbal or dietary supplements with varying degrees of regularity and product knowledge. Over 60 percent of Americans take a multivitamin, a practice which we've learned crosses over to use of single-letter vitamins and minerals, as well as herbals and other dietary supplements. Cutting across demographics, the consumer is in the early learning phase of supplement

---

[3] See Appendix I for more information on *Supplement Report.*

purchase and use. Despite the fact that some supplement brands and products have been available in the United States for decades, consumer brand recognition is extremely low.

BRAND AWARENESS

The Hartman Group has witnessed low brand awareness firsthand in focus group and individual interview research where consumers, when asked about what supplement brand they purchase, respond by hitting themselves on the forehead, exclaiming something such as, "It's the one with the leaf on it! It's Nature something!" Other common responses follow the line of "Well, I buy Ginseng and St. John's Wort. That's what I buy . . . I don't know what brand they are. . . ."

As noted earlier when discussing The Hartman Group's study *Vitamins, Minerals, Herbals, and Dietary Supplements: Phase II*, unaided brand awareness and trust of manufacturers in the supplement category hovers at a very low rate (see figure 13-1). It is easy to understand how brand confusion might occur, as The Hartman Group's *Supplement Report* currently tracks over ten major U.S. supplement brands that include the word "Nature." Brand name directories list dozens of other supplement brands using "Nature" or "Natural" on their labels.

Simultaneous to low brand recognition is the explosion of supplement availability through nearly every retail and sales channel imaginable (see table 13-1 and figure 13-2). Supplements are small, easily shipped, and regularly purchased; therefore, sales of these products are evolving to include direct mail and the Internet. Along with physical retail settings, these virtual channels are growing sales quickly as consumers relentlessly seek out products perceived to be high in quality, value and convenience. Wide-scale availability combined with a seemingly inexhaustible desire by the consumer to experiment with self-health promotion has fueled the growth of the supplement market as a whole: Consequently, and perhaps not surprisingly, among 150 top supplement brands sold in the United States through all channels, the top-selling brands are private label store brands and Spring Valley (the Wal-Mart brand). (See table 13-2.) The prevalence of such price and convenience brands underscores the movement of large numbers of health-seeking experimental shoppers into the supplement category.

Figure 13-1. Best, Most Trusted Vitamin, Mineral, Herbal, and Supplement Manufacturers (Unaided survey responses mentioned by at least 1 percent of 2,346 supplement user respondents)

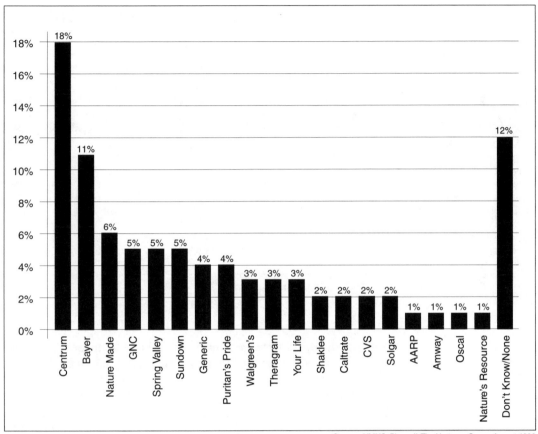

Source: *VMHS: Phase II*, The Hartman Group, August 1998

Table 13-1. Third Quarter 1998 Total U.S. Sales of Vitamins, Minerals, Herbals and Supplements by All Channels, with Average Price per Individual Purchase by Channel

	# of Purchases			Distribution of Volume	
	000's	% Total Purchases	Avg. Price/ Purchase	$000's	% Total Sales
Total VMHS	**224,070**	**100%**	**$10.15**	**$2,274,311**	**100%**
Pharmacy/Drug Store	49,393	22%	$8.04	$397,120	17%
Mass Market Store	49,301	22%	$7.18	$353,981	16%
Grocery Store/Supermarket	36,790	16%	$6.90	$253,851	11%
Direct Mail/Catalog	21,038	9%	$14.28	$300,423	13%
Direct from Sales Representative	13,272	6%	$23.19	$307,778	14%
Health Food Store	11,499	5%	$13.52	$155,466	7%
Vitamin/Supplement Store	9,419	4%	$14.02	$132,054	6%
Club Store	8,908	4%	$11.77	$104,847	5%
Health Care Practitioner	3,105	1%	$21.92	$68,062	3%
Natural Health Food Supermarket	2,254	1%	$10.30	$23,216	1%
Insurance Company/HMO	1,437	1%	$7.01	$10,073	0%
Over the Internet	898	0%	$6.16	$5,532	0%
Infomercial/Direct from TV	97	0%	$34.69	$3,365	0%
All Others	8,243	4%	$7.87	$64,872	3%
		100%			100%

Source: *Supplement Report*, The Hartman Group

Table 13-2. Top 15 Vitamin, Mineral, Herbal and Supplement Brands by Purchase with Average Purchase Price, Total U.S. Market, Third Quarter 1998

		# of Purchases		
		000's	% Total Purchases	Avg. Price/ Purchase
	Total VMHS	**224,070**	**100%**	**$10.15**
1	Store Brand/Private Label	42,121	19%	$8.36
2	Spring Valley	18,472	8%	$6.14
3	Centrum	12,949	6%	$8.81
4	Sundown	11,685	5%	$7.38
5	Nature Made	7,562	3%	$7.42
6	Puritan's Pride	6,580	3%	$9.92
7	One-A-Day	5,589	2%	$6.97
8	Your Life	5,492	2%	$8.15
9	GNC	5,162	2%	$15.50
10	Walgreen's	4,649	2%	$7.13
11	Shaklee	3,956	2%	$18.80
12	CVS	3,697	2%	$6.05
13	Prescription	3,673	2%	$11.75
14	One Source	3,501	2%	$5.94
15	Nature's Way	3,472	2%	$8.25

Source: *Supplement Report*, The Hartman Group

Figure 13-2. Purchases and Pricing per Purchase Channel, VMHS, Third Quarter 1998

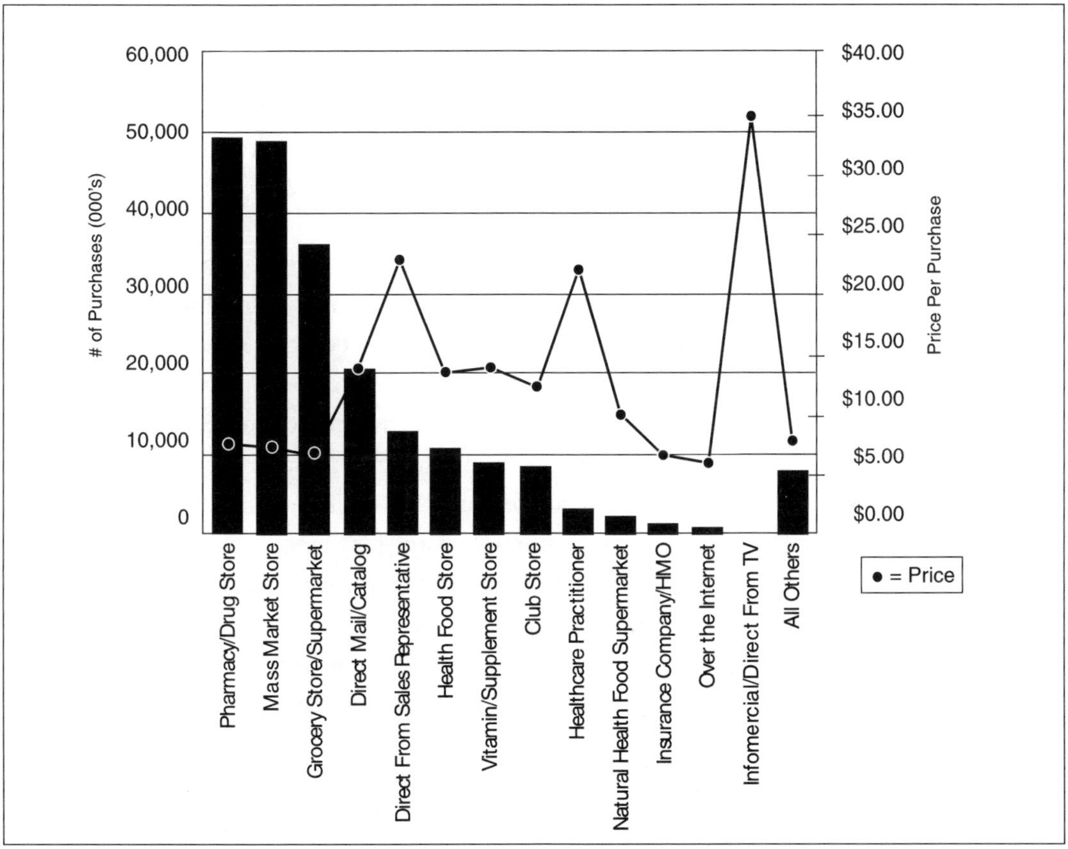

Strategically, vitamin and pharmaceutical producers are leveraging established brand equity and looking for the conversion of vitamin and mineral users into herbal and related supplement users. Currently some 60 percent of Americans take a multivitamin, while only about 25 percent regularly purchase and use herbals and other supplements. Simultaneous to the entry of mainstream vitamin and pharmaceutical giants into the supplement mass market, we see established "natural market" supplement brands and manufacturers competing for mainstream shelf space. National advertising appearing on television and radio spots reminds consumers that supplements are now available under familiar brand names, from established supplement manufacturers and from brand-specific ingredient marketers.

THE INGREDIENT AND BRAND LABYRINTH

With the entry of conventional pharmaceutical brands into the supplement market, the brand battle has begun: Like pioneers in the organic and natural food and beverage categories, the difficult tasks of pioneering a consumer product category and then maintaining a defensible foothold on large playing fields now awaits long-time players in the supplement market. Communicating the quality of the company (and thus the brand) of a long-time producer of supplements is an expensive and daunting task when faced with the requirements of mainstream brand building, pull-through and promotion costs. In some ways, partnerships based on financial brawn, such as the recent sale of Solgar to American Home Products (AHP), point to the realities of competing on a long-term basis for some companies. The entry of conventional brands into the supplement market is also legitimizing a market that formerly was held at arm's length. The power of consumer demand and the size of the market have brought in very large players.

An alternative to competing on financial terms is focusing strategically on channels or consumer niches—a strategy upon which some companies can thrive. The Hartman Group believes that the next generation of supplement companies will evolve into marketing companies that focus intensely on consumer health niches, such as those centered around arthritis or cancer. The needs and requirements of the ever-demanding consumer will require better and better relationship marketing.

However, growing numbers of supplement consumers, many with little brand allegiance, currently navigate the supplement ingredient and product labyrinth and purchase at will. This is despite their confessed lack of knowledge beyond what they glean from self-education, mass media and their immediate social network about what health conditions are treated by products.

Similar to consumers, supplement producers and marketers face a market of enormous size and scope: While one ingredient represents its own market and may only currently be purchased by less than 1 percent of the U.S. population—consumers who shop in different patterns, for different reasons and with varying knowledge and confidence—a 1 percent increase in product purchase and use can mean tens of millions of dollars in product growth. With proper attention to the demographics and prevalence of a health condition among the general population, a product that treats a specific health condition and is scientifically proven to be safe and effective can be constructed to drive an entire company's sales and marketing efforts. For example, several such companies currently source, produce, and market garlic-related products. Figure 13-3 demonstrates the range of decision choices open to raw material suppliers considering the launch of branded ingredient products.

Figure 13-3. Branding Opportunities for Raw Materials Suppliers in the U.S. Vitamin, Mineral, Herbal and Dietary Supplement Market

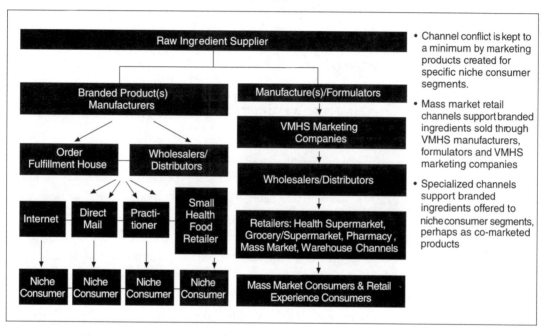

- Channel conflict is kept to a minimum by marketing products created for specific niche consumer segments.

- Mass market retail channels support branded ingredients sold through VMHS manufacturers, formulators and VMHS marketing companies

- Specialized channels support branded ingredients offered to niche consumer segments, perhaps as co-marketed products

To consider the total market open to today's supplement manufacturers, multiply single product market potential by 100 ingredients and consider the task faced in branding by the largest supplement companies, who dominate in the "natural" category and produce or market hundreds of products. Many of these companies maintain separate brands and brand management teams beneath a corporate umbrella that may or may not be apparent as the actual supplement producer. Such companies may maintain healthy margins and a presence in strategic channels such as health food stores, health food supermarkets, direct sales, or sales through health care practitioners.

Companies with diverse SKUs seeking entrance into mainstream supermarket, mass market and pharmacy retail channels face the difficult task of building brand awareness, trust, and communicating a health-oriented brand story to a confused and sometimes cynical mainstream shopper. At the same time, these firms must provide pull-through and promotional funds to promote their products through powerful grocery and pharmacy channels. Other firms, ranging from raw material suppliers selling branded ingredients to pure supplement marketing companies, face similar issues when faced with entering and tapping into the large volume of purchases made through mainstream retail channels. In this context, the brand battle really begins. How do supplement producers and marketers gather and retain new mainstream consumers?

COMMUNICATING THE BRAND AND COMPANY TO THE CONSUMER

We must remember that the supplement consumer is in the early learning phases of purchasing and using products in an ever-expanding health and wellness category. Just as with organic and natural foods, this is a new category to the conventional shopper. Even when it seems safe to say that there are perhaps two to three hundred core product ingredients from which stem thousands of single, multiple and proprietary combinations of product types, a single new ingredient enters the mass media and a "super-media" event drives a new ingredient-specific product onto a wide range of shelves, causing supplier turmoil and retail glut. Consumers may perhaps purchase the product and move it off of retail shelves and into their homes where the product enters the social network for trial use and recommendation.

This is a predictable event in the context of producing and selling supplements in the U.S. market. At its foundation, brand building in such a market requires laying a direct line of communication and trust between the producer of the brand that is marketing established and new products and the consumer who is purchasing and using the product in this dynamic and emerging market. David Aaker, brand guru notes:

"The most important part of a brand's identity is its core identity or essence. This essence is the brand's promise to customers, its growth aspirations, and the summarized expression of the supporting corporate or company culture. Most brands will have an extended identity which is the public manifestation of the brand personality, and is often visible in any marketing strategy. Core identity and extended identity must have synergy if brand equity is to impact earnings. This synergy creates a brand that is more than a product—it is an organization, a person, and a symbol."[4]

Aaker has seven questions which brand builders should ask themselves:

1. Does the brand have a resonant identity?
2. Does the brand system have synergy?
3. Are there any silver bullets?[5]
4. Is there cultural coherence?
5. Can the brand's promise be delivered?
6. Is there a brand personality?
7. Are there any brand symbols?

Importantly, one can ask these seven questions about many of the brands currently available in the supplement market—or in other wellness product categories. What identity do these brands have? How many supplement companies actually are able to communicate their corporate image via the branded supplement? Can the brand's promise, presumably centered on health and wellness promotion, be delivered?

The overriding question remains: What are consumers looking for in the supplement products they purchase? The Hartman Group has determined that underlying consumer purchase and use of supplements is a fragmented participation in the national quest for health and wellness, and while no one formula exists for how brands can be connected to this general trend, several very important points have arisen:[6]

---

[4] David Aaker (1998), in *Build Brand Value*, 1998 Conference Report, published by Venture Strategy Group, San Francisco, CA, p. 1.
[5] A "silver bullet" is a brand or sub-brand within a brand system created to alter or improve the image of an organizational or "parent" brand, as noted by David Aaker in *Build Brand Value*, 1998 Conference Report.
[6] *Natural Sensibility: A Study of America's Changing Culture and Lifestyle*, The Hartman Group, Fall 1998. See Appendix I.

Time and Place are of the Essence: In the context of shrinking available time, consumers indicate both directly and indirectly in attitudinal surveys and interviews designed to uncover behavior, that retail settings, where they can temporarily immerse themselves in the shopping experience they seek, are critical in tipping the balance toward both supplement and other natural product purchases.

I Tried it and I like It: Social networks are of enormous importance in how natural products and services are purchased and used. The diffusion of supplement purchase and use into more conventional consumer segments is the direct result of consumers communicating to each other about products they are using to treat their personal health. The high purchase prices still retained in the multi-level marketing and direct from sales representative categories underscore the power of social purchase behavior.

Displaced Trust: Consumers indicate strongly that they wish traditional sources of health information, such as physicians and pharmacists, were more knowledgeable about supplements. They trust these sources, but do not necessarily think that these practitioners provide the advice sought after.[7]

Table 13-3 shows common VMHS users' attitudes and beliefs that are important to understand when marketing to these consumers.

Table 13-3. VMHS User Attitudes and Beliefs, Ranked by Top Agreement Among VMHS User Respondents (among 27 statements)

Statement	Percent Who Agree
I wish I were more knowledgeable about vitamins, minerals, and supplements.	63%
I wish my (primary care) physician could tell me more about vitamins, minerals, and herbal supplements.	56%
When I go to a store to buy vitamins, minerals and herbal supplements, I usually know beforehand what brand I want to purchase.	54%
You get more benefits from using vitamins, minerals, and herbal supplements as you get older.	53%

Continued on next page

---

[7] *U.S. Consumer Use of Vitamins, Minerals, Herbals, and Dietary Supplements: Phase II*, The Hartman Group, August 1998. See Appendix I.

Statement	Percent Who Agree
Many vitamin, minerals, and supplement manufacturers make exaggerated claims and can not be trusted.	50%
I wish there was more independent, third-party information available about vitamins, minerals and herbal supplements.	50%
Herbal supplements should be more closely regulated by the Food and Drug Administration.	47%
I am concerned about using supplements in combination with prescription medications.	44%
Herbal supplements can be harmful if taken too long or too often.	30%
I worry less about effects from herbal supplements and remedies than prescription drugs.	29%

Source: *U.S. Consumer Use of Vitamins, Minerals, Herbals and Dietary Supplements: Phase II*, The Hartman Group, Fall 1998

Consumers shop piecemeal when it comes to natural products and supplements. Consequently, they may purchase supplements, if available, at any number of settings. Underneath such behavior, however, has arisen a familiar pattern, constructed from hundreds of hours of interviews and many national surveys conducted by The Hartman Group (see figure 13-4). In this scenario, the supplement purchaser, typically already a vitamin and mineral user, may shop initially in a health food store or health supermarket, seeking personal advice from a store employee on an herbal or dietary supplement. Once comfortable with the use of the supplement product(s) they seek knowledge about, the shopper begins price and value shopping, perhaps migrating to larger natural supermarkets, or mainstream supermarkets, pharmacies or mass-market stores. Finally, they may move on to purchasing via direct mail or Internet. Conversely, entire segments of consumers avoid health food stores and health supermarkets entirely and purchase only in mass retail settings, perhaps relying on a personal need to experiment with supplement use or a confidence inspired by mass-media information, social networks, and a growing awareness that supplement products can be used to promote both general health and wellness and specific health conditions.

Figure 13-4. Typical Usage and Purchase Pattern of Supplement Consumers

Use of Mulit-Vitamins Begins	Use of Multi-Vitamins and Single Letter Vitamins or Minerals (Vitamins C, E, etc.)	Use of Multi-Vitamin, Single Letter Vitamins, & Minerals and Experimentation & Awareness of Herbal & Dietary Supplement	Multi-Product User: Uses Vitamins or Minerals, and Specific Herbal and Dietary Supplements regularly
USAGE BEHAVIOR		→	
PURCHASE BEHAVIOR Self-education starts: Consumer may purchase via health food store or supplement specialty retailer (the informative retailers)	Self-education process continues but consumer may begin to seek new purchasing locations (large health food supermarkets, drug store/pharmacies: Price seeking starts)	Education on VMHS becomes greater: Now seeking price, a trusted retailer or brand. May begin to seek out direct mail or Internet for both price and convenience	Now purchasing VMHS via Direct Mail, Internet, or Trusted Retailer: Shopping on price and convenience or retail experience

Overall, consumers indicate that they are eager to trust a convenient purchase location and source, and moreover a purchase location that seeks to exceed their expectations about commonplace shopping—whether physical or virtual. The popularity of supplement sales via direct sales representatives and the higher prices paid for such products certainly speaks highly to the impact of personal selling and the power of social networks in marketing supplements. Underlying all of these factors is the current phenomenon of store and private label brands outselling all other brands. The power of place, combined with the traditional key buying factors of availability, cost, and perceived value, drive the current strength of store-branded supplements.

BUILDING THE BRAND AND THE COMPANY

In such a diverse and fragmented market, supplement marketers are faced with many alternatives for positioning and marketing their companies, and thus their brands, to the end-consumer. In the competitive arena faced by these marketers, concentrating on core competencies and strengthening barriers to entry are critical for long-term success.

It is important to ask whether the company has a core identity, production story, history, symbol and essence that can be communicated easily. These factors matter if the niche market relies in selling to consumers who largely self-educate and shop for their supplements in the natural channel. But do complex stories about product quality and production make a difference if the conventional customer is simply making purchasing decisions based on price and convenience?

New supplement consumers in general, like many new natural product and services customers, bear little resemblance to the committed, self-educating "natural" consumer. Instead, this new consumer is pandemographic, short on time, hungry for knowledge, and probably looking for a retail brand to trust. This profile will evolve with the emerging market as it matures over time. For now, consumers are currently seeking out a familiar list of benefits from the supplement products they purchase:

- Efficacy and performance (perceived and actual)
- Value and quality
- Price and availability

In time, the consumer will also be shopping the brand and company that is able to embody their particular health and wellness lifestyle and the authentic natural experiences they are seeking. The brand's *service* and *performance* will become paramount. The supplement category is an innovation and is almost entirely new to those who shop in it. Brand building that focuses on the retail lifestyle of health and wellness which consumers are incorporating piecemeal into their busy lives will succeed temporarily. Communicating and building a brand's underlying *cultural essence*, that of the company producing the product, will become a key component of long-term success.

Who will lead in the new brand building? One possible scenario lies in category management of the entire health category, whereby natural brands offer their own supplement product lines and work with key retailers to bring the entire health and wellness category to the new consumer. Natural brands that have been established and have penetrated conventional channels have a significant leg up on conventional competitors, so new rules of marketing may apply. Celestial Seasoning's entry into the supplement market, as part of building a portfolio of products around the company's historic tea name, is just such an example. The company is leveraging its existing—albeit small—brand equity in the conventional market. While few natural brands cut across food, beverage and supplement categories, such scenarios may increasingly gain popularity, specifically in the large supermarket and pharmacy channels. These natural companies can leverage whatever brand identity they may have built up over the years as a trusted natural health or wellness company.

In such a scenario, the portfolio of products offered by an umbrella health brand may reduce the risk of purchase for today's harried but health-focused shopper. Consumer trust of the supplier of physical health and wellness may equate to simplified purchase decisions, which can lead to significant corporate brand equity and value. Where is the Healthy Choice of natural brands? The answers lies at the heart of the food and the environment paradox and the small size and current fragmentation of natural manufacturers.

At the same time in various other channels, strategic partnerships, acquisitions and co-marketing arrangements constructed by supplement producers and marketers and focused on the power of retail settings (physical or virtual) will spell out long-term success. Retail proximity to the consumer, building brand trust and understanding why consumers are using supplements will build true brand equity. The consumer is currently purchasing supplements as part of an overall health and wellness lifestyle. Brands connected to the retail experience, constructed as spring boards toward brand allegiance and the trusted producer of the brand, will become extremely powerful in determining which supplement products consumer repeatedly purchase, use and recommend as they construct health regimes of increasing sophistication.

CHAPTER 14

New Horizons: Managing the Wellness Category

Much of The Hartman Group's work over the past ten years leads directly to this chapter. Our analysis of the environment in the 1980s that determined the terms by which consumers purchase and use environmentally enhanced products and services was a direct in-road toward analysis of consumer participation in the natural product marketplace in the 1990s.

THE WELLNESS CATEGORY

While Americans still voice attitudinal concerns for protecting their physical environment (water, flora and fauna, soil), The Hartman Group increasingly sees that the most consistent purchase behavior by consumers in the various food, beverage, supplement, and alternative medicine categories relates to wellness. As seen in figure 14-1, the consumer is centrally located in what we call the wellness category. Elements discussed throughout this book—including consumers' Natural Sensibility, the construction of personal wellness regimes, and the elements of authenticity, place, experience, tradition—all fall together as aspects of why consumers purchase and use these various products and services.

Figure 14-1. The Wellness Category

The American shopper is changing with the changing times. This evolution centers on increasing concerns about personal health and wellness, diet and nutrition, shrinking available time and an ever-widening availability of retail formats in which to experiment with the pursuit of lifestyle shopping experiences. Products and services offered to these consumers comprise the wellness category.

While wellness category products and services are increasingly available through conventional retail channels, such channels are only in the earliest stages of capitalizing on consumer participation in the newly forming wellness category. Many large food retailers have begun to integrate natural and organic products into their stores or have developed segregated "natural centers." Unfortunately with many of these conventional retailers, the foundation understanding of why consumers are purchasing these wellness subcategory products, and the efforts needed to make these subcategories a success, are also still in the early phases of development.

The wellness category currently makes up much more than just organic and natural foods: Conventional shoppers are now purchasing a large number of products that could be managed with both conventional and innovative category management techniques as an entirely new category of products and services. These products and services have a direct bearing on the future success and image of all conventional retailers as they enter a new century.

The dynamically growing wellness category is made up of natural and organic, diet, low/no fat, functional, fortified and specialty food and beverage; dietary supplements; sports nutrition products; and alternative health care products and services. The greatest success so far in marketing these products while providing an authentic retail experience lies in the hands of traditional health food stores and larger scale health food supermarkets such as Whole Foods and Wild Oats markets.

Whole Foods Market

Whole Foods Market owns and operates the nation's largest chain of natural and organic food supermarkets. Current stores average 24,000 square feet in size and $14.5 million in annual sales. Whole Foods is developing larger stores with 30,000 to 40,000 square feet of space. Whole Foods stores offer one-stop shopping for customers seeking high-quality natural and organic foods as well as products to support a natural lifestyle.

Figure 14-2. Whole Foods Market, Sales Growth 1993–1997

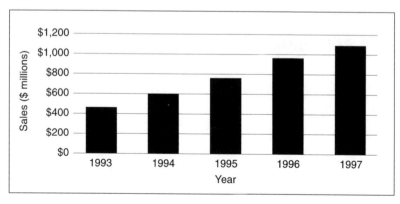

- Purchased supplement manufacturer Amrion in 1997
- 365-Everyday Value private label program initiated in 1997
- In-store Kiosks, website
- In-store Experiences: massage, ready-to-eat foods

Wild Oats Markets

Wild Oats operates the second-largest chain of natural and organic supermarkets in the United States. The company operates fifty-two stores in twelve states and Canada. Larger stores offer a complete shopping alternative to conventional supermarkets, with an average of 25,000 SKUs of natural and specialty foods, groceries, deli and juice bar items, prepared foods to go, natural meats and seafood, natural supplements and body care products.

Figure 14-3. Wild Oats Markets, Sales Growth 1993–1997

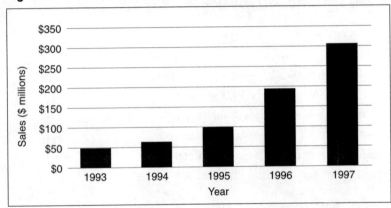

- Free nutritional consultations in markets and on website

- Informational brochures, health lectures, cooking classes

- Extensive food courts with healthy offerings

- Commitment to bulk product availability

- Sourcing goals: 80 percent organic produce; free-range, drug-free meat; earth- and body-friendly soaps, detergents and shampoos; cruelty-free body care products; rBGH-free dairy products.

THE RANGE OF OPTIONS

The notion that conventional retailers will evolve to become more like Whole Foods is plausible as long as consumer demand is visible to stimulate such changes. Currently, to keep pace with the evolving lifestyles sought after by wellness shoppers and the ever-changing and increasingly competitive retail environment, there are a range of retail experiences and wellness category products and services that conventional retailers can offer to the changing consumer.

Retailers can select from a range of store enhancements, category management innovations, and customer specific programs in order to achieve chain objectives centered on growing profitably with wellness trends (see figures 14-4 through 14-8).

Figure 14-4. Wellness Customer Research

There are a range of both conventional and innovative market research tools for use in defining, managing, and promoting the Wellness Category:

Traditional Consumer Research:

- In-store survey
- Loyalty card analysis

Innovative Consumer Research:

- In-home interviewing
- Internet communication
- Analysis of customer shopping experience

◄─────────────────────────────►

Consumer Research and Relationship Marketing:

Retailers can implement a range of consumer research and relationship building techniques to identify evolving wellness demographics, lifestyle behaviors and attitudes as they relate to the retail experience.

Figure 14-5. Wellness Products and Services

There are a range of conventional, natural, and related SKUs that can be defined to make up the Wellness Category:

Conventional Healthy:

- Healthy Choice
- Tropicana
- Multi-vitamins

True Natural:

- Organic Food and Beverage
- Functional Foods
- Herbal Supplements

◄─────────────────────────────►

Consumer Research and Relationship Marketing:

Retailers can identify a wide variety of conventional, natural, and organic food and beverage in the Wellness Category. Retailers can also identify Wellness services which complement wellness products.

Figure 14-6. Wellness Category Management

There are a range of conventional and innovative category management tools and techniques to use to manage and promote the Wellness Category:

Traditional Category Management:

- Analysis of pdduct placement and movement
- Traffic building, Transaction building
- Category profitability

Innovative Category Management:

- Consumer mind map integration
- Customer Pofitability/Loyalty, Relationship Building

◄─────────────────────────────►

Category Management Tools and Techniques:

Retailers can combine analysis of consumer research and relationship marketing with traditional category management tools.

Figure 14-7. Wellness Retail Setting

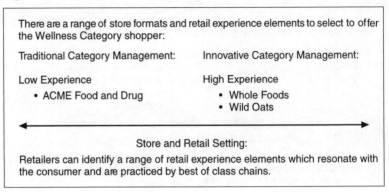

Figure 14-8. Wellness Category Experience

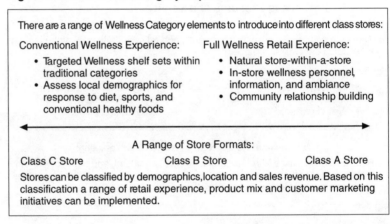

WELLNESS CATEGORY MANAGEMENT

The range of options available for use in wellness category management are similar to those found and used in traditional category management, except that a key component lies in communicating, analyzing and understanding consumer trends in health and wellness. Importantly, whereas traditional category management acknowledges the importance of consumers in the term "efficient consumer response," it is really focused on the industrial movement of large volumes of conventional products. The wellness category can be seen as defined specifically by consumer needs and desires. Some assumptions can be made about the wellness category in conventional channels:

- Consumers currently shop traditional grocery outlets, purchasing wellness products, yet this category is typically not managed as a strategic profit center.
- The wellness category can be defined as a strategic business unit.
- Wellness category products and services, because of their relative newness in conventional retail settings, are managed as groups of SKUs in separate categories and subcategories. Whereas traditional category management focuses on the overall return on investment for "the category," definitional and even placement confusion within stores makes for an unclear return on investment in the wellness category.
- The wellness category can be better managed through development and implementation of wellness category management techniques.

In particular, conventional marketers and retailers must continue to understand the wellness shopper's lifestyle goals and the experience they seek—the experience in which they come to identify with specific sets of products and services based on collective, shared experiences that result from personal health goals. Implementing new category management techniques to better reflect the customer's changing ways will lead to long-term profitability in the decades ahead.

The wellness category itself is not strictly the domain of physical retailers such as those found in health food, pharmacy, grocery or mass-market channels. The increasing importance of direct-to-consumer distribution, most evident in the direct mail channel, and now in the growing presence of the Internet, implies that building a wellness category can be done through many different channels, as long as time-honored customer relationship building is carried through.

Amazon.com, which is successfully building a book retail business centered squarely around individual customer service, is a logical model for the sale of various shelf-stable and easily shipped natural, organic and related food, beverage, supplement, and personal care products. The advent of large online health products retailers, such as DrugStore.com, implies that the wellness category will see long-term growth and expansion through a wide variety of retail channels.

Concluding Remarks

The various natural, environmentally enhanced, and sustainably manufactured products and services that make up "the wellness market" evoke important lifestyle experiences for a large number and variety of American consumers. The pursuit of wellness, and the construction of individual wellness regimes, is a common goal among consumers seeking respite and differentiation from an increasingly complex society. Based on greater sophistication in manufacturing and retailing, and the complex array of natural products and services available to offer, manufacturers and merchandisers can now interact on a more personal level with consumers to create more customized lifestyle shopping and product use experiences.

While food and beverage, dietary supplement, and health practice and service sectors have received the lion's share of attention in this book, there are many related products and services connected to the "natural" and wellness market which have not been examined. Legitimate markets are developing rapidly for forest products grown, harvested and produced under timber certification standards which parallel certification processes used to produce certified organic foods and beverages. The deregulation of the American electrical utility market now means that consumers can select their provider of electricity based not only on price per kilowatt but also on the perceived "green-ness" of the power producer they choose. Electric and hybrid electric cars as well as alternative fuel vehicles are increasingly available. Ecosystem management, the broad science whereby land, animal and water systems are managed as a sustainable whole, is gradually becoming the rule and not the exception at the federal and state government levels. Ecosystem management has broad implications for how many Americans recreate and earn livings in rural environments.

Eco-tourism, which funnels money from spending vacationers to the scenic economy they visit, is a popular form of travel both in the United States and internationally. In finance, consumers now have over 144 choices of socially responsible funds into which they can invest their money: These funds invest in companies based on the company's financial performance and its assessed impact on the environment, or its position on various issues such as gun control, alcohol, gambling, animal testing and so on. Green building and innovations designed to improve the overall "health" of both residential and commercial structures—as well as their impact on energy use, site selection and the expanded use of greener building materials and specifications—is gaining more and more momentum.

Developments in life sciences (formerly known as plant sciences) in biotechnology (biotech) and genetically modified organisms (GMOs) have become potent and controversial phenomena in conventional agricultural research. Life science developments based on advances in genetic sciences and the invention of gene manipulation tools has seen rising exposure in mass media. While the buying public harbors a vast spectrum of attitudes toward biotechnology, it is also difficult for them to weigh the tradeoffs involved when a biotechnological feat can, for example, reduce the amount of toxic chemicals that would otherwise be applied to a crop. For example, the 1997 *Food and the Environment* report found that 60 percent of environmentally inclined consumers "support plant biotechnology as a tool in agriculture if it reduces the amount of synthetic pesticide used," while 40 percent are more leery of the technology even when it ameliorates the food-related environmental danger they are most concerned about: pesticide contamination. But while pesticides are a "simple and visceral" health concern to understand, biotechnology is a seemingly silent science, highly complex, and only visible when examined by the media or watchdog nonprofits. Once there is greater public awareness of biotechnology issues, costs and benefits, considerable research will be needed to determine how consumers feel about the diverse bio-technical manipulations which can currently be applied to food production processes. In our opinion, much of the issues surrounding the success of biotech-influenced products will be determined in the arena of public opinion.

While consumer food, beverage, personal care and nutritional products and health services currently make up the greatest visible wellness market, it is clear that there are many related green markets comprising small, but growing pieces of huge conventional industrial and service sectors. Companies that rise to the single challenge of co-evolving with changing wellness consumers will undergo a difficult process, because producing and marketing to new and changing tastes is a complex challenge. Nevertheless, market winners will be those organizations that develop an intimate and ongoing understanding of consumers and their attitudes, behaviors, and shopping habits in the context of wellness. Such a reading on the consumer pulse may well form the dividing line between those product and service organizations that will succeed and those that will fall beside the way in the decades ahead.

For manufacturers, authenticity can be created by communicating effectively the laudable—and real—production practices and benefits that distinguish their products. For retailers, communicating the activities that are expended on the shoppers' behalf to authenticate and procure products of superior environmental performance can be a source of authenticity. The ability of manufacturers to think beyond organic, natural or environmentally enhanced in order to encompass the consumer's broad-stroke quest for personal health and wellness is a fundamental component of the wellness market's evolution. During times of market change, it is important to remember that those who were the established leaders in the previous era will have the hardest time responding to the new. In the midst of this change and consumer evolution, new market opportunities abound.

Appendices

APPENDIX I

Studies Cited

Food and the Environment: The Consumer Perspective, Phase I, Summer 1996

Study Background and Methodology

The first of its kind, *Food and the Environment: Phase I* was conducted to assess U.S. consumer perceptions and attitudes toward a broad array of earth-sustainable food and agricultural products and production methods.

Food and the Environment: Phase I was conducted as a mail study survey in 1996 by The Hartman Group and NFO Worldwide (National Family Opinion). Results are from a nationally representative sample drawn from NFO's panel of 475,000 households. In February 1996, an eight-page questionnaire was sent to the principal grocery shopper in 2,900 households, yielding 1,879 completed questionnaires. The data was cleaned to exclude respondents missing a high number of attributes. The first cleaning left 1,882 (96.5 percent) remaining. Data imputation was conducted on remaining sample analysis to replace missing values. The data was further cleaned to exclude respondents who recorded same rating for 80 percent of attributes. The second cleaning resulted in a total workable sample of 1,766.

Analysis employed used Factor Analysis procedures to identify key themes in the data. Factor solutions were rotated using orthogonal (varimax) and oblique (Harris-Kaiser) methodologies to identify underlying attribute patterns. Thirty of ninety-eight attributes were selected for use in segmentation analysis. The segmentation analysis procedure was performed on the ninety-eight attitudinal attributes to better identify and understand potential target groups:

- Standardization of data was used to minimize scale effects
- Hierarchical clustering technique (Ward's) was used to create starting points for the segmentation
- Iterative partitioning techniques (K-Means) was used to assign individuals to groups with the nearest values
- Segmentation procedures resulted in six identifiable separate groupings

Food and the Environment: The Consumer Perspective, Phase II, Winter 1997

Study Background and Methodology

Following Phase I, Phase II of *Food and the Environment* took a much closer look at the half of the U.S. population that has an orientation toward purchasing and using agricultural products produced using earth-sustainable methodologies.

In Winter 1997, The Hartman Group conducted a follow-up survey among households that had participated in the Phase I study. NFO conducted field and tabulation of a mail survey among 903 NFO households who had been previously identified in Phase I as one of four target segments of the population:

- True Naturals
- New Green Mainstream
- Affluent Healers
- Young Recyclers

On July 16, 1996, a twelve-page questionnaire was mailed to the primary grocery shopper in these households. On August 19, 1996, after allowing for an answering period, the returns were closed for machine tabulation. At that time, there were 715 households returning, representing 79 percent of the total mailing to households. In order to find underlying themes in the data, a Factor Analysis was performed on the forty-eight separate question items which made up Question 37 on the Phase II questionnaire as well as on the fifty-six separate question items which made up Question 10 on the Phase I questionnaire. The iterated principal factor method of factor extraction was employed using each variable's maximum correlation with the other variables as starting values for the commonalties. To assist in factor interpretation, the loadings were then orthogonally rotated using the varimax method. The regression method was used to obtain factor scores. Factorization was done on the correlation matrix. In an effort to assess the relationship between attitudes measured in Phase 1 and those measured in Phase 2, a canonical correlation analysis was performed.

Food and the Environment: The Consumer Perspective, Phase III, December 1998

Study Background and Methodology

Phase Three of *Food and the Environment* re-examined the U.S. population to assess changes in attitudes and perceptions toward food and the environment.

In May 1998, The Hartman Group conducted a follow-up survey via NFO utilizing the exact attitudinal questions fielded and analyzed in Phase I and II of Food and the Environment. Segmentation and analysis techniques similar to those undertaken in 1996 and 1997 were used to segment the U.S. population as relates to previous segmentations:

- True Naturals
- New Green Mainstream
- Affluent Healers
- Young Recyclers
- The Overwhelmed
- The Unconcerned

A twelve-page booklet with a $1.00 incentive was mailed to a representative sample of the population. On May 7, 1998, 3,700 questionnaires were mailed. A total of 2,039 usable returns were received, corresponding to 55 percent of the outgoing questionnaires. Questionnaire collection was closed on June 15, 1998. The returns were weighted to maintain population representation of age, household size, geographic division, market size and household income. A discriminant analysis was used on responses to create a mathematical function used to determine to which of the six *Food and the Environment* segments a respondent would most likely belong. The next table compares the incidence of the 1996–97 *Food and the Environment* segments versus the 1998 segments.

	F&E '96–'97		F&E '98	
Group	Sample Size	Incidence	Sample Size	Incidence
1. Unconcerned	314	17.7%	460	25.2%
2. New Green Mainstream	410	23.1%	310	17.0%
3. Overwhelmed	536	30.2%	408	22.4%
4. Affluent Healers	220	12.4%	200	11.0%
5. Young Recyclers	176	9.9%	244	13.4%
6. True Naturals	120	6.8%	201	11.0%
Total	**1776**	**100.0%**	**1823**	**100.0%**

Ecolabels: The Key to Consumer Support, Summer 1997 (Prepared for the Food Alliance, Portland, OR)

Survey Background and Methodology

In *Ecolabels: The Key to Consumer Support*, The Hartman Group explored ecolabeling as a specific retail tactic for effectively delivering sustainably produced goods and services to the segments of the consumer base outlined in Phases I and II of *Food and the Environment*. The report is divided into two sections: Section One outlines consumer attitudes as understood through a survey of consumer perceptions of ecolabels, and was designed to quantitatively assess consumer attitudes toward ecolabels for sustainably produced agricultural products. The survey consisted of a self-administered questionnaire, which was mailed to 600 environmentally sensitive consumers. Respondents represent a sample of individuals participating in the Consumer Behavior Index (CBI). The CBI is a continuous market research panel implemented and run via a collaboration between the nonprofit organization Mothers and Others for a Livable Planet and The Hartman Group. The CBI is the first "green panel" of its kind in the United States and regularly surveys thousands of environmentally conscious consumers. The information gathered provides a deeper understanding of green consumer purchase behavior and how this behavior relates to environmentally related product or service improvements. This consumer perspective is essential to designing and implementing a focused and effective ecolabeling program.

Section Two of the *Ecolabels* report explores the definition and function of ecolabeling programs as they exist today and provides suggestions for making such labeling initiatives more effective.

The Evolving Organic Marketplace, Winter 1997

Survey Background and Methodology

The Hartman Group's August 1997 organic survey polled 1,000 Americans in a nationally representative sampling. The survey sought to assess the understanding consumers have of organic products and what it means for a product to be organic. More than forty questions tested respondents about their attitudes, preferences, definitions, use and purchase patterns with regard to organic products. In order to assess purchase interest, the survey utilized a negatively phrased statement technique, in which respondents were asked to indicate their degree of agreement or disagreement with the statement (For example, "I am not very interested in buying organic products." This negative phrasing technique generally produces more thoughtful and conservative responses in surveys.) Consumer segments were differentiated based on three prestipulated criteria: respondents' reported buying interest, their unassisted mentions of products purchased, and their reported priorities regarding organic purchase criteria.

U.S. Consumer Use of Vitamins, Minerals, Herbals, and Dietary Supplements: Phase I, March 1998

U.S. Consumer Use of Vitamins, Minerals, Herbals, and Dietary Supplements: Multi-Product Users, March 1998

Survey Backgrounds and Methodologies

VMHS: Phase I and its resulting special report, *VMHS: Multi-Product Users*, result from the first phase of a supplement study conducted by The Hartman Group in 1997–98. The objective of Phase I was to determine the baseline demographics and usage patterns of U.S. consumer households of twenty-five vitamins and minerals and seventy-two different herbal and supplement products. A unique and powerful feature of the study lies in the number of households surveyed: some 43,442 households returned the survey. Such a large sample size allows for statistically reliable estimates, accurate to within one-fifth of one percent, on U.S. household usage even with products that are used by as little as 1 percent of user households. NFO Worldwide was contracted for fielding and tabulation of Phase I data, which was collected during the months of November and December, 1997. On November 1 and November 15, 1997, a mail questionnaire was mailed to 60,000 NFO panel households. The NFO cross-sectional panel consists of 550,000 households previously selected to conform to the latest available U.S. census data for the nine geographical divisions and within each division by population density, age of homemaker, annual household income and household size. A total of 43,442 households returned the survey, representing 72 percent of the total mailing households. Of these, 29,611 (or 68 percent of total returns) were consider qualifiers, i.e. they contained a household member who had used vitamins, minerals or supplements in the past six months (not in cooking or food preparation).

Statistical methods used for analysis include:

- **Correspondence mapping:** allowing for identification of products used by various demographic groups.
- **Q-factor/cluster analysis:** allows for analysis of what products are most commonly associated in use with other products by specific demographic clusters.

U.S. Consumer Use of Vitamins, Minerals, Herbals, and Dietary Supplements: Phase II, August 1998

Survey Background and Methodology

Phase II of the *U.S. Consumer Use of Vitamins, Minerals, Herbals and Dietary Supplements* study (*VMHS: Phase II*) builds on information gained by The Hartman Group in *VMHS: Phase I*. While *VMHS: Phase I* presented information from the general population, *VMHS: Phase II* examined the behaviors and attitudes of users and their households who had used vitamins, minerals, herbals and dietary supplements (VMHS) for the past six months. Information on usage behavior, brands and brand switching, stated importance, and product ratings was included in the analysis. An eight-page booklet, fielded and tabbed by NFO Worldwide, was mailed to respondents who completed the *VMHS: Phase I* survey. On February 20, 1998, 3,100 questionnaires were mailed. A total of 2,346 usable returns were received, corresponding to 75 percent of the outgoing questionnaires. Questionnaire collection was closed on March 30, 1998. As mentioned, the sample for this study consisted of respondents who had used any vitamins, minerals, herbals or dietary supplements as dietary supplements (not in cooking or food preparation) in the past six months. Approximately three-quarters (77 percent) of the sample were female (1,790 respondents) and 23 percent were male (543 respondents).

Respondents were questioned on several VMHS subjects, including the following:

- Duration and frequency of VMHS use
- Average doses of VMHS consumed per week
- Expected time to see results from using VMHS
- Forms of VMHS preferred
- Reasons why specific VMHS are used
- Importance of characteristics of VMHS
- How VMHS rate on key characteristics
- Attitudes toward VMHS
- Sources used to learn about VMHS and the trustworthiness of these sources
- Importance of VMHS brands
- VMHS purchasing behavior

Returns were weighted to maintain population representation of age, household size, geographic division, market size and household income. Statistical methods used for analysis include:

- Q-factor/cluster analysis: allows for analysis of what products are most commonly associated in use with other products by specific demographic clusters.
- Standardization of data was used to minimize scale effects
- Hierarchical clustering technique (Ward's) was used to create starting points for the segmentation
- Iterative partitioning techniques (K-Means) was used to assign individuals to groups with the nearest values

Integrated Health Care: Consumer Use and Attitudes, November 1998

Survey Background and Methodology

The *Integrated Health Care* study was designed to measure consumer attitudes, habits and practices about health care and in particular about alternative health care services and products. One of the primary research objectives of the integrated health study was to identify alternative medicine/health care consumer segments in order to further understand the alternative medicine and health care market. Alternative medicine consumer segments were derived using health management behaviors located in different sections of the questionnaire. In May 1998, The Hartman Group contracted NFO Worldwide to field a mail survey among NFO panelists. The study results are based on a representative sample of 2,039 households who responded to the questionnaire.

Via NFO, a twelve-page booklet with a $1.00 incentive was mailed to a representative sample of the population. On May 7, 1998, 3,700 questionnaires were mailed. A total of 2,039 usable returns were received, corresponding to 55 percent of the outgoing questionnaires. Questionnaire collection was closed on June 15, 1998. The returns were weighted to maintain population representation of age, household size, geographic division, market size and household income. Segmentation analysis was performed on the twenty-eight alternative health management practices or products tested in the study, using both hierarchical and iterative partitioning methodologies.

Natural Sensibility: A Study of America's Changing Culture and Lifestyle, August 1998

Survey Background and Methodology

The data for *Natural Sensibility* was gathered in the form of over 1000 hours of in-depth, one-on-one interviews with consumers in four major metropolitan markets: Seattle, San Francisco, Chicago, and New York. This strategy was an attempt to account for possible regional differences in behavior among consumers in the natural products arena.

Respondents were recruited by research firms in each of these cities and were screened for at least minimal participation in the natural products arena. Since the goal of our study was to understand how people come to use natural products and services, we determined that it would be inefficient and costly to interview non-participants. Future research may be done to learn more about those people who have yet to incorporate any natural products or services into their daily lives. While we are confident that the findings presented here are representative of what is happening in the natural products arena, these results are not, statistically speaking, generalizable to the entire U.S. consumer population. While this caution may alarm those with a penchant for significance tests, we pursued this strategy out of a strong desire for methodological rigor. Quite simply, this approach was best suited to our goal: To provide a context or background with which to interpret the growing consumer involvement in the natural products arena. Remember, we were not trying to predict individual consumer behavior. Instead, we were trying to gain a clearer picture of the larger world within which individual consumers participate.

Interviews were approximately one hour in length and conducted by trained professionals—psychologists, anthropologists, and sociologists—at research facilities with audio and video-recording capabilities. Interviewers were instructed, whenever possible, to ask how instead of why. Answers to "why" questions often involve some element of post-hoc interpretation and justification for a given behavior or scenario ("Well, I take Echinacea because I don't like getting sick"). On the other hand, "how" questions are more likely to reveal the common, practical foundations to behaviors and actions ("Well, I first took Echinacea when a co-worker gave it to me and now it's part of my daily routine"). Ethnomethodologists have employed this trick for years as a way of getting to the bottom of how things really happen in the "real world." While some readers may feel this is a trivial point, the results and implications can sometimes be dramatic.

Audio recordings of the interviews were transcribed, coded, and analyzed with computer software programs designed to facilitate systematical analysis of qualitative research data. The data—approximately 800 pages of conversations, notes, and observations—were coded individually by two Hartman Group researchers to correct for intercoder-reliability errors. Finally, additional analyses of videotape recordings were performed to clarify any ambiguities resulting from audio transcribing.

Natural Products Census *Supplement Report*
An Ongoing Consumer Study

From annual industry summaries of vitamins, minerals, herbs, and dietary supplements purchased and used by U.S. consumers to targeted monthly and quarterly reports which describe the supplement market by overall size, brand, category and distribution channel, Natural Products Census and its underlying *Supplement Report* is considered the first U.S. information source to track both consumer use and purchase of supplements at the individual level.

Supplement Report builds upon a full year of supplement category research. Following identification of U.S. supplement consumers, a panel of over 10,000 individuals (composed of users in the supplement category) was recruited via NFO Worldwide for continuous reporting on their purchase and use of supplement products. These individuals compose the *Supplement Report* consumer panel.

Supplement Report provides information on:

- Over 132 different vitamins, minerals, herbs, and supplements
- Over 130 different brands
- 13 distribution channels, including natural products retailers, mass market retailers, direct mail, multi-level marketing, and the Internet
- Pricing, product forms, dosages used, and frequency of use for each product
- Over 58 health reasons for use
- 17 demographic categories broken down into 144 potential respondent variables (such as income, age, region)

Supplement Report is designed to shed light on not only who is purchasing dietary supplements, but also which individuals within each household are using supplements, and why: that is, which health concerns lead people to choose which individual supplements.

Information from *Supplement Report* is based on weekly reporting by a group of approximately 10,000 U.S. individuals using vitamins, minerals, herbs, or other supplements. Panel members report every purchase of dietary supplements, detailing the brand they purchased, the price they paid, and where they purchased the product, among other variables. In addition, use of dietary supplements by every member of the household is recorded, including reasons for use, frequency of use, and dosages.

The study is designed to provide longitudinal data and projected data with predictive value for market size and sales growth for individual products, as well as for product categories of vitamins, minerals, herbals, and dietary supplements. By subscribing to *Supplement Report* information, manufacturers and marketers are able to:

- Understand the size of the market for individual supplement products, both in terms of number of users and sales dollars
- Anticipate sales growth potential for supplement products
- Conduct brand comparisons and market share analysis
- Develop a complete demographic profile of users of their product
- Target marketing programs based on accurate understanding for the reasons consumers use different supplements
- Do competitive tracking

A variety of subscription and report packages are available, designed to meet a variety of marketing information needs. Companies can elect to subscribe to full electronic access and a variety of printed reports, or select from individual data sets, depending on company research objectives and budgets. Based on subscription levels, companies are able to get immediate answers to specific questions, at every stage of business development and marketing planning. Cross-tabs, charts, and graphs are easily prepared on the following topics:

Supplement Purchases	Supplement Usage
Demographics of purchasers (age, income, education, lifestage, etc.)	Household demographics
Regionality	Demographics of individual users within households
Channels	Regionality
Pricing	Health concerns/reasons for use
Brands purchased	Dosages, frequency of use

Supplement Report data is provided along with Quanvert software, an easy-to-use, interactive tabulation program, which runs under Windows with a point-and-click style interface. Output can be printed directly or converted to Excel, SPSS, SAS, or ASCII de-limited file formats for additional analysis or visualization. Data files are provided on diskette or via e-mail each period. Software installation, plus user training, is provided on-site by Hartman Group technical staff. Templates reflecting the client" specific information needs will be provided.

These reports can be combined with The Hartman Group's strategic consulting services. Such services include:

- New product development
- New product market analysis
- Brand development strategies
- Channel analysis
- Strategic models and methods

The Hartman Group: Understanding the Wellness Category

The Hartman Group combines years of experience in reporting on and interpreting the natural products marketplace, the American consumer, and the participation of these consumers in the wellness category. We bring our clients new depth in understanding product, category and sector-wide trends in the natural products industry, as well as a window into the constantly changing American culture.

The Hartman Group assists clients to better understand how an increasing consumer emphasis on health, fitness and nutrition influences target markets and how these factors can be incorporated into innovative marketing and corporate strategies. From consumer and trade market research reports to strategic consulting and comprehensive business forums, we provide an accurate, insightful view on the dynamic natural products marketplace. Whether a company is a primary producer, a manufacturer, a distributor or a retailer, our reports, custom market research and strategic consulting will provide key information and insights on which to base actionable decisions.

The Hartman Group Strategic Consulting

Building upon years of experience in top-line business analysis and strategic marketing advice to natural products and conventional consumer goods companies, Hartman Group Strategic Consulting provides assessment, insights and strategic decision platforms to help clients produce, distribute and promote their products and services to areas with the greatest demand.

From brand management, positioning and strategy to distribution theory and value-chain analysis, our customized proprietary studies on consumer and trade behavior seek to uncover market opportunities for our clients.

The Hartman Group provides top-line strategic marketing advice of the highest quality.

The Hartman Group Mission: To help our clients formulate, evaluate and implement better strategic marketing decisions in the natural and consumer product sectors.

Core Markets Served: Natural and Organic Products; Herbal and Dietary Supplements; Conventional Food and Beverage; Agriculture; Life Science and Fine Chemicals; Pharmaceutical; Health Care Services and Products; Consumer Packaged Goods; Financial Investment Community.

Key Services

N|sight

N/sight is the branding identity division of The Hartman Group. We believe a natural brand is a promise encompassing quality, trustworthiness and authenticity. *N/sight* provides in-depth focus on the dynamic relationship between changing consumers and the rapidly expanding natural products and services marketplace. In order to assist our clients in developing and maintaining competitive advantages, we provide:

- Data—Facts, figures, numbers, statistics
- Information—What the data *say*
- Knowledge—What the information *means*
- Wisdom—How to *apply* the knowledge

Hartman Group New Product Development and Market Analysis:

New Product Development: New Product Idea Generation and Product Innovation; New Product Concept Development, Screening, and Testing; Product Line Additions and Extensions; New Product Launch and

Tracking; New Product Sales Forecasting

New Product Market Analysis: Market Identification, Positioning and Strategy; Consumer Product Tests; Market Test/Trial; Market Projection; Market Assessment; Market Entry Decisions

Hartman Group Brand Development Strategies:

Building Natural Brands; Building New Brands; Brand Extensions and Sub-Brands; Private Labeling; Generic and Premium Brand Strategies; Ingredient Branding; Brand Positioning; Brand and Channel Strategies; Branding and Advertising

Hartman Group Channel Analysis Services:

Value Chain Analysis and Distribution Theory; Relationship Marketing and Strategic Partnerships; Natural Product Channels; Mass Marketing; Consumer-direct; Category Management

Hartman Group Sample Strategic Models and Methods:

Focus Groups; National Mail and Telephone Attitude and Usage Surveys; Panel Survey and Longitudinal Research Vehicles; Concept Tests; Conjoint Analysis; Delphi; Quality Function Development (QFD); Product Life-Cycle Models; Diffusion Modeling; Price Elasticity's and Optimization; Participant Analysis, Ethnography; Phenomenology; Content Analysis

Sample 1997–99 Projects

The Hartman Group's current clients include dietary and herbal supplement firms, pharmaceutical companies, organic and natural food and beverage firms, specialized retailers and raw material manufacturers and suppliers located in both the U.S. and internationally:

- A $14 billion grocery chain engages The Hartman Group for consulting on creating, managing and promoting the wellness category. Includes consumer analysis, retail delivery analysis, and plans for implementation.
- A $5 billion grocery chain engages The Hartman Group for consulting on creating, managing and promoting the wellness category. Includes consumer analysis, retail delivery analysis, and plans for implementation.

- A Fortune 50 agriculture and food products corporation seeks specialized consulting on ingredient branding in the functional food category. The scope of work includes proprietary consumer research coupled with market estimations, branding recommendations, value chain analysis and insights to long-term potential in this and other branded ingredient opportunities.

- A Fortune 50 pharmaceutical/agricultural/fine chemicals corporation seeks specialized research on the potential for an environmentally enhanced agricultural textile resource. The scope of work included proprietary consumer research coupled with work in value chain analysis, conjoint analysis of consumer response, branded ingredient research, branding recommendations and market estimations.

- A large natural grain processor engages The Hartman Group to analyze competitor supplier firms and the client in the context of the market, using primary research with provision of strategic plans for product introductions to trade segments.

- The Hartman Group performs proprietary consumer research and strategic analysis in a syndicated study undertaken with ten major dietary, herbal, and pharmaceutical manufacturers to understand usage, branding, and purchase behavior issues in the vitamins, minerals, herbals and dietary supplements market.

- A company introducing a dietary supplement product requires quantitative estimations of market size and consumer response for a product offered in a variety of formats. The scope of work included analysis of The Hartman Group's consumer and trade data to simulate market size and product format potential, estimations of market growth and impact of promotion.

- An Italian herbal and dietary supplements manufacturer is interested in entering the U.S. market and partnering or co-marketing products. The scope of work included a competitive analysis and recommendations on fifteen major U.S. natural products companies.

- A project involving the identification of investment opportunities in organic food and natural product companies for a Mexican venture capital group seeking to invest heavily in progressive enterprise.

- Work involving competitive analysis of companies involved in sales of vitamins, minerals, herbals and dietary supplements over the Internet
- Proprietary consumer research and analysis undertaken to determine the level of interest in a nutrition bar formulated for a specific demographic age segment

Strategic Consulting and Market Research

Client/Customer List, Including Proprietary Studies

Albertson's Inc.
Allergan Pharmaceuticals
American Home Products
Anheuser Busch
Archer-Daniels-Midland (ADM)
Avondale Mills
BASF
Bayer Corporation
BBDO Advertising
Beckman Instruments
Bristol-Myers Squibb
Canada Seabuckthorn Enterprises, Ltd.
Cascadian Farm
Capital Integral
Coleman Natural Products
DDB Needham
The Food Alliance
Food Marketing Institute
The Gap
General Mills
Grey Advertising
Hanes Hosiery
Henkel
Hoechst Celanese
Hoffmann-La Roche

International Institute for Sustainable Development
JTC International
Kellogg Foundation
Lee Jeans
Leiner Health Products
Levi Strauss
Mattel
McKinsey & Co. Inc.
Mead Johnson Nutritionals
Miller Brewing Company
Monsanto
Mothers and Others for a Livable Planet
NatureMark
Nature's Way Products, Inc.
New Organics, Inc.
Nike, Inc.
Ocean Nutrition
Patagonia
Rocky Mountain Flour
Ross Labs
Sara Lee Corporation
Shaklee
Smith Kline Beecham
Spectrum Naturals
Stemilt Growers
The Stop & Shop Companies, Inc.
Tom's of Maine
Traditional Medicinals
Twin Laboratories
UNOCAL
VF Corporation
Virkler Chemical
Warner Lambert
Weider Nutrition Group
Wrangler

Consumer Market Research and Trade Analysis

The Hartman Group's consumer market research and analysis group focuses on both annual consumer market research studies and specialized projects which seek to answer specific corporate branding, product development and natural product category questions.

Our annual consumer studies, each available for corporate participation, focus on the following natural product sectors and areas:

- Vitamins, Minerals, Herbals and Dietary Supplements
- Food and Beverage
- Organic Products
- Personal Care Products
- Integrated Medicine and Health Care
- Cultural Studies: Lifestyle Change and the Consumer's Natural Sensibility

These nationally representative consumer studies, fielded through NFO Worldwide (National Family Opinion), are based on state-of-the-art market research methodologies and practices. From initial focus group work to sophisticated mail, telephone, Internet studies and panel research, our work provides an incisive quantitative platform for fact-based strategic decision making.

Nationally representative studies fielded in the last two years, many with proprietary corporate participation and with resulting general publications include:

- *Food and the Environment: The Consumer Perspective, Phase I*, Summer 1996
- *Food and the Environment, The Consumer Perspective, Phase II*, Winter 1997
- *The Greening of Consumers: A Food Retailer's Guide*, Winter 1997 (Prepared for the Food Marketing Institute)
- *The Evolving Organic Marketplace*, Winter 1997
- *Ecolabels: The Key to Consumer Support*, Summer 1997 (Prepared for the Food Alliance, Portland, OR)
- *Mothers and Others Consumer Behavior Index*, Summer 1997 (Prepared for Mothers and Others for a Liveable Planet)
- *U.S. Consumer Use of Vitamins, Minerals, Herbals, and Dietary Supplements: Phase I*, March 1998

- *U.S. Consumer Use of Vitamins, Minerals, Herbals, and Dietary Supplements: Multi-Product Users*, March 1998
- *Natural Foods Merchandiser Market Overview of U.S. Natural Products Market*, June 1998
- *U.S. Consumer Use of Vitamins, Minerals, Herbals, and Dietary Supplements: Phase II*, August 1998
- *Natural Sensibility: A Study of America's Changing Culture and Lifestyle*, August 1998
- *Food and the Environment: The Consumer Perspective, Phase III*, December 1998
- *Integrated Health Care: Consumer Use and Attitudes*, November 1998
- Natural Products Census
  - *Supplement Report*, June 1998–present
  - *Supplement Market Perspective*, November 1998–present
  - *Supplement MarkeTrax*, November 1998–present
  - *Supplement MarketIndex*, November 1998–present
  - *Supplement Brand* or *Product Focus Reports*, November 1998–present

Regular Publications

N\sight

N/sight is a quarterly publication exploring the dynamics of the natural products marketplace. *N/sight* reviews consumer and trade information and trends occurring in the natural market from a strategic marketing perspective. Articles cover branding, consumer segmentations, retail marketing, and many other aspects as they relate to the supplement, personal care, integrated medicine, natural and organic food, and functional food sectors.

Natural Sensibility

Natural Sensibility is a free fax and email newsletter sent to over 2,000 Hartman Group clients and customers on a bi-monthly basis. This free publication provides provocative analysis of in-depth research findings as they relate to natural consumers and strategic marketing issues pertaining to the sales and manufacture of wellness products and services.

The Hartman Group—Biosketches

Harvey Hartman

As president and founder of The Hartman Group, a strategic consulting and marketing analysis company founded in 1989, Mr. Hartman oversees the company's varied market research, management consulting and marketing services. Mr. Hartman works personally with senior management, ranging from those working at Fortune 500 to small companies, to ensure that their expectations are exceeded in developing innovative strategic solutions. He currently consults on a wide range of topics concerning American cultural change and how consumer activities impact daily business products and services for a wide range of sectors, including but not limited to: the natural products marketplace, the alternative health care and mainstream health care market, food and beverage industries, and the pharmaceutical and personal care sectors.

In his work developing innovative marketing and environmental strategies, Mr. Hartman has developed methodologies by which clients can uncover valuable market opportunities based on a factual understanding of consumer purchase and usage patterns in numerous product categories. Consulting engagements undertaken from 1989 to the present have focused on brand strategy and development, product development and placement, category management, channel analysis and distribution theory. The Hartman Group specializes in integrating these strategic marketing decisions with its state-of-the-art market research collection and analysis techniques.

In consulting to and developing research methodologies for natural and mainstream consumer products sectors, Mr. Hartman has gained a clear understanding of the American "natural sensibility" and how this is impacting both lifestyles and large components of consumer business sectors. He has taken this understanding and currently lectures to audiences in business schools and professional organizations across the country. Mr. Hartman has taught courses on environmental business and marketing strategy at the University of California, Irvine Graduate School of Management, and the University of North Carolina, Greensboro. He has been a guest lecturer at Harvard Business School; the University of Washington Graduate Business School; the University of Rhode Island; Washington University; and the UCLA MBA Program.

Mr. Hartman has been a contributing columnist for such publications as inbusiness and *Total Quality Environmental Management*, and has co-authored several major studies, including *Natural Sensibility: A Study of America's Changing Culture and Lifestyle* (1998); *Integrated Health Care: Consumer Use and Attitudes* (1998); *U.S. Consumer Usage of Vitamins, Minerals and Herbal Supplements* (Phases One and Two, 1998); *The Evolving Organic Marketplace* (1997); *The Hartman Reports, Phases One* and *Two*; *Food and the Environment, A Consumer's Perspective* (1996 and 1997); *The Greening of Consumers: A Food Retailer's Guide* (prepared for Food Marketing Institute, 1997); and *The Hartman Environmental Marketing Strategies and Research Report* (1993).

In addition to his work in consulting, writing and lecturing, Mr. Hartman works on an ongoing basis with the New York based nonprofit, Mothers and Others for a Livable Planet, and has consulted to numerous government and NGO organizations such as the EPA, the FDA, USDA, World Wildlife Fund, Co-op America, The Food Alliance and the Corporation for the Northern Rockies. Mr. Hartman's specialty lies in helping organizations with strategic, multi-functional integration of business process and the environment as well as developing winning solutions and opportunities for clients in the areas of marketing, communications, new product development, environmental policy, operations design, organizational processes and strategic alliances. Prior to forming The Hartman Group in 1989, Mr. Hartman devoted his career to the high technology industry where he served in senior executive positions for Fortune 500 companies.

Education: BS, Business and Marketing, St. Louis University

David Wright—Strategic Marketing/Corporate Development
Mr. Wright's primary focus is in marketing research, consumer behavior, and the process by which sustainably produced natural resources are marketed. Mr. Wright has over ten years of professional writing and research experience centering on forest and agricultural marketing and products, forest ecology and management, private and public corporate business analysis, the energy industry and nonprofit management.

Education: MS Marketing, Forest Products, University of Washington
MF Master of Forestry, Yale School of Forestry and
Environmental Studies
BA English, University of Massachusetts

William Gottlieb—Director of Marketing Research

Mr. Gottlieb has twenty years of experience in the marketing research field, specializing in providing full-service quantitative research to businesses, public sector organizations and consumer marketing companies. Areas of expertise include research design, questionnaire development, field work/data collection, data processing and tabulation, analysis and reporting.

Education: MBA, University of Denver
BES, Johns Hopkins University

Mel Oyler—Strategic Consulting

Dr. Oyler has over ten years of successful integrated product development, product marketing, applications engineering, market discovery, and R&D experience. His background experience includes process design and innovation, strategic product planning, strategic market research, market requirement statements, competitive product positioning, technology road maps, new product definition and technical business preparations/training.

Education: Ph.D. Strategic Marketing, University of Washington
MS, Electrical and Computer Engineering, University of California, Davis
MS, Chemical Engineering, University of California, Davis

Tanya Pergola—Cultural Analysis and Consumer Behavior

Dr. Pergola's area of expertise is in statistics and methodology of sociological research. She is experienced in market research analysis and research consulting. She currently is a sociology instructor at the University of Washington and a researcher for the USGA.

Education: Ph.D. Sociology, University of Washington
MA, Sociology, University of Washington
BA, Sociology/Anthropology, special honors, Washington   & Lee University

Laurie Demeritt—Director of Marketing

Ms. Demeritt oversees and facilitates all marketing strategies. She is the liaison between all media representatives and The Hartman Group. Additionally, Ms. Demeritt is also responsible for special events including the Natural Products Marketing Summit. Previous experience includes marketing for a national sports organization and teaching environmental and language skills.

Education: MBA, Emphasis in Marketing and Environmental Management, University of Washington

BA, Political Science, Cornell University

Stephanie Gailing—Nutrition and Health Care Research Manager
Ms. Gailing combines her background in natural products marketing with her education in both nutrition and business management as The Hartman Group's Integrated Health Care Specialist. Ms. Gailing's previous experience includes operating her own natural products consulting company and retail store, technical writing for a dietary supplements company, research for a naturopathic physician and marketing for a homeopathic medicine manufacturer. She is currently completing her master's degree in nutrition at Bastyr University, where she is doing research on the relationship between consumers and dietary supplement information sources.

Education: MS, Nutrition, Bastyr University

BS, Cornell University

Charles M. Curtis—Project Consultant
Mr. Curtis' experience in project management, consulting and public relations include extensive report writing and client service work. As a project consultant, Mr. Curtis draws from a diverse education which encompasses degrees in economics and business with concentrations in environmental management, writing and marketing. Academic projects have included research reports on product extensions, technology transfer and options for strategic business reorganization. Mr. Curtis is currently implementing a client development program with members of the U.S. financial investment community.

Education: MBA, University of Washington School of Business

BA, Economics, Middlebury College

Robert Hashizume—Research Manager

Mr. Hashizume has experience in international trade and market research and new market development. He has managed mail survey, personal interviewing and focus-group research projects. His focus is on quantitative analysis and reporting.

Education: MS, Marketing—Forest Products, University of Washington
BS, Wood Science, University of British Columbia

Jarrett Paschel—Project Consultant

Dr. Paschel is experienced in planning, developing and designing computer-based survey research projects. Dr. Paschel has worked extensively on Web-based services and projects. He is currently a sociology instructor at the University of Washington and does freelance work with a major computer software company.

Education: Ph.D. Sociology, University of Washington
MA, Sociology, University of Washington
BA, Sociology, special honors, University of Texas, Austin

William Turner, Jr.—Project Consultant

Mr. Turner's previous experience as an investment project director and a budget analyst includes conducting project investment analyses, developing strategic pricing and forecasting labor rates. Mr. Turner is currently acting as adjunct professor at Seattle Pacific University while completing his PhD in Forest Economics at University of Washington focusing on portfolio theory, financial analysis, and resource supply and demand.

Education: PhD, Forest Economics, University of Washington
MA, Applied Economics, Seatt/le University
BS, Seattle Pacific University

Cindy Robideau—Accounting and Administrative Coordinator

Ms. Robideau has worked as an account coordinator and research analyst, experienced with primary and secondary research vehicles. Ms. Robideau currently oversees all office administration and bookkeeping activities for The Hartman Group.

Education: BA, Education, Purdue University.

Joelle Chizmar—Marketing Assistant

Ms. Chizmar implements all marketing projects for The Hartman Group, including all targeted consumer contact as well as distribution and maintenance of all publicity materials. Her previous experience includes working as an English educator in public schools, focusing on writing instruction. Ms. Chizmar is also responsible for nonprofit coordination as a result of her work with various nonprofit educational programs.

Education: BA, English, University of Illinois
                 BA, Education, Illinois State University

Bryce Patrick Hartman—Director Youth Research

Bryce combines his knowledge of Nintendo, soccer, baseball, and basketball to examine lifestyle trends among younger consumers. He is #53 on the Enatai Indians baseball team and #11 on the Enatai Eagles basketball team.

Education: Enatai Grade School, First Grade

APPENDIX III

Census Regions of the U.S.

East	North	South	West
New England	**East North Central**	**South Atlantic**	**Mountain**
Connecticut	Illinois	Delaware	Arizona
Maine	Indiana	District of Columbia	Colorado
Massachusetts	Michigan	Florida	Idaho
New Hampshire	Ohio	Georgia	Montana
Rhode Island	Wisconsin	Maryland	Nevada
Vermont		North Carolina	New Mexico
		South Carolina	Utah
		Virginia	Wyoming
		West Virginia	
Middle Atlantic	**West North Central**	**East South Central**	**Pacific**
New Jersey	Iowa	Alabama	California
New York	Kansas	Kentucky	Oregon
Pennsylvania	Minnesota	Mississippi	Washington
	Missouri	Tennessee	
	Nebraska		
	North Dakota		
	South Dakota		
		West South Central	
		Arkansas	
		Louisiana	
		Oklahoma	
		Texas	

PUBLICATION ORDER FORM

Publication	Available	Price	Quantity	Total
The Evolving Organic Marketplace	Now	$475	_____	$ _____
Vitamins, Minerals, Herbs and Supplements: A Year in Review	Now	$1,000	_____	$ _____
Vitamins, Minerals, Herbs and Supplements: Phase One	Now	$1,500	_____	$ _____
Vitamins, Minerals, Herbs and Supplements Multi-Product Users Report	Now	$750	_____	$ _____
Package Offer: VMHS One & Multi-Product Users Report	Now	$2,000	_____	$ _____
Vitamins, Minerals, Herbs and Supplements: Phase Two	Now	$3,500	_____	$ _____
Package Offer: VMHS One, Multi-Product Users Report & VMHS Two	Now	$5,000	_____	$ _____
Natural Sensibility: A Study of America's Changing Culture and Lifestyle	Now	$500	_____	$ _____
Food and the Environment: A Consumer's Perspective, Phase One	Now	$250	_____	$ _____
Food and the Environment: A Consumer's Perspective, Phase Two	Now	$250	_____	$ _____
Food and the Environment: A Consumer's Perspective, Phase Three	Now	$475	_____	$ _____
Package Offer: Food and the Environment, Phase One, Two and Three	Now	$750	_____	$ _____
Integrated Health Care: Consumer Use and Attitudes	Now	$1,000	_____	$ _____
Marketing to the New Natural Consumer: Understanding Trends in Wellness	Now	$39.95	_____	$ _____

Total Price: $

Total number of items ordered: _____

Bill To:

Name _____

Title _____

Company _____

Address _____

City, State, Zip _____

Country _____

Telephone _____

Fax _____

Send To (if different):

Name _____

Title _____

Company _____

Address _____

City, State, Zip _____

Country _____

Telephone _____

Fax _____

Payment by ☐ Check ☐ Visa ☐ MasterCard ☐ American Express

Credit card number _____ Expiration date _____ Signature _____

Please send order form to:

The Hartman Group
1621 114th Ave. SE, #105
Bellevue, WA 98004

Or fax form to:

(425) 452-9092

For more information please call:

(425) 452-0818 or
email: info@hartman-group.com
website: www.hartman-group.com